CHRIST
THE
YOGI

CHRIST THE YOGI

A Hindu Reflection on
The Gospel of John

RAVI RAVINDRA, PH.D.

INNER TRADITIONS
ROCHESTER, VERMONT

Inner Traditions International
One Park Street
Rochester, Vermont 05767
www.InnerTraditions.com

First Inner Traditions edition published 1998
Copyright © 1990, 1998 by Ravi Ravindra

LIBRARY OF CONGRESS CATALOGING-IN-PUBLICATION DATA
Ravindra, Ravi.
   [Yoga of the Christ]
   Christ the Yogi : a Hindu reflection on the Gospel of John / Ravi Ravindra.
     p. cm.
   Originally published: Yoga of the Christ. Shaftesbury, Dorset ; Rockport, Mass. : Element Books, 1990.
   Includes bibliographical references and indexes.
   ISBN 0-89281-671-6 (pbk. : alk. paper)
   1. Bible. N.T. John—Hindu interpretations. 2. Jesus Christ—Hindu interpretations. I. Title.
BS2615.2.R365   1998
226.5'06—dc21   98-21279
                                              CIP

Printed and bound in the United States

10 9 8 7 6 5 4 3 2

This book was typeset in Palantino with Serlio as the display typeface

CONTENTS

Acknowledgements   x
Preface   xi
Introduction   1

CHAPTER ONE

Verses
  1–9   Intelligence Beyond Time   13
10–13   All Who Receive the Word are Begotten by God   15
14–18   Eternity in Love with Time   17
19–34   The Witness as the Midwife of the Spirit   20
35–51   Preparation for Withstanding Truth   24

CHAPTER TWO

  1–11   Transformation: Water into Wine   31
12–25   Temple, Body and Spirit   33

CHAPTER THREE

  1–21   New Birth   38
22–36   None but the Groom has the Bride and the Fire   41

CHAPTER FOUR

  1–3   Beware of the Hollow Men   46
 4–15   The Inner Spring of Living Water   47
16–18   The Need for Inner Unity   50
19–24   The Worshippers whom the Father Seeks   51
25–42   The Secret Name of God   52
43–54   Belief of Signs and Wonders   55

CHAPTER FIVE

1–9	The Struggle between the Self and the Ego	57
10–17	Action and Rest from Action	59
18–30	Only He can be Just who Does Nothing by Himself	62
31–47	The Esoteric Message of the Tradition	64

CHAPTER SIX

1–13	The Bread from a Simple Heart	68
14–15	The Fear and Temptation of Becoming King	70
16–21	The Power of I AM	71
22–58	I AM as the Bread of Eternal Life	74
59–71	Levels of Struggle	81

CHAPTER SEVEN

1–13	Conflict between the Spirit and the World	84
14–32	My Teaching is not My Own	87
33–36	Where I AM, No One Can Come	90
37–52	Rivers of Living Water from the Belly	92

CHAPTER EIGHT

1–11	Adultery: Mixing of Levels	96
12–20	The Highest Person as the Witness Within	99
21–30	Without Knowing I AM, One Dies Missing the Mark	101
31–47	A Disciple is He who Lives the Teaching	104
48–59	Losing One's Mind Rightly	108

CHAPTER NINE

1–7	Spiritual Blindness is Natural	111
8–17	Sight as New Birth	114
18–34	Insight or More Sights?	116
35–41	The Sighted and the Sightless	118

CHAPTER TEN
1–21	Many Sheep and One Shepherd	121
22–42	The Father and You are One	124

CHAPTER ELEVEN
1–16	He whom Christ Loves, Dies to Himself	129
17–44	Awake, O Sleeper, Arise from the Dead	134
45–57	Alien People Clutching their Gods	138

CHAPTER TWELVE
1–8	Giving One's All to the Master	142
9–19	The Kingdom of Christ is Not of This World	143
20–36	Unless a Seed Dies it Bears no Fruit	144
37–43	Levels of Seeing	148
44–50	The Yoga of the Cross	151

CHAPTER THIRTEEN
1–17	Washing Off the Surface Self	153
18–32	The Trial of Judas	155
33–38	Only He who Knows can Love	163

CHAPTER FOURTEEN
1–14	I AM the Way and the Truth and the Life	165
15–26	Those who Love can Come to Truth	167
27–31	He who Has Nothing will not Die	169

CHAPTER FIFTEEN
1–6	Right Order – Internal and External	172
7–13	Love from Above, Obedience from Below	175
14–17	Levels of Disciples	177
18–25	Leave the World in Order to Change It	179
26–27	The Eternal Witness from the Beginning	181

CHAPTER SIXTEEN

1–6	The Scandal of the Cross	183
7–15	The Inner Guide	185
16–23	Death and New Birth	187
23–28	Participating in the Mind of Christ	188

CHAPTER SEVENTEEN

1–13	The Work of the Father	191
14–26	Consecration in Truth	194

CHAPTER EIGHTEEN

1–12	The Overwhelming Force of I AM	197
13–27	The Trial of Peter	200
28–40	The King of the Inner Kingdom	203

CHAPTER NINETEEN

1–22	The Crown of Thorns and the Inner Kingdom	206
23–42	Delivering the Spirit to the One Whom He Loved	209

CHAPTER TWENTY

1–18	I Sleep, but My Heart Waketh	215
19–31	The Spirit of Truth as the Subtle Body of Christ	220

CHAPTER TWENTY-ONE

1–14	A New Beginning	226
15–19	The Lamb of Christ among the Wolves of the World	229
20–25	Let Not Him Who Seeks Cease until He Finds	232

Bibliography	235
Index of References	237
Index of Subjects	242

To The Crucifer,
First-born Son of
Our Common Father

'He who is near me is near the fire,
and he who is far from me is far from the Kingdom.'

–The Gospel of Thomas

ACKNOWLEDGEMENTS

A person incurs many debts in attempting a work of this kind, often without realising the specific contribution of others. So many sages, teachers, scholars and friends have contributed to what I understand about, in and with the Gospel that it is impossible to list them all. I shall content myself with an expression of general gratitude to all who have assisted directly or indirectly.

In particular, however, I wish to mention Professor A. Hilary Armstrong, the Plotinus scholar, with whom I studied the Gospel According to St John word by word a decade ago. Also, some of the students in a course I have taught for a few years under the title of 'A Comparative Study of Christianity and Other Religions', most of whom have come from a variety of Christian backgrounds, have been very helpful with their responses to my feelings and comments about the Gospel. In addition, a research grant from Dalhousie University is gratefully acknowledged, as is the generous support of Mr. Patrick J. Guiry.

This book, if it had been written at all, would have been quite different in substance and form, without the tireless and selfless help of my friend Priscilla Murray; I acknowledge her contribution with delight.

PREFACE

It is gratifying to acknowledge the reception given to the first printing of *Christ the Yogi*.[1] It was widely reviewed and I continue to receive letters from complete strangers as well as from friends, both scholars and non-scholars, who have been very moved and helped by my reflections on the *Gospel According to St. John*. I have myself continued to ponder over and to take delight in the marvellous wisdom of the Gospel. It is more amazing than I have succeeded in conveying. If I were to rewrite this book now, no doubt I would say several things a little differently, here and there, but the substance would be the same. I feel amply rewarded if *Christ the Yogi* helps some people to read or re-read the Gospel with more attention and with more love.

As is to be expected, some reviewers have been quite critical of the book. A few feel that I should not have done what I tried to do, or at least not in the way I did it. Some reviewers have found fault with one or another interpretation or suggestion of mine or with some assumptions in the book. I have neither the competence nor the wish to counter their arguments. In fact I do not wish to argue at all. I tried to describe what I see in the Gospel and to indicate the direction which is opened up by it in a search for inner transformation. Others might well see much more profoundly and clearly. For me, scriptures are not weapons of scholarly warfare; I hope to be transformed by them towards a greater clarity of perception, simplicity of feeling and wholeness of being.

Some reviewers were offended by what they regarded to be 'spilling Ganges water into the Jordan'. It is certainly true that my eyes have been affected by the light reflected from the Ganga. It is also true that the world I live in now and most of the people I encounter have been more influenced by teachings either spoken loudly or whispered on the banks of the Jordan. If the ancient texts are going to have contemporary relevance, both the Ganga and the Jordan will have to be kept simultaneously in view. The author could not have arrived where he is now without flying over many rivers, including the Ganga and the Jordan. A view from an aeroplane surely does reveal different aspects of our planet than does one from a camel by the Jordan or from a bullock cart by the Ganga.

For some readers it is difficult to accept the suggestion that Christ is the way but Jesus is a way; whereas for some others that very suggestion is liberating and helpful for coming to terms with religious pluralism in the world.

Numerous stylistic changes are needed in order to make the language of the book obviously inclusive of both males and females. But that would have to wait for another edition. However, the intention throughout the book is to be inclusive, not only as concerns gender but also with respect to religious and cultural traditions.

1. *Christ the Yogi* has also been published in 1991 as *Le Yoga du Christ* in French, by La Table Ronde in Paris, with a preface by Arnaud Desjardins, in a series called *'Les Chemin de la Sagesse'*, and in Portuguese in 1992 as *Yoga de Christo,* by Editora Teosofica in Brasilia, Brazil.

INTRODUCTION

The only reason that I, an outsider to the Christian tradition and not particularly learned in it, write about one of its most sacred texts is my love for it. The first time I encountered it, nearly a quarter of a century ago, I was much moved by The Gospel According to St John. Since then I have read this gospel many times; always it leaves me in an uplifted internal state; I feel myself called by a mysterious and higher voice.

In our contemporary pluralistic world, where a cross-cultural communication has increasingly become a matter of necessity for global survival, a new consciousness is emerging. One of the major features of this new consciousness is going to be a non-sectarian spirituality. A universal spirituality is at the very root of all traditions, but is continually lost in theological exclusivism, or in scholastic partiality, or in evangelical enthusiasm, and needs to be rediscovered and restated anew again and again. Anybody who would approach a major work of a religious tradition with a global perspective, and with an effort to discover the universal truths in it, will aid the development of the new consciousness in the right direction.

Since I was brought up in India, my psyche is naturally Indian in its early formation, without my being able to say exactly what that means in the present context. When I read the Gospel According to St John, I am struck by many similarities with the Indian traditions, and of course by many differences. But that is not the focus of the present book; here I am more interested in discovering the heart of the Gospel to the extent that it will reveal itself to me. In trying to understand the Gospel, here and there I have found some Indian texts specifically helpful in offering a new way of looking at a metaphor or in enlarging the appreciation of something that has already been understood. I am persuaded that the major division in the human psyche is not horizontal or regional, dividing the Eastern from the Western soul; rather it is vertical and global, separating the few from the many, and the spiritual, inner and symbolical way of understanding from the material, outer and literal one – culturally as well as in each human soul. Still, it is a relevant fact that my whole vision has been shaped to some extent by Indian culture, even though no individual is completely determined by his cultural background.

My understanding of the Hindu tradition is that it aims at *sanatana dharma* (eternal order) of which at its best it is one representation, and that the tradition is most fulfilled only when it succeeds in leading one to the Truth beyond itself and beyond oneself, to experience It and become one with It. One is born *prakrita* (natural, common, unformed); one must attempt to die *samskrita* (well sculpted, cultured, educated). The truly educated person, the formation of which is the real aim and meaning of any spiritual path, of any *yoga*, is he who is internally rightly ordered, and, in the words of the *Bhagavad Gita* (6:29), 'sees the Self in everyone, and everyone in the Self, seeing everywhere impartially'. Everywhere, the one Truth and one Being, or simply the One, has manifested itself in many truths, myriad beings and many selves, corresponding to different times, places, cultures, religions and needs. Each language has its own particular genius, and some things can be expressed in it in a way which is especially profound and engaging; nevertheless no language has a monopoly on depth of discourse, nor does any particular language exhaust all possibilities of communication. In fact, at its best, as one sees in love, and in the utterances of so many mystics and sages, a language may most succeed as it carries one to the silence beyond any articulation. Similarly, each religious and spiritual tradition has its own beauty and emphasis, and certain truths are most profoundly expressed in it, and perhaps in it alone. Nevertheless, no tradition exhausts all possibilities of The Vastness, as no Being exhausts all modalities of Being.

No two spiritual paths can be exactly the same, even though there may be many parallels and areas of agreement between them. Each path has its own specific centre of gravity. And the most important thing from a practical religious point of view is to be actually searching for and responding to a way, a path of inner integration; that alone can lead to salvation or freedom or truth. Still, even the practice of a path, and not only its theory, can be illumined by a light coming from another tradition. What is important to appreciate is that no spiritual path can be true if it is essentially devised here below by human reasoning. A true path depends on the Will of Heaven; it originates from Above. There cannot be a way from here to There, unless it be laid from There to here. In these matters, more than elsewhere, it is true as the Gospel says (John 3:27) that 'No one can lay hold on anything unless it is given him from on high'.

The way of Jesus Christ is through the Christ himself, that is to say, through the *I* which is 'the only Son of God', which is 'one with the Father', which is 'the Word that was in the Beginning, with God, and was God' (John 3:16; 10:30; 1:1). Having completely emptied himself of himself, so that the word we hear is not his and is instead the Word of the Father who sent him (John 14:24), having become a transmitting conduit without any personal distortions, he could say, 'I am not myself the source of the words I speak: it is the Father who dwells in me doing his own work' (John 14:10). Such an *I*, in supreme identity with the Father, is the one which can say, 'I AM the Way, the Truth and the Life; no one comes to the Father except through me' (John 14:6). Whether the Father had incarnated himself in the body of Jesus of Nazareth, or whether Jesus became one with the Father, is not necessary for us to resolve here, especially when we recall the Gospel saying (John 3:13) that 'no one went up into Heaven except the one who came down from Heaven'.

However, it is important to guard against a lowering of the level of insight: the significant truth, which alone has the power to lead to eternal life, resides in the egoless 'supreme identity' in which 'the Father and I are one', and less in any exclusive identification of the Father with this specific person or that. In the Indian tradition, particularly in the *Upanishads*, the deepest self of every human being, the very kernel of a person, the *Atman*, is said to be beyond any limiting particularity, and identically one with *Brahman*, the Absolute, the essence of all there is. Furthermore, the way to *Brahman* is through the *Atman*. This is equally true in the *Bhagavad Gita*, where the overall mode of discourse is much closer in its theistic metaphor to that in the Gospels: Krishna, the incarnate God, repeatedly says that he is seated in the heart of everyone, and a person can come to know him and participate in his being by following his own essential being. Anyone who speaks from that core of oneself, which is possible only when one has surrendered all of one's relatively

3

superficial selves to the service of this one Self, constitutes a bridge, a way, from here to There.

The way, however, is not the goal; and a person can too easily get excessively attached to a particular way or a teacher. More especially, when someone is actively opposed to other teachers and other ways, he commits a sin against the Holy Spirit in limiting its possibilities to the particular mode of expression which he has somehow, usually by an accident of birth in a particular culture, encountered. Thus one practises idolatry in another form even though one may be against the idols of other people. The ever-present sense of exclusivism of the way and the saviour, so pervasive in Christianity, is in my judgement based on a misunderstanding of the sacred texts, by interpreting at the surface what is spoken from the depth, and is not worthy of Jesus Christ who completely denied his self, and emptied himself of any feeling of particularity, as well as distinction from God. 'A certain ruler asked him, "Good teacher, what shall I do to inherit eternal life?" And Jesus said unto him, "Why call me good? None is good but God alone"' (Luke 18:18–19).

In addition to the point of view implied in the remarks above, this book is written with certain further assumptions and attitudes, which together specify what may be called the 'method of vertical reasoning'.

The first assumption is that the Gospel According to St John is not on test. If anyone or anything is on test, it is we ourselves and our sensitivity. The text has proved itself: many times, in many places and to many very intelligent and sensitive people. It constitutes one of the most sacred texts of a great religion, and has provided spiritual nourishment to an entire culture over centuries. If it does not speak to us, alas! too bad for us! It is not for nothing that so many great teachers have said words to the effect that 'you have ears but do not hear; you have eyes but do not see.' If we cannot hear, we must surely be hardened and closed of heart, and set in a defensive posture of narrow-mindedness. There are some people in whom such a posture has been formed in reaction to the insensitivity and aggression of some of those who proclaim adherence, or opposition, to the

Gospel and its message. Still, if one can be a little freed of such reactions, the beauty of the Gospel will be apparent.

The second assumption is that the Gospel has come down to us from a higher mind than ours. If there is something in it which we do not understand, the difficulty is likely to be in us and in our limitations. One cannot be blind to the fact that there are several places where the later editors, compilers, translators and others with various interests have added words or stories into the Gospel which change the original meaning or intention. This was perhaps done sometimes unintentionally and sometimes with a view to a doctrinal dispute. Wherever scholarship has revealed alterations or additions in the text, a note will be made if appropriate and helpful in understanding the heart of the matter. Otherwise, in our attempts to make some sense of the text, whenever there is any question about its intelligence, we have no doubt that the Gospel comes from a higher intelligence than ours. In fact, precisely at the point where our best efforts do not yield a satisfactory sense in the Gospel, there is an opportunity for us to listen with quietness and humility so that we may hear what we are not usually accustomed to hear, and allow the Gospel to work its magic in lifting us above ourselves. I am convinced that the Scriptures and the teachers are not among us for them to be intelligible to us while we remain as we are; on the contrary, I believe that they are here so that we may become higher than we ordinarily are. All religions everywhere insist that we do not live as we might: from our right mind. Thus we live in sin, or in sorrow or in illusion or in a dream-like sleepy state; and not in grace, with joy, in reality, wakeful. The teachings from Above, of which the Scriptures are an example, cannot be for the purpose of adding more knowledge or comfort or dreams to our sleepy state; we assume that they can nudge us a little towards wakefulness if we do not undo their effect by dragging them down to our level, at which we win or lose theological arguments, convert others to our doctrines, and exercise control over them.

The third assumption is that the Gospel belongs to the whole world, and in particular to those who feel called by it and find some help in it, even though they are not nominally Christian and have no need of so labelling themselves. It is a great classic of world spirituality, and too important to be relegated to an exclusively sectarian reading. I detect a curious attitude among many of the Christians I have met, scholars and non-scholars alike. They find it a little odd that anybody who is not a Christian should be seriously reading Christian books. It is understandable to them that one might read such books to become a Christian, or even in order to engage in polemics against Christianity, but one must choose and take sides. Commitment to Christ seems to imply for them either an enthusiastic to mild commitment against other teachers and teachings, or a certain degree of tolerance and allowance for co-existence of other religions, but not very often any conviction that these other teachings could be useful for one's own salvation. And those Christians who find something of value in other teachings often find it necessary to put Christianity down and to deny that they are Christians. Perhaps this either/or attitude arises from an over-literal interpretation of a fragment of a saying of Jesus Christ, namely, 'He who is not with me is against me' (Matthew 12:30; Luke 11:23). For myself, I am happy to find light wherever I can, without thereby having to deny other sources of illumination or other colours of the spectrum, which together can more fully express the glory and abundance of The Vastness than any one can alone.

The fourth assumption is that there is a definite meaning to spiritual sensitivity, which perhaps all human beings have in a rudimentary form and which is highly developed in some. This spiritual sense is able to comprehend subtle ideas, suggestions and phenomena which are not comprehensible to the other senses and the rational mind. To me it appears obvious that scholarship, erudition and mental acumen by themselves are not sufficient for approaching the Scriptures, although they justly have a high place, and could be most illuminating. However, this extra dimension of spiritual sensitivity seems to be a much more important requirement. As is said in another tradition, just as a donkey bearing a sandalwood load knows its weight but not its fragrance, so also is a scholar who knows the texts of the Scriptures but not their significance. It is clear, on the other hand, that ignorance of what scholarship has to say about any matter pertaining to the Scriptures is by itself no guarantee of spiritual sensitivity! My interest in the Gospel is not doctrinal or dogmatic in the ordinary sense of these words. Nevertheless, one may recognise and understand what Jesus the Christ said, 'Whoever chooses to do the will of God will know about the doctrine – namely, whether it comes from God or is merely my own' (John 7:17).

There are many levels of quality of being Christian – from Jesus the Christ to Torquemada the inquisitor. In pointing to this wide variation my purpose is not to belittle Christianity or to elevate it; a similar qualitative range exists in every other religious tradition. My interest in this book is to discover a subtler and less churchly level in the Gospel than usual, to which many thoughtful and sensitive Christians, as well as non-Christians, are lost simply because there is not an appreciation of the various levels of being within each human being, and the corresponding levels within Christianity. As one grows spiritually, it is natural and necessary to be free of the level of religion which one knows and in which one dwells; in clinging to that level, one accepts a stunting of the natural process of development. Unfortunately, far too often there is a fixed, externalistic notion of what Christianity is; and it does not permit people, especially disgruntled ex-Christians, to see the immense spiritual wealth of Christianity and its dynamic elasticity adequate to the full measure of the most developed soul. Many years ago in one of my classes, while disputing an interpretation of one of the parables in the Gospels, an ordained minister of a Protestant church had pronounced that 'Mysticism has nothing to do with Christianity; it is just a Catholic heresy.' To be sure, he later regretted having made that remark, and wished to withdraw it because, as he said, he had spoken unconsciously. After the class, another participant, a Sufi Muslim and now a quite well-known Professor of Religion, said to me with tears in his eyes, 'How sad! So many Christians don't know what treasures there are in the Gospels.'

This book is written in the hope of letting the inner Christ grow in us; for me it is a form of prayer and meditation. I am called by, and heartily endorse, what the seventeenth-century mystic Angelus Silesius (translator: Frederick Franck) wrote:

> Christ could be born
> a thousand times in Galilee—
> but all in vain
> until He is born in me.

The reader will not find in this book an academic or historical analysis of any particularities of John's Gospel, of the kind published in professional journals dealing with biblical studies. Here I am interested in the spiritual heart of the Gospel rather than the details of any facts about it. As far as I am aware, I do not belong to any specific school of Johannine interpretation. Those well versed in biblical scholarship, which has an immensely sophisticated intellectual tradition behind it, may find some specific remarks and interpretations too well known to them, and some others too rash and without the customary scholarly caution. I have no intention in this book to enter into a debate or a detailed discussion of the minutiae of the relevant scholarship. There are fine commentaries available for this purpose; the one by Raymond Brown in the Anchor Bible Series, although nearly two decades old, is unsurpassed in its genre. Also, I wish to look at the Gospel unburdened by any particular churchly point of view. One reader has said that what I have here is a compendium of almost all the heresies which have been condemned by the Church down the ages! But he did add that, all considered, some of these points of view should not have been condemned after all. Above all, I wish my point of view to be that of a lover – first of all of the Spirit and secondly of John's Gospel. Apart from my delight in it, I read the Gospel as scripture providing spiritual nourishment.

All factual, informational and textual material and the translation from the original languages, of the scriptural passages as well as of the specific words and phrases singled out for emphasis in my comments, rely on the work of others, referred to in the Bibliography at the end of the book. As one would expect, these scholars do not agree with each other concerning all details and nuances; wherever there was a choice, I have made selections suitable for my purposes.

The Gospel According to St John is different from the other gospels in its overall point of view concerning Jesus Christ and his mission on the earth. It is much more cosmological in scale and mystical in nature than the other canonical gospels which are all called the synoptic gospels owing to the fact that they, in contrast to John, can together be regarded as revealing the same vision. John's Gospel has been for a very long time considered as more inner or spiritual or esoteric. Clement of Alexandria (about AD 150–215) said about this Gospel: 'Last of all [meaning after the other evangelists] John, perceiving that the external facts had been made plain in the gospel, being urged by his friends, and inspired by the Spirit, composed a spiritual gospel.'

It is not clear who wrote this Gospel. The Church tradition for centuries has identified the author with the Beloved Disciple mentioned in the Gospel itself, and him with John, son of Zebedee. It is doubtful that it was written by one of the apostles who witnessed the events himself; however, the Gospel may have been based on some eyewitness accounts which circulated orally for decades among a school of early Christians. The direct evidence, such as it is, regarding the time of composition of the Gospel, points on the whole to a date between AD 80 and 120, after the other three gospels. However, this is not at all certain. The Gospel could have been written as early as AD 70, and could thus be the first gospel to be written. In any case, this and other related questions, although of enormous scholarly interest, are not the concern of this book.

Many scholars seem to be in agreement that some alterations and additions have been made in the text as it has come down to us. For the purpose of the comments made in this book, however, the standard arrangement of chapters and verses in the Gospel will be followed. The comments are arranged by sections, not by individual verses, but in strict order, and the complete text is given. After much consideration, I decided to use this method rather than a thematic approach. The major reason is that there is an integrity to the text as it has been accepted for many centuries, and I found it a useful discipline to have to wrestle with each verse, even difficult ones which are likely to be less accounted for in a commentary focusing on specific topics. It will become obvious to the reader which verses have not yielded anything to me and which have been left unremarked. My advice to the reader is to read a particular section of the Gospel text and to meditate on it for a while before reading my comments on it. It is also helpful to have any one of the many standard commentaries on the Gospel, some of which are listed in the Bibliography, to refer to, both for gaining the sort of information and interpretation which have not been of interest to me here, and by way of contrast. The reader is also urged to make liberal use of the index where the references to the remarks scattered throughout the book on specific themes, such as virgin birth, baptism, witness, disciple, belief, sin, I AM, and the like, are gathered together with reference to the appropriate section of the Gospel and my comments.

———————

Among the distinctive features of the Gospel According to St John are two which may be remarked upon here. Much more than the other gospels, this one has a special propensity for highlighting contrasts: between light and darkness, between one who is from Above and one who is from below, between God and the world, between good and evil, between spirit and flesh, and the like. Secondly, the author seems to be self-consciously setting out a parallel in many places between the Old Testament and the New Testament. For example, there are similar scale and style in the opening lines of the Book of Genesis and the present Gospel, and a complete parallel between the sacrifice of Jesus Christ as the Lamb of God and the lamb sacrificed by the Israelites at the Passover feast; as the latter has to do with physical freedom from bondage, the former with spiritual freedom from sin.

In general, John is much less concerned with the actual historical events in the life of Jesus Christ and more with his spiritual teachings. There is no mention at all about the birth of Jesus or his childhood, nor of his father Joseph. Although his mother is mentioned in the Gospel, she is never identified as Mary. The author is not particularly interested in such biographical or historical details. The first reference to Jesus Christ on the earth is the sighting of him by John the Baptiser, who recognises him as the Chosen One of God, and as the Lamb of God, previsioning his sacrifice for the sake of mankind.

There can be no doubt about the symbolic nature of the various events and miracles mentioned in this Gospel. Two of the most important miracles performed by Christ, namely the raising of Lazarus from the dead, and the transforming of water into wine at Cana, are not even mentioned in any of the other gospels. This is especially puzzling in the case of the former miracle: by any ordinary or literal standards the bringing of a dead person to life has to be considered the most stunning miracle of all, and one about which it is difficult to avoid public notice. There will be occasions, in the appropriate places in the discussion of the text, for fuller remarks about these miracles; here it may be briefly noted that these are ways of speaking about transformation of being and the forging of an internal integration so that those who were like the dead found a new and a more abundant life.

That such miracles may have actually and externally taken place, indicating the possession by Jesus Christ of supernatural powers, is entirely possible. Why not? We hardly know all there is to know about nature; and there may be principles and forces available only in heightened states of consciousness, as attested universally in all cultures. However, what interests me here is the greatest miracle of all: transformation of being. Rather than the external transformation of water into wine, what I find vastly more engaging is the fact that by the action of Christ Saul could be internally transformed into Paul.

Soon after the descent of the Holy Spirit on his head, seen spiritually by John the Baptiser, Jesus Christ begins to teach. It is the teaching that engages John; and in this Gospel one finds mainly long discourses, and only a few short sayings or parables. The teaching of Jesus Christ exists for exactly the same purpose as do all other authentic teachings: to show mankind a way of transformation of being so that one may live not self-centred, as one does, but God-centred. The true teaching does not originate from this person or that, but only from God; and he alone who is one with Him can reveal it. 'The teaching that I give is not my own; it is the teaching of Him who sent me' (John 7:16).

According to the *Shatapatha Brahmana* (I,7,2,1–5), when a man is born, simultaneously with him are born obligations to the Gods, to the sages, to the ancestors, and to the community of fellow men. Out of these, the obligation to the sages is met by studying the Veda (literally, 'sacred knowledge'); this is how we repay our debt to them. Now we are living at a special moment in world history: for the first time it seems to be possible for us to be free from our cultural isolation, and to become heirs to the wisdom and truth as much of the Christ as of Lao Tze, of Krishna or of the Buddha, if we would. In the global village that we live in, as we have access to the words and teachings of more sages, our obligations are also increased. I hope to meet a part of my obligation to the Christian sages by studying the Gospel According to St John, which represents the Christian Veda *par excellence*.

However, in paying our debts to the sages and the saints, we must not forget a yet higher obligation: that to the Vastness beyond. It is This that the sages behold and to which they themselves are beholden; they show us that the Kingdom is neither in this place nor in that, but in each individual soul that is centred in the present moment on the only One who is. As Christ said, 'Believe me, woman, an hour is coming when you will worship the Father neither on this mountain, nor in Jerusalem. An hour is coming, and is already here, when those who are real worshippers will worship the Father in Spirit and in truth. Indeed it is just such worshippers the Father seeks. God is Spirit and those who worship Him must worship in Spirit and in truth' (John 4:21,23–24).

CHAPTER

— 1 —

Intelligence Beyond Time

> In the Beginning was the Word, and the Word was with God,
> and the Word was God. He was present to God in the Begin-
> ning. Through him all things came into being, and apart from
> him nothing came to be. What came to be in him was Life;
> and Life was the Light of mankind. And the Light shines on
> in Darkness, and the Darkness has not overcome it (1:1–5).

The great Prologue (1:1–18) is an independent hymn, with a
formal poetic structure, and was almost certainly adapted later
as an overture to the Gospel According to St John. This hymn
gives a cosmological and mystical dimension to this Gospel, setting it apart from the others.

Right away, we are faced with a very great difficulty: how to
speak about timeless realities in the language of time. When
we hear 'In the Beginning . . .' we are likely to think in the
dimension of time alone, extended into the past along the linear
axis of time. However, all mystical and mythological literature
understands a different dimension of consciousness, in which
one has a perspective of eternity, which is not in opposition to
time but independent of it. This eternal vision does not speak
of reality in the past or in the future, but in its suchness in the
present *now*, when alone the eternal manifests itself in time. The
True Word not only *was*, in the past, It *is* at the present moment.
Whenever the Word is present to God, It is with God, and *is*
God. Eternal is the Word.

What is translated as 'Word' is *logos* in the original Greek.
Among other things, *logos* means intelligence, wisdom, God,
spirit, fire and order. In the present hymn, it clearly signifies the
Intelligence which is beyond time, which was present before

anything was made in the entire creation, and is present now and shall be evermore, for nothing whatever of time alone, of darkness, can overcome It. As Krishna says in the *Bhagavad Gita* (2:17), 'Yes, that is indestructible by which this universe was spun. That eternal being is not destroyed by anyone.'

Everything that has come into existence has done so through this eternal Intelligence, without which nothing could be created. The whole cosmos is the handiwork of God, who as the *Bhagavad Gita* (13:15–17) puts it, is 'external, yet inside creatures, immobile and yet moving, too subtle to be explained, distant yet near . . . the goal of wisdom . . . the very light of lights . . . seated in everyone's heart.' All those who participate in this Intelligence beyond time, find Eternal Life which is the true Illumination of anyone's heart.

There is hardly a question of gender in the realm of this Eternal Intelligence. Neither male nor female, this Intelligence is best referred to as 'It', as long as one remembers, as with the Hindu notion of *Brahman*, or the Chinese notion of *Tao*, that we are not talking of anything which is sub-gender and which has not yet developed to the degree which qualifies for the differentiation of the sexes. On the contrary, we are in the realm of the essential wholeness which is super-gender and has not yet limited itself to one or the other sex.

In a certain sense, there is a constant struggle in the soul of every creature between the tendencies of light and those of darkness, between that which comes from Above and that which pulls one down. In the midst of this struggle, each one can be assured by the scripture that the eternal Light continues to shine, summoning us to be rightly ordered and to dwell in the wisdom of the True Word.

> There was a man named John, sent from God; he came as a witness to testify to the Light, so that through him all men might believe. He was not himself the Light; he came to bear witness to the Light. The Light was in being, Light absolute, enlightening every man born into the world (1:6–9).

These verses do not originally belong to the Prologue; they are more prosaic than the other verses and their content is intrusive and out of place, more like a parenthetical addition by an editor of the hymn. Still, there are two very important notions introduced here, of extreme significance from the perspective of the later Gospel. These are the notions of being a witness and of believing. We will need to return to these on several occasions later; here only a few remarks will be made concerning them.

According to the present gospel, John the Baptiser was the first witness of the special status of Jesus Christ. He was the one who saw the Spirit descend like a dove on Jesus Christ, and recognised him to be God's Chosen One; that is to say, he was the first person to realise and to testify that Jesus is the Christ. In other gospels, that first realisation, although perhaps not to the same full degree, is vouchsafed to Mary or to the shepherds or to the magi; but here only to John the Baptiser who was sent from God. This divine messenger was also responsible for baptising Jesus, that is for marking through a significant rite his ascent to another level of truth – perhaps the highest level possible for any human being, the level of being the 'Chosen One of God', or, as the Christian tradition has held, being the 'Son of God' or, as Jesus Christ himself said, being 'one with the Father'.

There cannot be any question about the very high level of spiritual development of John the Baptiser, even though the Gospels do not say very much about him after his fulfilment of these crucial functions in the life of Jesus Christ. What is also important is to underscore the function of a midwife that is performed by a witness who enables the realisation in actuality of something which is potentially there to be born.

To *believe*, which is connected with the English word *beloved*, in John's Gospel is not far in meaning from *to recognise* and *to see*. In fact, understanding and believing are practically interchangeable in this gospel.

All Who Receive the Word are Begotten by God

The Word was in the world, and through him the world was made, yet the world did not know who he was. To his own he came, yet his own did not accept him. But to all who did receive him, to those who have yielded him their allegiance, he gave the right to become children of God, begotten not by blood, nor by carnal desire, nor by man's willing, but by God (1:10–13).

15

We have a remarkable statement here, suggesting that the Word has always been in the world. This should not be at all surprising, for the Word is with God, and is God, and thus is wherever God is, that is everywhere – including the world. However, the Word remains distinct from the world which does not know him and does not receive him; thus the world, in general, is cut off from God's grace even though it has been made by Him. However, it is possible to relate, in various degrees, with the wisdom and love of God, and not be driven wholly by the blind necessity attaching to matter, including the psychic matter of the soul.

Only a few human beings make the requisite effort, and have the necessary subtlety, purity, wisdom and grace, to receive the Word. John's Gospel, like the other gospels, is thoroughly permeated with the notion of a hierarchy of human beings, according to their openness and receptivity to the Word and their actual impregnation by the Spirit so that the Word is embodied in them. Anyone who accepts the Logos in the core of his heart undergoes a radical change of being, a new birth. Whatever his human patrimony, the new being in him has been begotten by God, and is a child of God. This, after all, is the only real purpose of all the incarnations and descents (avatars) of God: to help us all, all those who yearn for it and are called, to give birth in our soul to a child of God.

This birth is, of course, a virgin birth that is to say a spiritual birth and not that of the flesh. So it was with Mary (Luke 1:28–38;46–47). 'Rejoice, O highly favoured daughter!' said the angel Gabriel. 'The Lord is with you. Blessed are you among women.' Like all those who genuinely hear words from Above, Mary was surprised and troubled. 'Do not fear, Mary. You have found favour with God. You shall conceive and bear a son and give him the name Jesus. Great will be his dignity and he will be called Son of the Most High'. 'How can this be since I do not know man?' 'The Holy Spirit will come upon you and the power of the Most High will overshadow you; and for that reason the holy child to be born will be called "Son of God".' Mary's acceptance is total: 'Here am I. I am the servant of the Lord. Let it be done to me as you say.' In her obedience is her joy: 'My being proclaims the greatness of the Lord, my spirit finds joy in God my saviour.'

The scripture proclaims constantly the need to hear subtly, and to guard against a lowering of level by a literal-mindedness which is always an indication of a shallow mind. The virgin birth has no more to do with the physical virginity than being born again has to do with a physical re-entering into the womb. But the mind that understands at that level of physicality alone is always there. Each one of us has our Nicodemus, demanding to know at his own level: 'How can a man be born again once he is old? Can he return to his mother's womb and be born over again?' (John 3:4).

It is hard to see how a literal, sex-related, impregnation of Mary by the Holy Spirit can possibly be intended by the Gospel writer. The masculine association with the Holy Spirit in English is derived from the corresponding Latin, *Spiritus Sanctus*. This in its turn is the translation of the Greek word *Pneuma*, which is neuter. Although the Gospels are written in Greek, in the circles of Jesus and his disciples the language of ordinary usage was Aramaic, whereas Hebrew was used for sacred purposes. The two words from Hebrew which are both translated into Greek as *Pneuma* are *rhuh* and *shekinah*. However, both of these words in Hebrew are feminine. There is a passage in the Gospel of Philip (II,3) which is pertinent to this: 'Mary conceived by the Holy Spirit.' They are in error. They do not know what they are saying. When did a woman ever conceive by a woman? Mary is the virgin whom no power defiled . . . And the Lord would not have said, 'My Father who is in heaven' (Matthew 16:17) unless he had had another father, but he would have said simply 'My Father'.

'Give ear and try to understand,' said Jesus to the crowd (Matthew 15:10).

Eternity in Love with Time

The Word became flesh and dwelt in us, and we have seen his glory, such glory as befits the Father's only Son, full of grace and truth (1:14).

Here we encounter the central core of spirituality, the very heart of the practice: the Incarnation. Precisely because of its profundity, it is a mystery, highly cherished wherever the word mystery has not been denuded of its spiritual power. We have become habituated to the notion of mystery as in a murder mystery or a detective novel, in which the solution is found either when we accidentally stumble upon a missing clue or when we cleverly deduce it from other information. But, as far as spiritual mysteries are concerned, no amount of data or clues or information or cleverness at reasoning can lead us in solving the mystery. Spiritual mysteries always remain mysteries; they cannot be solved, simply because their mysteriousness is not a result of any missing data; it arises from their fullness which cannot be wholly comprehended by our ordinary mind. On the other hand, if we let such a mystery play its proper role, and by submitting to it in contemplation we allow it to work in us, we can ourselves be raised to the level of a higher mind, and higher still, without end. At that vantage point, the mystery is not solved, but the knots of the mind are resolved. And the mystery has been instrumental in this movement as a *koan* can be in the practice of Zen. A genuine mystery carries with it the living water for a true baptism, an initiation to another level of being, a new birth.

> Then came, at a predetermined moment, a moment in time and of time,
> A moment not out of time, but in time, in what we call history: transacting, bisecting the world of time, a moment in time but not like a moment of time,
> A moment in time but time was made through that moment: for without the meaning there is no time, and that moment of time gave the meaning.
>
> (T. S. Eliot: *Choruses from the Rock*, 1934; VII)

Here then is the point of intersection between eternity and time, an extraordinary manifestation of the Spirit in flesh, God himself incarnate in human form – for the explicit purpose of leading human beings to divinity. And he dwelt in us (literally, 'he pitched his tent in us'), participating in us, in the tabernacle of our own body. This incarnation in the human being shows the commonality of the Word with us in form if not wholly in substance. Closer to God than ourselves, he is like our older brother, our common Father's first-born Son. And the fact of human incarnation must be taken seriously: one must not ignore either the link with eternity or with time; both Spirit and flesh must be honoured. 'Flesh' here means the whole man, including the physical body, emotions and mind. Thus Jesus Christ is both God and man. And furthermore, we within ourselves must not ignore the possibility of this dual paternity: born of the will of man as we are, in order to be truly human we must also be begotten by God. As one of the Vedas puts it, at the end of his journey a man becomes the son of two mothers. That is why He sent His own Son, full of grace and truth, for him to dwell not only *among* us, as the usual translations have it, but *in* us, as it literally says in the original Greek, divinising all those who let the Logos abide in them: 'While he was speaking thus a woman from the crowd called out "Blest is the womb that bore you and the breasts that nursed you!" "Rather," Jesus replied, "blest are they who hear the Word of God and keep it"' (Luke 11:27–28).

> John testified to him by proclaiming: 'This is he of whom I said, "The one who comes after me ranks ahead of me, for he was before me"' (1:15).

This verse, more or less a paraphrase of verse 30, belongs to the same group as verses 6–9 above; it interrupts the flow of the hymn, and has probably been added by a later editor. However, attention may be drawn to the quality of insight into the level of Jesus Christ that John the Baptiser shows, while displaying a remarkable self-awareness and impartiality.

> Out of his fullness we have all received grace upon grace; for while the Law was given through Moses, grace and truth came through Jesus Christ. No one has ever seen God; but the only one, himself God, the nearest to the Father's heart, has made him known (1:16–18).

A distinction is made here between what we obtain lawfully, as a just reward for what we have undertaken and carried out, and something which overflows towards us freely from its own fullness. The first one is the domain of the law and tradition, personified by the great prophet Moses to whom the Torah was given by God on Mount Sinai. That is the domain of law (*dharma*) and justice, with the consequent reward and punishment. Every action (*karma*) here is basically controlled by either desire or fear – which, furthermore, are merely two sides of the same coin – and will have its results, good or bad, in time, either in this life or in the life to come. At its own level, the law is valid and needs to be given its due. Nevertheless, there is something radically different, and completely other: a realm of freedom from all law, action, desire and fear. That is the kingdom of God. And the possibility of coming to that kingdom, the transformation enabling that state of freedom, is brought by Jesus Christ, who said, 'My kingdom is not of this world' (John 18:36). His domain is that of grace, truth and love, not opposed to action, tradition or justice, but beyond them. Since no one knows the Father but the Son and those to whom he reveals him, he calls without ceasing, 'Come unto me, all you that labour and are heavy laden, and I will give you rest' (Matthew 11:27–28).

This persistent tension between tradition and freedom appears elsewhere as well. It shows up as the tension between the law and love, between obligation and grace, justice and compassion. Krishna advises Arjuna to go beyond the domain of the Vedas which deal with action and their consequences, and not with total freedom. 'Abandoning all concerns of law, come to me alone; I shall liberate you from all evil, do not worry' (*Bhagavad Gita* 18:66). But Krishna is no more against the Vedas than Jesus Christ is against the Torah. Traditions have their place; the great avatars even come to fulfil them. But they are not bound by any tradition; in the very end of the tradition, they reveal its fulfilment. As St Paul says, 'If you are guided by the Spirit, you are not under the law' (Galatians 5:18).

The Witness as the Midwife of the Spirit

The testimony John gave when the Jews of Jerusalem sent a deputation of priests and Levites to ask, 'Who are you?' was the direct statement, 'I am not the Messiah.' They questioned him further, 'Who then? Elijah?' 'I am not Elijah,' he answered. 'Are you the Prophet?' 'No,' he replied (1:19–21).

Finally they said to him: 'Tell us who you are, so that we can give some answer to those who sent us. What do you have to say for yourself?' He said, quoting the prophet

Isaiah, 'I am a voice crying aloud in the wilderness: make straight the way of the Lord!' (1:22–23).

Those whom the Pharisees had sent proceeded to question him further: 'If you are not the Messiah, nor Elijah, nor the Prophet, why do you baptise?' John answered them: 'I baptise with water. There is one among you whom you do not recognise – the one who is to come after me – the strap of whose sandal I am not worthy to unfasten.' This happened in Bethany, across the Jordan, where John was baptising (1:24–28).

The next day, when John caught sight of Jesus coming toward him, he exclaimed: 'Look there is the Lamb of God who takes away the sin of the world! It is he of whom I said: 'After me is to come a man who ranks ahead of me, because he was before me.' I confess I did not recognise him, though the very reason I came baptising with water was that he might be revealed to Israel' (1:29–31).

John gave this testimony also: 'I saw the Spirit descend like a dove from the sky, and it came to rest on him. But I did not recognise him. The one who sent me to baptise with water told me, "When you see the Spirit descend and rest on someone, it is he who is to baptise with the Holy Spirit." Now I have seen for myself and have testified, "This is God's Chosen One"' (1:32–34).

Each one of us is at one time or another confronted with a direct question about our true nature: 'Who am I?' and 'What can I really say for myself?' If we are not hasty in replying and do not take the question lightly, this is the most potent and the most profound question we can face; it cuts radically through any mask that we may wear or which others may impose upon us out of their need or fantasy. John, who is clearly a great teacher – great enough that Jesus Christ himself was baptised by him, and that he could have been taken for the Messiah – knows himself very well and impartially. He knows his proper place and function and accepts them without vanity or complaint. He knows that his function is that of integrated discernment, conscience and will in a human being, in preparing for and recognising the arrival of the true master from above the tumultuous wilderness of the conflicting desires and ideas of the multitude.

Speaking in the context of the interior of a human being, a point of view to which we shall return repeatedly for we wish to understand the Gospel spiritually and not simply externally, John the Baptiser has the function played by *buddhi* in the *Bhagavad Gita*. According to the hierarchy of being in the *Bhagavad Gita* (see for example 3:42), above the senses is *manas* (ordinary mind), and above the *manas* is *buddhi* (integrated intelligence). Above the *buddhi* is *Atman* (Self, Spirit). *Buddhi* constitutes the subtlest and the highest part of human individuality which still belongs to *prakriti* (nature) which is the realm of causality and the laws, or in the language of John's Gospel is the domain of this world. This integrated intelligence, *buddhi*, stands between the human mind and the Spirit, between what is below and what is Above, between the individual and the cosmic. This is the only part in the human psyche which can see the Spirit, and recognise its true nature and bear witness to it. The multitude, acting at the level of the fickle senses, or the priests and the scribes, at the level of the ordinary mind, cannot hear the Word or see the Christ.

John the Baptiser was special, right from birth. He was born, like Jesus, by a miraculous intervention of God, of a kinswoman of Mary. Even in the womb he was filled with the Holy Spirit and sensed the presence of the Christ in Mary's womb (Luke 1:13–17,44). That the being of John was almost that of Jesus Christ is clear from the fact that when people saw the miraculous power of Jesus many of them, including King Herod, thought that John the Baptiser had been raised from the dead (Mark 6:14–16). Still, in spite of his manifest ability to see the workings of the Spirit, John remained within the level of the world – individuality, materiality, causality, law, nature – and was not from Above, even though he was also sent by God, as is everyone. He was not at the level of the *Atman*, the Son of God. We have the unequivocal testimony of Jesus Christ himself: 'I assure you, there is no man born of woman greater than John. Yet the least born into the kingdom of God is greater than he' (Luke 7:28). This is also the meaning of the statement that John baptised with water and not with fire or Spirit. The truth, the teaching and the initiation given by John and Jesus Christ belong to two entirely different levels, symbolised in the Gospel by water and Spirit respectively. A person who has had only one birth, that from woman, as long as he is not also begotten by God, can rise from the level of the earth at most to that of water, and not to the level of fire or Spirit.

There is an emphasis in the Gospel on the difficulty of recognising and appreciating the true nature of Jesus Christ. Even John, whose whole mission and teaching seems to be for the purpose of preparing Israel (one possible meaning of which is 'one who sees') to see truly the subtler level of Christ, fails to recognise him. Even when he sees the Spirit descend on him and remain there, John does not appreciate the significance of his own spiritual vision until he is able to be in communication with a still higher energy, God.

The Gospel writer here draws a parallel between Jesus Christ as the Lamb of God and the lamb sacrificed by the Israelites at the Passover feast; the latter has to do with physical freedom from bondage, the former with spiritual freedom from sin. Each one of us is some sort of lamb: we are born as lambs of nature in any case – to be raised, fattened and killed, a hundred million of us each year – but we could also become lambs of God.

The word for 'sin' in the original Greek is *amartia* which literally means 'to miss the mark'. The Son of God has come into the world to show the right path so that those who would follow his way would not miss the mark, and would be able to fulfil their purpose on the earth. If we interpret these verses to mean that our sins have already been taken away by Jesus Christ and that we are required to do nothing to receive his teaching and to live accordingly, we fool ourselves and lull ourselves to the very sleep from which Christ came to wake us up.

The Holy Spirit descended on the head of Jesus initiating him and making him the Chosen One of God. This is when Jesus became the Christ. The difference between John, who was also filled with the Holy Spirit as we have been told elsewhere (Luke 1:15), and Jesus is that the latter was, after this sacred moment, constantly in touch with the Holy Spirit who rested with him, as symbolised by the dove settling and remaining on his head. In other words, Jesus underwent a radical and permanent transformation of being: born of flesh, he was also begotten by God; being so completely filled with the Spirit, he became the Son of God.

It may be remarked here, somewhat parenthetically, that many ancient traditions are in agreement that the higher energies enter into a human being from above himself and through an opening at the top of his head. This opening is called in the classical yoga literature the *Brahman* gate, through which the energies from the Brahman world, the world of the Absolute, enter into an individual organism. This is also the reason why the *sahasrara chakra*, the centre of the subtlest energy in a human being is said to be located a little above the head. The second birth, or the transformation of consciousness, is like an alchemical transmutation of being and is always accompanied by subtle physiological and chemical changes, recognisable externally by trained and sensitive eyes.

Preparation for Withstanding Truth

The next day John was there again with two of his disciples. As he watched Jesus walk by he said, 'Look! There is the Lamb of God!' The two disciples heard what he said, and followed Jesus. When Jesus turned around and noticed them following him, he asked them, 'What are you looking for?' They said to him, 'Rabbi (which means a teacher), where do you dwell?' 'Come and see,' he answered. So they went to see where he dwelt and abode with him that day, for it was about the tenth hour (1:35–39).

One of the two who had followed him after hearing John was Simon Peter's brother Andrew. The first thing he did was to seek out his brother Simon and tell him, 'We have found the Messiah (which means the Christ)!' He brought him to Jesus who looked at him and said, 'You are Simon, son of John; your name shall be Cephas (that is, Peter, the Rock) (1:40–42).

The next day he wanted to set out for Galilee, but first he came upon Philip. 'Follow me,' Jesus said to him. Now Philip was from Bethsaida, the same town as Andrew and Peter. Philip sought out Nathanael and told him, 'We have found the one Moses spoke of in the law, and the Prophets too – Jesus, son of Joseph, from Nazareth.' Nathanael's response to that was, 'Can anything good come from Nazareth?' Philip replied, 'Come, see for yourself' (1:43–46).

When Jesus saw Nathanael coming toward him, he remarked: 'This man is a true Israelite. There is no guile in him.' 'How do you know me?' Nathanael asked him. 'Before

24

Philip called you,' Jesus answered, 'I saw you under the fig tree.' 'Rabbi,' said Nathanael, 'you are the Son of God; you are the king of Israel.' Jesus responded: 'Do you believe just because I told you I saw you under the fig tree? You will see much greater things than that' (1:47–50).

He went on to tell them, 'In truth, in very truth I tell you all, you shall see the sky opened and the angels of God ascending and descending on the Son of Man' (1:51).

Only two of the disciples of John were advanced enough to be told the sacrificial nature of the mission of Jesus Christ, the Lamb of God. And they heard an inner call which summoned them to follow the Word made flesh and to participate in his work. There are repeated references in the Gospel to 'looking', 'seeing', 'witnessing' and other words suggesting direct perception. The two disciples of John immediately recognised in Jesus a great teacher; however, it was only after they stayed with him for a little while that they came to realise that he was the Christ.

It is clear that Jesus Christ became the teacher of a very select band of pupils whom he gathered around himself, perhaps no more than two dozen in all, male and female. He was not really interested in teaching the masses who could not understand him nor follow him. It is true that occasionally he was involved in large public events where there were a lot of people. He may have done so either in order to cast a wider net to see if there were any with suitable preparation or potential whom he should call as disciples, or for showing something specific to his followers. But always it was he himself who was in command of the sacred and initiatic master–disciple relationship. Not everyone who wished to come could be accepted, 'for many are called, but few are chosen' (Matthew 22:14). As he told his disciples towards the end of his life, 'It was not you who chose me, it was I who chose you to go forth and bear fruit' (John 15:16). Also, it was essentially for the sake of these disciples' education and illumination that he worked and suffered. Speaking of his disciples, he said in his last prayer to God, 'For these I pray – not for the world, but for these you have given me for they are really yours' (John 17:9).

Others may be helped by the disciples in turn, but not directly by Jesus Christ himself who baptised with fire and Spirit only those who were ripe for it. As for the others, who could not go beyond baptism with water, we are told in John 4:2, that Jesus Christ himself did not baptise anyone but his disciples did. He is too far above the multitude to reach them directly; his influence can be brought down only through intermediaries, occupying the rungs of the ladder of being in between the multitude and Christ himself, in bearable doses. Truth is something for which we have to be prepared: not only to *understand* it but also to *withstand* it. The sort of truth in question here is not a matter of some proposition or another which one accepts or believes in blindly, but is a matter of seeing directly, experiencing it oneself and living it. Without proper preparation, an exposure to higher truth and the corresponding energies can be dangerous to the body and the psyche which cannot bear it, as has been attested by a great deal of systematic mystical literature, particularly in yoga. This is also true of some of the experiences with consciousness-altering drugs: a person may be given a vision of a truth about the human situation which is ordinarily hidden from him, but which he cannot bear without preparation because he reacts to such truths too personally. In such cases, often involving paranoia, a person is likely to lose his mental balance and get physically ill.

There is a well-known story in India which speaks about the necessity of proper preparation for a vision of spiritual truth. It is said that a very great sage Bhagirth performed severe spiritual austerities for the sake of the suffering humanity. When the higher forces were pleased with him, he was granted his wish: the descent to the earth of the sacred river Ganga which flows in Heaven. However, it was anticipated that the earth could not bear the impact of the mighty river descending from Heaven and would be shattered. In order to protect the earth from disintegration, Shiva – the master of yoga and transformation – undertook to mitigate the force of the descent of Ganga by letting her land on his head, from where she flows down to the earth in seven life-giving streams.

The immediate disciples of Jesus Christ were already sufficiently prepared before being accepted by him, and then further trained by him, to withstand the descent of the Spirit of Truth – bringing the life-giving waters from heaven – not only for their own personal sake but for the sake of the entire parched humanity. The word 'disciple' is intimately related to the word 'discipline', and in this gospel to be a believer is the same thing as to be a disciple. Without this discipline, this yoga of Jesus Christ, the disciples can neither receive nor bear the Spirit of Truth. 'If you love me, you will obey my commands. I will ask the Father and He will send you another guide to be with you always: the Spirit of Truth whom the world cannot accept, since it neither sees it nor recognises it; but you can recognise it because it remains with you and will be within you' (John 14:15–17).

The two disciples of John who followed Jesus Christ were obviously well trained by the Baptiser, who seems to have understood his life's mission as preparing the way for the acceptance of the Word. It is interesting to note that John himself does not become a disciple of the Christ even when he recognises him as the Son of God. John seems to be completely clear about his own capacities and limitations, and about his own specific work and responsibility which he must undertake corresponding to his own inner law (*svadharma*). Everyone's *svadharma* is set in his heart by God as His own path, as Krishna says in the *Bhagavad Gita*: one can come to God following his own deepest calling, and by that alone. As with Jesus Christ, the work John must do corresponds to his innermost being, and therefore to God. It is not done for the sake of his own ego or according to his likes or dislikes. It is God's work, and he is God's own because he is able to listen to His will and obey it; he cannot abandon his own calling and follow another's without betraying himself and God. 'Better to follow one's own *svadharma*, however humble, than to follow another's, though great. By engaging in the work prescribed by one's own inner calling, one does not miss the mark' (*Bhagavad Gita* 18:47).

There is a great deal of importance attached to kinship and friendship in the circles of Jesus Christ. His mother and brothers played important parts throughout his life; it was James, one of his brothers, who was the leader of the Christians in Jerusalem after the Crucifixion; he may have been one of his disciples. Among his disciples were Andrew along with his brother Simon Peter, and James and his brother John, sons of Zebedee. James and John were fishing partners with Simon Peter. Another disciple, Philip, was from the same town as Andrew and Peter and in all likelihood was their friend. Philip, in his turn, was eager to introduce his friend Nathanael to Jesus

Christ. The inner circle around Jesus Christ seems to have been constituted primarily by the family members, friends, and friends of friends. This is not surprising, for one should expect an essential kinship and a unity of purpose among those dedicated to the same cause. And these relationships constituted a sort of spiritual preparation. Still, it was always clear that the really significant relationship was neither biological nor social, but a sacred one in the service of God. 'Who are my mother and my brothers? Whoever does the will of God is brother and sister and mother to me' (Mark 3:33,35).

The first thing Andrew did, after he recognised that Jesus was the Christ, was to seek out his brother Simon and tell him. Simon seems to be the only one to recognise not only the greatness of Jesus Christ but also his own terrifying distance from this greatness. According to the account given in Luke 5:1–11, when Simon saw the power of Christ he was so struck by his inadequacy in the face of what was demanded of him that he was seized by terror, and said, 'Depart from me, O Lord, for I am a sinful man.' This very realisation and acknowledgement of his nothingness elicits from Jesus Christ not only reassurance and acceptance as a disciple, but also the bestowal of a new name. The giving of a new name is in many ancient traditions, including the biblical one, an acknowledgement of a changed level of being or a new relationship with God. In these traditions, the name is not merely a label attached superficially to a person; it signifies his essential being and power. When there is a radical transformation of that being and of the corresponding power, a new name is called for: Abram is then called Abraham, Jacob is called Israel, and Saul becomes Paul. Simon, which literally means 'heard', is now named by Christ as Peter, the Rock-man! On the solidity of the knowledge of one's nothingness, a new being of an entirely different quality can be born.

His call to Philip is a good illustration of an immediate two-way recognition between the Master and the pupil. Philip shows no concern for his personal comforts or familiar social and family relationships. He abandons everything to follow the one who is revealed to his insight as beckoning him to the very end and purpose of his tradition. Having been disciplined well by the law and the teachings of the prophets, he is prepared to stake his all for the sake of the Spirit. Neither the Master nor the pupil has any hesitation at all; the sacred relationship is established right away and the teaching is begun. Each one knows the need for the other: without dwelling with Christ and participating in his work, the disciples have no significance to their lives; on the other hand, without disciples to teach and to transform, Jesus Christ has no *function*. Krishna needs Arjuna as much as Arjuna needs Krishna: both of them together engage in divine work. Without God it cannot be done; without man it will not be done.

Nathanael is not quite as freed of the social castes and status; he still has illusions about the trappings of civilisation being necessary for a true teacher; he cannot quite believe that an insignificant town like Nazareth could produce anyone worthwhile. Philip appeals to Nathanael's own direct perception, independent of contemporary conventions, and Christ speaks to his essential innocence and purity, below the surface web of acquired ideas and expectations. From that vantage point, freed of the concerns about social origins, Nathanael sees that he is in the presence of the Son of God. He seems to be somewhat overwhelmed by his discovery and almost overstates his perceptions. Christ admonishes him to keep his balance, and to give right weight to his present insights which are bound to deepen and enlarge with further work. Uncontrolled enthusiasm is as much an impediment to spiritual development as undisciplined thought.

Then Jesus Christ tells his disciples his true mission: with the use of a direct parallel to Jacob's ladder, he declares his purpose to be to show them that he himself, in this very body of a son of man, is a link between Heaven and earth, and to prepare them to be such links themselves within their own beings. He is not taken by any suggestion of becoming externally the king of Israel. Son of God as he is, here he insists upon being also the Son of Man. It is for the integration of these two aspects in the right order that he has incarnated himself, so that the energies from on high, the very forces which are said to be carried by angels, may descend and renew the world, and the energies from below may ascend to play their proper role in the maintenance of the cosmos. According to the Gospel of Mary (BG 8502, I;8), Jesus greeted them all saying 'Peace be with you. Receive my peace to yourself. Beware that no one lead you astray saying, "Lo here!" or "Lo there!" For the Son of Man is within you. Follow after him! Those who seek him will find him.'

According to traditional literature, in actual spiritual practice these energies are experienced as ascending and descending along the central axis of the body, which, by a strict correspondence between the microcosmos and the macrocosmos, is the ground where all levels of energy in the cosmos have their play. Jesus Christ reminds Nathanael that when within himself is established the proper rhythm of the movement of higher energies, he will realise that the sort of occult power of clairvoyance displayed by Christ need not have so overwhelmed him, for it is a mere trifle compared with the vast untapped potentialities of the Son of Man.

The Son of God instructs and invites the son of man to become the Son of Man, to realise his dual paternity and participate with him in the cosmic *yajna* – sacrifice involving an exchange of energies between different levels of reality – for accomplishing divine work. 'With this *yajna* you shall nourish the gods, and let the gods nourish you. By this reciprocal sustenance you shall achieve the highest good' (*Bhagavad Gita* 3:11).

CHAPTER

— 2 —

Transformation: Water into Wine

On the third day there was a wedding at Cana in Galilee, and the mother of Jesus was there. Jesus and his disciples had likewise been invited to the celebration (2:1–2).

At a certain point the wine ran out, and Jesus' mother told him, 'They have no more wine.' Jesus replied, 'Your concern, mother, is not mine. My hour has not yet come.' His mother told those waiting on tables, 'Do whatever he tells you.' As prescribed for Jewish ceremonial washings, there were at hand six stone water jars, each one holding fifteen to twenty-five gallons. 'Fill those jars with water,' Jesus ordered, at which they filled them to the brim. 'Now,' he said, 'draw some out and take it to the master of the feast.' They did as he instructed them. The master of the feast tasted the water made wine, without knowing where it had come from; only the waiters knew since they had drawn the water. Then the master of the feast called the groom over and remarked to him: 'People usually serve the choice wine first; then when the guests have been drinking awhile, a lesser vintage. What you have done is keep the choice wine until now' (2:3–10).

Jesus performed this first of his signs at Cana in Galilee. Thus did he reveal his glory, and his disciples believed in him (2:11).

It is interesting to note that in this gospel the narrative begins from the moment of the descent of the Holy Spirit on the head of Jesus, and not from the moment of his nativity. The writer of this gospel is exclusively interested in the teaching given by the Christ after his spiritual birth, rather than in the events related with his physical birth. A new order of creation is being brought about by the Incarnated Word and it parallels the original creation as narrated in the Book of Genesis. So far, the disciples sense the spiritual greatness of Jesus Christ, but do not understand its implications. Now, on the third day after his own new birth, marked by his annointing by the Spirit, he is ready to teach the disciples through the manifestation of the powers which are a prerogative of the new being in him. It is important to bear in mind, as the gospel hints at the end of this story, that this sign was given specifically for the sake of the disciples and not for the others gathered at the wedding.

This is the occasion when there is a parting of the ways between the concerns of his worldly being and his spiritual being, and from this moment onward everything in the life of Jesus Christ is placed unconditionally at the service of the Spirit. His earthly mother Mary, although not so named anywhere in this gospel, is there, as is his Heavenly Mother, the Holy Spirit (*Shekinah*, the word for Spirit in Hebrew, is feminine). Mary has her concerns and Shekinah has hers – not contradictory or even incompatible, but different. 'Your concern, mother, is not mine.' Mary herself, however, recognises the working of a superior level in Jesus Christ, and submits to it, waiting for his initiative and instructing the servants to obey him.

Jesus Christ is a little uncertain whether the time is yet ripe for the disciples to see an expression of unusual power and to understand its due significance, without either being over-whelmed by it or indulging in excessive doubting and criticism – which are the two natural reactions of the ordinary mind in the face of anything unusual which it does not understand at its own level. But a real master seizes every opportunity for teaching if he senses that the pupils can profit from it. In this case, the disciples did understand, which in the language of this gospel is synonymous with believing, what the proper place of such occult phenomena and powers is. The others, the waiters along with the brothers of Jesus and perhaps Mary herself, did not see the miracle; otherwise, they would have very likely reacted with superficial and sentimental believing in the powers of Jesus Christ. It is even possible that some of the disciples, who directly or indirectly inspired the synoptic gospels, also were not aware of this miracle because no other gospel mentions it.

Given the very common tendency in this gospel to suggest more than one level of meaning, one would be completely justi-fied in looking at the whole story symbolically as well, or even primarily as an allegory, suggesting the transformation of being from the level of water, which was the level of John the Baptiser, to another level, that of the Spirit, initiated for the disciples by Jesus Christ. After this initiation, the disciples would also be begotten by the Spirit, and they *believe in him*, that is to say they understand him and follow him in order to prepare themselves to participate in his work fully.

Temple, Body and Spirit

After this he went down to Capernaum, along with his mother and brothers and his disciples but they stayed there only a few days. As the Jewish Passover was near, Jesus went up to Jerusalem. In the temple precinct he found dealers in oxen, sheep and pigeons, and money-changers seated at their tables. He made a whip of cords and drove sheep and oxen alike out of the temple. He upset the tables of the money-changers scattering their coins. He told those who were selling pigeons: 'Get them out of here! Stop turning my Father's house into a market place!' His disciples recalled the words of Scripture: 'Zeal for thy house consumes me' (2:12–17).

At this the Jews reacted, 'What sign can you show us as authorising you to do these things?' 'Destroy this temple', Jesus replied, 'and in three days I will raise it again.' They retorted, 'This temple took forty-six years to build, and you are going to "raise it again in three days"!' But the temple he was speaking of was his body. Only after Jesus had been raised from the dead did his disciples recall that he had said this, and come to believe the Scripture and the word he had spoken (2:18–22).

While he was in Jerusalem during the Passover festival, many believed in his name, for they could see the signs he was performing. For his part, Jesus would not trust himself to them because he knew them all. He needed no one to give him testimony about human nature; he was well aware of what was in man's heart (2:23–25).

It is clear within the narrative that the cleansing involved is not merely of an external temple. It is constantly emphasised in the Gospels that people around Jesus Christ, including his close disciples, found it very hard to comprehend what he was trying to communicate. This is not surprising, for the level of Christ is so much higher than the others. Also, again and again it is stressed that the multitude is untrustworthy and can be easily swayed this way or that by a show of power of one kind or another. Clearly, Jesus Christ is not easily taken in by their display of allegiance to him; he knows human beings too well for that. He works and waits patiently for the quiet and slow ripening of the disciples, until they are radically transformed in their being, which some of his close disciples finally are when the Spirit of Truth enters into them after the death of Jesus. Until then they are not prepared enough to understand him; then they saw that neither the Scripture nor Jesus Christ had spoken about the temple in the ordinary sense. A teacher takes what is around and is usual and infuses it with extraordinary meaning with intimations of subtler realities hidden from the crowd who have ears but do not hear.

There are at least three levels of increasing subtlety in the meaning of the 'temple'. The first one is the external temple in Jerusalem, built out of stone and wood, serving as the place of gathering and worship for the people. This is all that the multitude understands, as is shown by the subsequent questioning. There are the animals to be sacrificed and bargains to be struck – with fellow men and with God. It is the sphere of gaining and losing, of desire and fear, of reward and punishment; in a nutshell, this is the realm of the world. And there are long-standing practices and conventions of the temple in the world which cannot be easily changed. So, what authority has Jesus Christ to bring about this drastic break with tradition? He, of course, does not really speak their language even though outwardly he seems to, for his concerns are quite other. He would say later, in another context of a large gap in the levels of understanding, 'My kingdom is not of this world!' (John 18:36) Certainly the temple precincts always need to be cleaned and cleansed, and Jesus and his disciples may have done their share, but the baptism that Christ was about had its concern with another realm.

Then there is the body as the temple of the Spirit. For any action to be undertaken in the world, even the Word has to acquire a body, including the mind. The psychosomatic organism is the potential instrument through which the Spirit may act. But for the right order to be established, so that the body-mind may obey the Spirit, one's attachment to the lower world needs to be sacrificed for the sake of the higher; that is what can make it sacred. (Sacrifice is derived from the Latin *sacre* + *facere* which means literally "to make sacred".) That is why the oxen, sheep and pigeons were sacrificed, as a vicarious substitute for the interior sacrifice. But the Lamb of God is not interested in the sacrifice of external lambs, but of oneself. It is the cleansing of a disciple's own body and psyche that engages him, so that each one of them may become a fit vessel for the Spirit.

Every action of Jesus Christ is a part of the teaching to the disciples. Here the concern is with the interiorisation of external animal sacrifice practised in the temple. In another tradition, we find the oldest verses of the most ancient Upanishad, the *Brihadaranyaka* Upanishad (I. 1:1–2), already identifying the sacrificial animal, in this case a horse, with the world, and then with the worldliness within oneself; and 'he desired, let this body of mine be fit for sacrifice and let me have a self through this' (BU I. 2:7). The same is true in this gospel: the sacrificial lamb is the hold that the world has on oneself; freedom from that is the true sacrifice. Only when one is liberated from the worldly self can one acquire a truer self. It is the worldly self which is the merchant trying to make a bargain with God; it will even agree to do the will of God if it is profitable in this world or the next. Even some of the disciples of Jesus Christ were concerned with rewards in Heaven and the special places they might occupy there. As long as this bargaining goes on inside a person, he is not truly in love with God, and cannot serve Him unselfishly.

The whole situation reminded the disciples of some words in Psalm 69, namely 'Zeal for thy house consumes me'. It is worth recalling a larger portion from this long psalm:

> Save me, O God;
>> for the waters have risen up to my neck.
> I sink in muddy depths and have no foothold;
> I am swept into deep water, and the flood carries me away.
> I am wearied with crying out, my throat is sore,
>> my eyes grow dim as I wait for God to help me. . . .
> For in thy service I have suffered reproach;
>> I dare not show my face for shame. . . .
> I have become a stranger to my brothers,

an alien to my own mother's sons;
Zeal for thy temple consumes me;
   Those who reproach thee reproach me.
I have broken my spirit with fasting,
   only to lay myself open to many reproaches.
I have made sackcloth my clothing
   and have become a byword among them. . . .
But by thy saving power, O God, lift me high
   above my pain and distress,
   then I will praise God's name in song
   and glorify him with thanksgiving;
that will please the Lord more than the offering of oxen,
   or bullocks with horn and cloven hoof.
See and rejoice, you humble folk,
   take heart, you seekers after God;
For the Lord listens to the poor
   and does not despise those bound to his service.
                 (Psalm 69: 1–3, 7–11, 29–33)

Here we get a glimpse, aided by the disciples' associations, of the internal struggle which goes on between the natural self and the spiritual self in the same person, and of the utter desolation experienced by a seeker of God in the dark night of his soul. The disciples are taught and shown the many austerities which they must undertake and the ignominy which they must suffer in their attempts to purge their body-mind of all impurity so that they could serve God without holding back and without bargaining with Him. An aspirant is almost annihilated in the depths of his despair and fears fatal drowning in his sorrow until he thoroughly humbles himself and totally surrenders to God. When the natural self is in complete obedience to the spiritual self, one is rightly ordered; then one knows that after the destruction of the bodily temple, the real self, the very person, will rise again in eternal life.

But what rises after death is not the physical body; we must therefore seek yet subtler meaning of the temple. St Paul says,

Perhaps someone will say, 'How are the dead to be raised up? What kind of body will they have?' A nonsensical question! The seed you sow does not germinate unless it dies. When you sow, you do not sow the full-blown plant, but a kernel of wheat or some other grain. God gives body to it as he pleases – to each seed its own fruition. Not all bodily nature is the same. Men have one kind of body, animals another. Birds are of their kind, fish are of theirs. There are heavenly bodies, and there are earthly bodies. The splendour of the heavenly bodies is one thing, that of the earthly another. The sun has a splendour of its own, so has the moon, and the stars have theirs. Even among the stars, one differs from another in brightness. So it is with the resurrection of the dead. What is sown in the earth is subject to decay, what rises is incorruptible. What is sown is ignoble, what rises is glorious. Weakness is sown, strength rises up. A natural body is put down and a spiritual body comes up. If there is a natural body, be sure there is also a spiritual body. (1 Corinthians 15:35–44).

The subtler temple, the 'self' of the Upanishad quoted above, will rise from within the bodily temple, and in this true individuality God can reside and say I AM.

CHAPTER

— 3 —

New Birth

A certain Pharisee named Nicodemus, a member of the Jewish
Council, came to him at night. 'Rabbi,' he said, 'we know you
are a teacher come from God, for no man can perform signs
and wonders such as you perform unless God is with him.'
Jesus answered: 'In truth, in very truth I tell you, no one can
see the kingdom of God unless he is begotten from Above'
(3:1–3).

'How can a man be born again once he is old?' asked
Nicodemus. 'Can he return to his mother's womb and be born
over again?' Jesus replied: 'In truth, in very truth I tell you, no
one can enter the kingdom of God without being begotten of
water and Spirit. Flesh begets flesh, Spirit begets spirit. Do not
be surprised that I tell you that you must all be begotten from
Above. The wind blows where it will. You hear the sound it
makes but you do not know where it comes from, or where it
goes. So it is with everyone begotten of the Spirit' (3:4–8).

'How can such a thing happen?' asked Nicodemus. Jesus
responded, 'You are a famous teacher of Israel, yet you are
ignorant of such things. In very truth I tell you, we speak of
what we know, and testify to what we have seen, but you do
not accept our testimony. If you do not believe when I tell
you about earthly things, how are you to believe when I tell
you about the things of Heaven? And no one has gone up to
Heaven except he who came down from Heaven. Moreover,
as Moses lifted up the serpent in the wilderness, so must the
Son of Man be lifted up in order that all who believe may have
Eternal Life in him. Indeed, God so loved the world that He
gave His only Son, that whoever believes in him may not die
but may have Eternal Life'(3:9–16).

'God did not send the Son into the world to condemn
the world, but that the world might be saved through him.

Whoever believes in him avoids condemnation, but whoever does not believe is already condemned for not believing in the name of God's only Son. The judgement of condemnation is this: the Light came into the world, but men loved darkness rather than Light because their deeds were wicked. Everyone who practises evil hates the Light; he does not come near it for fear his deeds will be exposed. But he who acts in truth comes into the Light, to make clear that his deeds are done in God' (3:17–21).

Nicodemus is a man with position and status in his community, a man of social importance. (Literally, in Greek, *Nicodemus* means *'ruler'*.) He is also someone partially awake to his real need and to his difficulty. He senses that Jesus Christ is a teacher sent from God and he wishes to follow him. But being a member of the governing religious council, the *Sanhedrin*, he is understandably reticent. Such councils throughout human history, no matter what their religious affiliation, have often had concerns which are more worldly than spiritual. The world has to do with reward and punishment, even if these rewards are ecclesiastical or in heaven, whereas the Spirit has to do with freedom, and above all with freedom from the desire for rewards and the fear of punishment. Truth does not come, nor does the teaching leading to salvation, in conventionally acceptable packages. Nicodemus faces his internal and external dilemma cleverly: he comes at night, in the cloak of darkness, avoiding notice by fellow dignitaries but seeking instruction and light wherever he might find them. Unlike the disciples of Christ, he is unable to risk his all for the one thing that he needs and a part of him wants.

What Nicodemus needs, as he is told by Jesus Christ, is not simply to see the signs and wonders, but to see the Kingdom of God. But he cannot do this, nor can anyone else, unless a new being is born in him, begotten both by water and by Spirit, the levels of John the Baptiser and of Jesus Christ, or of *buddhi* and *Atman*, as we have already seen. Nicodemus is puzzled: is the new birth like the familiar physical one, an actual emergence from the womb? Is this still possible for Nicodemus or is he too old for this journey into an unknown land? He is told, as are we, that the new birth is like the old but also different. It is like the old in that it is a definite birth in which a new being is born with its own, albeit subtle, body. But the new being is born from a different parentage and in a different manner: it is not by carnal intercourse nor from the physical womb. The conception takes place by receiving the seed of the Spirit in the womb of the heart; and the birth is an inner, spiritual, virgin birth.

There are two parts to a grown-up human being: one part generated by flesh and the other generated by Spirit. The first part is easy to see, the other is subtler and harder to see with ordinary fleshly eyes which can hardly even see the wind, not to speak of the Spirit. The Greek word used for both wind and Spirit is *pneuma*, also meaning 'breath', which in many spiritual disciplines, especially in yoga, plays a crucial role in connecting the world of the flesh with the world of the Spirit. As the worldly breath is transformed into the breath of the Spirit, through the yoga of Christ, a lamb of the world can become the Lamb of God.

It is worth drawing attention to the necessity stressed by Jesus Christ of the purification and initiation at the level of water. As has been remarked earlier in the commentary on John 1:19–28, the level of water is that of *buddhi*, the integrated intelligence. Krishna advises Arjuna in the *Bhagavad Gita* (2:49; 10:10), 'to seek refuge in *buddhi*'. 'To them who are constantly integrated worshipping me with love, I give that *buddhi yoga* by which they may draw near to me.' Unless one is integrated within, well within the natural self, one's energies are not unified and one is unable to receive and withstand the descent of the Spirit (*Atman*).

For Nicodemus the question is an existential one: how can this spiritual birth take place in him? Not only a man of social importance, Nicodemus is also a learned being, himself a teacher in the community; still he is told by Jesus Christ that he is not able to understand and follow him, for the level at which Christ is speaking is too far above the one for which Nicodemus has been prepared by his scriptural learning and priestly office. If he does not understand even the relatively simple things, from the point of view of Jesus Christ, how can he be shown subtler realities, those of Heaven? Because he has not been begotten by the Spirit which is in Heaven, he has not acquired the spiritual body which can enter into Heaven. Born a son of man, like Jesus himself, he did not attain the capability, unlike Jesus and later his close associates, to be lifted up into Eternal Life. However,

Nicodemus can continue to play an honourable, religious and social role in the community, and can even be a well-wisher and a helper of Christ although not his disciple. He understood his situation and his limitations, and seems to have gone his way with Christ's blessings, to remain a friend but outside the initiatory circle of Jesus Christ to which, as it can be seen again and again, very few were admitted. Within the citadel of the orthodoxy and social hierarchy, to which none of Christ's close disciples seem to have belonged, Niocodemus later suffered ridicule in defending Jesus Christ's right to be heard before being judged; and helped, along with another secret admirer, to bury Jesus after his crucifixion (John 7:50; 19:39).

Even though God is so far above the world, still out of His love for His creation He sends His apostles to help those who yearn for truth and right order and do not wish to be lost in the wilderness of the world. 'Whenever there is withering of *dharma* (order, righteousness) and an increase of *adharma*, I generate myself on the earth. For the protection of the holy, for the destruction of the evil-doers, for establishing *dharma* I come into being age after age' (*Bhagavad Gita* 4:7–8). The ladder is always descending from Heaven so that those who are able may ascend up to Heaven. Jesus Christ is an apostle of God; in turn he prepares other apostles who teach others, in a continuous chain of being. The Son of God is not here to judge or condemn the world but to help those who seek Light. Not to accept the spiritual light, but to prefer darkness is sadly the natural inclination of the multitude which thus condemns itself. To the degree one can struggle against the downward tendencies of one's own natural self, one can rise in the ladder of spiritual being, and come more and more into the Light. What stands in our way is that we want to do our own will and not the will of God. Thus we remain exiled from God, suffering in our ego-made hell. As the *Theologia Germanica* (Chapter 34) says, 'nothing burneth in hell except self-will.' He who comes into the Light does not work for himself or by himself; his deeds are done in God.

None but the Groom has the Bride and the Fire

After his stay in Jerusalem, Jesus and his disciples went

to Judaea, where he remained with them for some time and baptised. Meanwhile John, who had not yet been thrown into prison, was also baptising, at Aenon near Salim, where there was plenty of water, and people were constantly coming for baptism. Some of John's disciples had fallen into a dispute with Jews about purification; so they came to him, and said, 'Rabbi, the man who was with you across the Jordan – the one about whom you have been testifying – is baptising now and everyone is flocking to him.' John answered, 'No one can lay hold on anything unless it is given him from on high. You yourselves are witnesses to the fact that I said: "I am not the Messiah, but have been sent before him." None but the groom has the bride. The groom's best man waits there listening for him and is overjoyed to hear his voice. That is my joy and it is complete. He must wax while I must wane' (3:22–30).

He who comes from Above is above all others; he who is from the earth belongs to the earth and uses speech of the earth. He who has come from Heaven bears witness to what he has seen and heard, yet no one accepts his witness. To accept his witness is to attest that God speaks the truth; for he whom God sent utters the words of God, so measureless is God's gift of the Spirit. The Father loves the Son and has entrusted him with all authority. He who puts his faith in the Son has hold of eternal life, but he who disobeys the Son shall not see that life; God's wrath rests upon him (3:31–36).

It was now the time for Jesus Christ to consolidate the teaching he had been imparting to his disciples, and he took them away from the big city of Jerusalem to the Judaean wilderness where he initiated them into further understanding. Meanwhile John, with an abundance of purified and integrated intelligence, was preparing more and more disciples and giving them his teaching of *buddhi yoga*, at the level of water, so that some of them would be able to be initiated at the level of the Spirit. He taught in complete harmony with himself, knowing his proper place, purpose and function, at the fountain (the literal meaning of *Aenon*) of peace (which is the literal meaning of Salim), without competition with his own manifestly superior protégé whom he himself had baptised and initiated. John's joy at the wonderful greatness of Jesus Christ was that of a loving father seeing his own son grow up and surpass him and wax strong among men, or that of a teacher whose pupil has outgrown him in understanding. John was wholly clear that in the festival of love none but the groom has the bride. The others are there as helpers, friends, parents and the groom's best man; all are needed for the wedding feast.

God's work is not done by one person alone, however exalted, nor in one exclusive manner. Only small minds are concerned with exclusivity; they cannot be content knowing only that they are on a right path, but they must also convince themselves that all other paths are wrong or inferior! The dispute between the disciples of John and the others may be of such a nature, demanding to know whose baptism is right – that of Jesus Christ or that of John? If the evolutionary character of a transformational teaching is not understood, then each person wishes to be personally taught by the greatest teacher, without wondering whether he is capable of the highest initiation. On the other hand, one may also see here a question posed to John by his own disciples about their readiness yet to be initiated by Jesus Christ. He, of course, blesses their graduation, as it were, and the consequent separation from himself reminding them what he has consistently said about the extraordinary nature of Jesus Christ and his spiritual kinship with God. John must accomplish what he came to do, just as Jesus must do his part in the sacred work.

In this gospel in particular there is a sharp contrast between Heaven and earth, and between the one who comes from Above and the one who comes from below. These are two radically different levels, and everything about them is different – words, initiations, qualities and characteristics. Within each one of these realms there are further levels. John the Baptiser is the greatest teacher, higher than anyone born of woman, yet he remains in the domain of causality, here below. In the spiritual realm of freedom also there are levels: no one can come to the Father directly, for He is too high, except the Son. We can be connected with the Father only through the Son, who also does not initiate anybody but the prepared few. In practice, within the lower realm of the world, one must be educated and prepared by an appropriate teacher so that one could later be a disciple of Christ, which is the same as believing in him, and being begotten by the Spirit.

As long as one is not prepared adequately, as long as one does not have a sufficiently integrated intelligence, one cannot even hear the Christ, and the question of believing him or disbelieving him does not even arise. Those who are prepared enough to be able to hear him and see him, then have the question: are they sufficiently trained and internally unified to be able to carry out his instructions? If yes, they believe in him and are his disciples, otherwise they do not believe in him and find themselves disobeying him – not because they want to, but because they cannot help it. This is why they suffer. 'If I had not come to them and spoken to them, they would not be guilty of sin; now, however, their sin cannot be excused' (John 15: 22). Their own conscience is what now tortures them; they know what is the right thing to do but they cannot do it, for their different parts are internally at war with each other. They see the mark, and know how far off the mark (literally the Greek original *amartia*, translated as 'sin') they really are. We hear the anguished recognition by St Paul:

> We know that the law is spiritual, whereas I am weak flesh sold into the slavery of sin. I cannot even understand my own actions. I do not do what I want to do but what I hate. When I act against my own wish, by that very fact I agree that the law is good. This indicates that it is not I who do it but sin that resides in me. I know that no good dwells in me, that is, in my flesh; the desire to do right is there but not the power. What happens is that I do, not the good that I will to do but the evil I do not intend. But if I do what is against my wish, it is not I who do it, but sin that dwells in me. This means that even though I want to do what is right, a law that leads to wrongdoing is always ready at hand. My inner self agrees with the law of God, but I see in my body's members another law at war with the law of my mind; this makes me the prisoner of the law of sin in my members. What a wretched man I am! Who can free me from this body under the power of death? All praise to God, through Jesus Christ our Lord! So with my mind I serve the law of God but with my flesh the law of sin (Romans 7:14–25)

44

The rest of us are not even aware of our distance from the true mark, and the struggle between our two natures. We exist in blissful ignorance, not in the joy of grace and Eternal Life. When we begin to wake up, however dimly, to our real situation, we are terrified, and suffer the wrath of God. Whenever we get a glimpse of ourselves in truth, that is, when we look at ourselves from above, we see our inadequacy before God, for 'how can a man be just in God's sight?' (Job 25:4). So much of the mystical literature in the world expresses the agony of those who have come near enough to God to see the face of the Beloved, but have then been separated; they suffer in the dark night of their soul, the ecstasy of union having turned into the desolation of parting. Often the reassurance and comfort flowing from the nearness of God turns into the dread of His judgement when one is separated. It is frequently said, for example in Psalm 111:10, that 'fear of the Lord is the beginning of wisdom.' It may also be said truly that wisdom is the beginning of the fear of the Lord.

One must not take the Son lightly; unless one is prepared to withstand his vision and his fire, one runs the risk of being burned. Jesus said, 'He who is near me is near the fire, and he who is far from me is far from the Kingdom'(Gospel of Thomas II,2:82). The preparation given by the baptism of John is necessary for the right *metanoia* – which literally means a 'radical reorientation', a complete turning around, although it is usually translated as 'repentance'. As John said,

> 'I baptise you in water for the sake of *metanoia*, but the one who comes after me is more powerful than I. I am not even fit to carry his sandals. He it is who will baptise you in the Holy Spirit and fire. His winnowing fan is in his hand. He will clear the threshing floor and gather his grain into the barn, but the chaff he will burn in unquenchable fire' (Matthew 3:11–12).

Unless one is purified and rightly prepared, one steps into the fire at one's peril: 'I came to set the world on fire. How I wish it were already kindled! I have a baptism to undergo; what anguish I feel till it is accomplished' (Luke 12:49–50).

CHAPTER
— 4 —

Beware of the Hollow Men

Now when Jesus learned that the Pharisees heard that he was winning over and baptising more disciples than John (in fact, however, it was not he himself who baptised, but his disciples), he left Judaea and started back for Galilee again (4:1–3).

We are told that Jesus Christ himself was not baptising, that is to say, he himself was not teaching and initiating anyone other than the select band of his own close disciples. One meaning of 'baptism' in the original Greek is immersion in sufferings. Christ's baptism is very demanding, requiring discipline and strength to endure it; it could not be suffered by many. Nevertheless, many people were coming under his influence, either owing to the striking impression created by his miraculous powers, which are naturally associated with any great spiritual master, or by a more direct contact with his disciples. This was causing concern to the keepers of the established church and tradition. John the Baptiser had been trouble enough, insisting on the priority of the integrated intelligence or the higher mind (*buddhi*) over the rational mind of the traditional learning of the priests (at the level of *manas*) or of the multitude, at the level of the senses. Still, John belonged to the level just above their own, and they could at least understand what he was saying even though they could not follow him in practice. Jesus Christ, on the other hand, spoke from a still higher level which was completely incomprehensible to most of them.

According to traditional doctrines, a human being is basically a creature of three worlds or levels: the world at the level to which he himself essentially belongs, and the world above and the world below, for these are the only two that he can communicate with and know in some measure. The other levels are either too far below him or too far above, and he can have only some vague sense of them either by a theoretical extrapolation or by faith in the authority of those scriptures or people who can speak with direct knowledge. If a person has neither the requisite being and sensitivity to have a direct contact with the level of the Christ, nor the mental ability to allow a theoretical possibility for that level to exist, nor the faith in the tradition that speaks of such realities, he is not going to make any room for it. Such a one is likely to be indifferent to the Spirit, and to remain a simple and hollow man. However, those who are expected to know of such matters professionally or otherwise, but do not in fact understand, such as the clergy or the teachers who know the words of the Scriptures but not necessarily their substance, are particularly threatened by someone who knows whereof he speaks. Concerned with their own control and power, it is mainly the quantitative consideration that interests them; any hint of a quality higher than themselves makes them uneasy. And they lash back with all the fury and vengence of the hollow men seeking to destroy what they do not understand.

This is also true inwardly, for each one of us has our own hollow man. Unless the mind is properly trained in humility and steadiness with respect to the Spirit, it wants to quantify and reduce the higher level which threatens its supremacy and control. So the mind constantly engages in analysing and speculating or in enthusiastic believing or doubting, wishing to proclaim and sell or to destroy that which comes from Above. The danger is less from the crowds or the senses; they neither understand nor care, and are easily swayed this way or that. Real destructive force is unleashed by those who partially understand, in one dimension of the mind, either emotionally or rationally, as was demonstrated by the constant vehemence of the priestly class against Jesus Christ: 'I know that you are descendants of Abraham; yet you seek to kill me because my word finds no place in you' (John 8:37).

The Inner Spring of Living Water

He had to pass through Samaria, and his journey brought

him to a Samaritan town named Sychar near the plot of
land which Jacob had given to his son Joseph. This was
the site of Jacob's well. Jesus, tired from his journey, sat
down at the well. The hour was about noon. (His disciples
had gone off to the town to buy food.) When a Samaritan
woman came to draw water, Jesus said to her, 'Give me
a drink.' The Samaritan woman said to him, 'You are a
Jew. How can you ask me, a Samaritan and a woman, for
a drink?' (Jews and Samaritans, it should be noted, have
nothing to do with each other.) Jesus replied: 'If only you
recognized God's gift, and who it is that is asking you for
a drink, you would have asked him instead, and he would
have given you living water' (4:4–10).

'Sir,' the woman said, 'you do not have a bucket and this
well is deep. How can you give me "living water"? Are
you a greater man than our ancestor Jacob who gave us
this well and drank from it with his sons and his flocks?'
Jesus replied: 'Everyone who drinks this water will be
thirsty again. But whoever drinks the water I give him
will never be thirsty. The water that I shall give him will
be an inner spring always welling up for Eternal Life.'
The woman said to him, 'Give me this water, sir, so that
I shall not grow thirsty and have to keep coming here to
draw water' (4:11–16).

The Samaritan woman was a seeker after God. She returned
periodically to draw spiritual sustenance and to be renewed
at Jacob's well on a sacred mountain. In ancient lands even
today, for example in India, near naturally inviting features
such as wells or ponds or grottoes, outside a village but not
too far, little shrines arise and holy men begin to live near the
place. They engage in their own meditations and prayers and
teach those who come to them seeking guidance. The village
folk often bring some food as an offering to sustain those who
have dedicated their life to God; and an occasional one among
the villagers is himself called by the Spirit and begins to live
with those whose concerns are no longer wholly worldly. Some
such holy person, likely in the tradition and spiritual lineage
of Jacob, had taught near the well to which the people from
the neighbouring village would have come to fetch water. This
teacher must have been fortunate in having a student like the

Samaritan woman who seems to have had a simple and essential quality of being and a deep spiritual gift.

The two parenthetical remarks, namely that the Jews and the Samaritans had nothing to do with each other, and that the disciples of Jesus had gone to the town to buy food, essentially contradict each other. In any case, whatever the historical relevance of these remarks, it is clear throughout the Gospel that neither Jesus Christ himself, nor any of his disciples, is particularly concerned with what racial, social or religious group anyone belongs to. In the deepest sense, his path is not sectarian. He is clearly interested in engaging the woman in an exchange and asks her to tell him about the teaching she is following, in the metaphor of asking for a drink of the water she has drawn.

There is a progressive revelation by Jesus Christ to the Samaritan woman, corresponding to her ability to recognise and to receive. First of all, she sees only the outermost layer and takes him to be a Jew and a male, who should not, according to the acceptable social conventions, have anything to do with her, a Samaritan and a woman. Jesus Christ invites her to see a little more deeply so that she could recognise his true nature, and therefore be able to receive the truer teaching, the living water, leading to Eternal Life. She is dimly aware and becomes immediately more reverent, but wonders how could this man have access to a truth greater than that of Jacob, the great patriarch who had wrestled with an angel of the Lord:

In the course of that night . . . Jacob was left there alone. Then some man wrestled with him until the break of dawn. When the man saw that he could not prevail over him, he struck Jacob's hip at its socket, so that the hip socket was wrenched as they wrestled. The man then said, 'Let me go, for it is day break.' But Jacob said, 'I will not let you go until you bless me.' 'What is your name?' the man asked. He answered, 'Jacob.' Then the man said, 'You shall no longer be spoken of as Jacob, but as Israel, because you have contended with the divine and human beings and have prevailed.' Jacob then asked him, 'Do tell me your name, please.' He answered, 'Why should you want to know my name?' With that he bade him farewell. Jacob named the place Peniel, 'Because I have seen God face to face,'he said, 'yet my life has been spared' (Genesis 32:23–31).

Jacob's wrestling with the mysterious higher force, as much within himself as outside, resulted in a permanent transformation of his being, underscored by the granting of a new name to him; furthermore, a name by which the whole of his tribe was destined to call itself and its land. Jacob was no small being, he had seen God face to face, and the seeker from Samaria rightly wondered if the person present before her could possibly be greater than the source teacher of the teaching she had been following. The teaching of Jesus Christ is not merely scriptural nor traditional in the usual sense of that word; it is original in that it deals with the very source and origin of Truth, the One, which is deep within oneself, as is Krishna who said, 'I am the eternal kernel of all beings' (*Bhagavad Gita* 7:10). If one understands it, one would discover this internal spring of Truth which naturally leads to Eternal Life. If one were situated at the very source of this life-giving water, one would not be thirsty again, nor would one need to keep searching here and there, understanding a little and forgetting again, having to draw the water of truth repeatedly. The woman was eager for the inner spring of life-giving water, which is Spirit brought by the baptism initiated by Christ, and asks for it without hesitation. But is she ready?

The Need for Inner Unity

Jesus said to her, 'Go home, call your husband, and then come back here.' 'I have no husband,' replied the woman. 'You are right in saying that you have no husband,' said Jesus. 'The fact is that you have had five, and the man you are now living with is not your husband. What you said is true' (4:16–18).

Is the seeker from Samaria ready yet for the highest truth? Does she have the requisite inner unity of being so that she has one master or husband? There is no suggestion of any moralistic judgement in this story; that is not what the mention of one

50

or many husbands is about. The word 'husband' in many languages, including Hebrew and English, also means master or lord. The literal sense of this word in old English was the master of the house. If there is not one single inner master, controlling and unifying all the conflicting desires, thoughts and wills, there cannot be a single purpose and a person's energies are dispersed, and one's house is divided. In the imagery of the *Bhagavad Gita* (2:41, 62–63), the *buddhi* of a dispersed person is many-branched, for only a resolute *buddhi* is single. The woman sees her inner situation clearly, she is aware of the dispersion and lack of steadiness in her attention, and she acknowledges it. This very acknowledgement forges in her, at least temporarily, an inner unity and prepares her to recognise Jesus Christ a little more deeply.

The Worshippers whom the Father Seeks

'Sir,' answered the woman, 'I can see you are a prophet. Our ancestors worshipped on this mountain, but you people claim that Jerusalem is the place where men ought to worship God.' Jesus told her, 'Believe me, woman, an hour is coming when you will worship the Father neither on this mountain nor in Jerusalem. [You people worship what you do not understand, while we understand what we worship; after all, salvation is from the Jews.] Yet an hour is coming, and is already here, when those who are real worshippers will worship the Father in Spirit and truth. Indeed, it is just such worshippers the Father seeks. God is Spirit, and those who worship Him must worship in Spirit and truth' (4:19–24).

She sees that she is in front of a prophet. She is also afraid, like everyone else in a similar situation in one's spiritual journey, to cast aside the security of the familiar surroundings and the ancestral teaching. Prophets always call those who would hear to come to a right alignment along the axis connecting heaven and earth. For the prophets of Judaea, this axis symbolically passed through Jerusalem. She, like the disciples and like Nicodemus, had to struggle with a literal and habitual understanding in order to make room for the inner spiritual

51

truth. Jesus Christ is not concerned with this mountain or that city, or any sectarian considerations (precisely the reason why the bracketed verse above must be regarded as a later addition, unjustifiably attributed to Jesus), but with God who is Spirit, not here or there in some exclusive place, but wherever the heart of a true seeker opens to worship in spirit and truth.

The Secret Name of God

The woman said to him: 'I know that the Messiah (that is Christ) is coming. When he is here, he will tell us everything.' Jesus said, 'I AM, I who am speaking to you now' (4:25–26).

His disciples, returning at this point, were surprised that Jesus was speaking with a woman. But none of them said, 'What do you want of him?' or 'Why are you talking with her?' The woman then left her water jar and went off into the town. She said to the people: 'Come and see someone who told me everything I ever did. Could this be the Messiah?' At that they set out from the town to meet him (4:27–30).

Meanwhile the disciples were urging him, 'Rabbi, eat something.' But he told them: 'I have food to eat of which you do not know.' At this the disciples said to one another, 'Do you suppose that someone has brought him something to eat?' Jesus explained to them, 'Doing the will of him who sent me and bringing his work to completion is my food. Do you not have a saying: "Four months more and it will be harvest!"? Listen to my saying: Open your eyes and see! The fields are already shining for harvest. The reaper collects his wages and gathers a yield for Eternal Life, that sower and reaper may rejoice together. For in this case what the proverb says is true – one man sows, another reaps. I sent you to reap a field in which you had not laboured. Others had laboured: you have come in for the fruits of their toil' (4:31–38).

Many Samaritans from that town believed in him on the strength of the woman's word of testimony: 'He told me everything I ever did.' The result was that, when these Samaritans came to him, they begged him to stay with them awhile. So he stayed there two days, and as result many more were convinced by what he told them himself. As they told the woman, 'We no longer believe because of your story. Now we have heard for ourselves and know that this man is indeed the Saviour of the World' (4:39–42).

Her insight is now deepened further; she is able to know that the Messiah is coming soon, and she is poised for the revelation, waiting attentively. She is ready and ripe, and the Christ reveals his true being to her: I AM!

There will be occasions later to speak about the use of *I AM* by Jesus Christ: suffice to mention here that both in the Old Testament as well as the New, and in particular in the Gospel According to St John, I AM is the divine name. As the Lord God said, in Isaiah 52:6, 'On that day my people shall know my name; that I AM is the one who speaks.' I AM serves essentially as a proper name of God, and he who will speak in His name, must have His authority, and must not use it for the purposes of his own vanity. Otherwise, one defies a commandment of God: 'You shall not take the name of the Lord, your God, in vain. For the Lord will not leave unpunished him who takes His name in vain' (Exodus 20:7). Babylon was destroyed for saying 'I AM, and there is none beside me' (Isaiah 47:8–10).

We must be constantly on guard to make sure that we do not ascribe to Jesus Christ any exclusivist egoistic use of the most sacred and mysterious name of God, I AM. That would be the real blasphemy, the charge of which the multitude of non-believers laid upon him and for which they tried to stone him (John 10:30–39). However, the multitude of believers in subsequent centuries have laid upon him the same blasphemous claim, thinking it to be an honour to him. Only he who has totally emptied himself of all his egoistic concerns and projects, he who is no longer the author of the words he uses, who does nothing by himself, who is completely one with the Father, in the obedience to Whose will he submitted himself to be crucified (Matthew 26:39; John 8:28, 50; 10:30;14:10; Galatians 6:14; Philippians 2:7), and such a one alone, can say with impunity I AM. This is what Jesus Christ did. During his earthly sojourn he showed this special and glorious state of complete identity with God, the state of I AM, for the sake of only a few people, even though others were sometimes incidentally present and not comprehending were overwhelmed by the great manifestation.

Having seen the ripeness of the seeker from Samaria, Jesus Christ displayed to her the state of I AM. She was deeply touched, and the disciples themselves, when they arrived on the scene, were struck by the specialness of the occasion and did not engage in the expected reaction of asking this or that question, for a sacred moment of spiritual exchange is delicate and extremely fragile. Soon a particular phase was over; she had had her fill from the presence of the Chosen One of God, and went running to the town, giving her testimony to his greatness.

The Samaritan woman must have had a standing as an honourable person in her community, and her word was accepted by many. But the many always wish something for free without having to pay for it by any internal discipline or sacrifice. Jesus Christ let himself be prevailed upon, perhaps for the sake of the one true seeker from Samaria whom he would have undoubtedly wanted to watch further, to stay in that town for two days. As has always happened, and happens even now with others, many people in the crowd proclaimed him the Saviour of the World. Equally easily, under other mass influences, many elsewhere declared him to be possessed by the devil and worthy of being stoned. Quite rightly, as was said earlier, in John 2:24–25, Jesus would not trust himself to the crowd for he was well aware what was in man's heart.

Jesus Christ himself seems to have been deeply nourished by the exchange with the seeker from Samaria. The only one thing for which he had come was to do the will of God and to complete His work. That is what sustained him; all other food was secondary, as he told his disciples. He had been immediately aware of the exceptional quality of the Samarian seeker and that she had been well prepared by someone else, and was ripe for the harvesting into Eternal Life. Ordinarily, the teacher has to sow the seeds and to nourish them until reaping, meanwhile waiting patiently during the 'four months until it will be harvest', as the saying went. In this case, he had seen with his inner eye that someone else had already laboured and readied the harvest, and he as the reaper could rejoice together with the sower. She was the first person, and not even a disciple prepared by himself, to be shown the extraordinary state of the I AM as a way to Eternal Life.

Belief of Signs and Wonders

When the two days were over, he set out for Galilee; for Jesus himself declared that a prophet is without honour in his own country. On his arrival in Galilee the Galileans gave him a welcome, because they had seen all that he did at the festival in Jerusalem; they had been at the festival themselves (4:43–45).

Once again he visited Cana-in-Galilee, where he had turned the water into wine. An officer in the royal service was there, whose son was lying ill in Capernaum. When he heard that Jesus had come from Judaea into Galilee, he came to him and begged him to to go down and cure his son, who was at the point of death. Jesus said to him, 'Will none of you ever believe without seeing signs and wonders?' The officer pleaded with him, 'Sir, come down before my boy dies.' Then Jesus said, 'Return home; your son will live.' The man believed what Jesus said and started for home. When he was on his way down his servants met him with the news, 'Your boy is going to live.' So he asked them what time it was when he began to recover. They said, 'Yesterday at one in the afternoon the fever left him.' The father noted that this was the exact time when Jesus had said to him, 'Your son will live,' and he and all his household became believers. This was now the second sign that Jesus performed after coming down from Judaea into Galilee (4:46–54).

There is no reason for us to believe that Jesus Christ was after any sort of worldly adulation or honour. In any case, the sugges-tion that a prophet has no honour in his own country hardly squares with the fact stated immediately after that remark that the Galileans, the folk from his own country, gave him a wel-come. Nevertheless, he was not truly honoured in his own region in the sense that no one there seems to have understood him enough to become his real follower and disciple to whom he could reveal himself in essence. The royal officer may be taken as a typical representative, impressed by the miraculous powers of Jesus Christ and interested in his healing capacities at the level of ordinary body and life only. Neither he, nor anybody else in that region, seems to have understood the real nature and mission of Jesus Christ in whom they believed as in a wonder worker and a magician. That level of understanding or belief is not what the Christ was looking for; that is not where his Father's work could be done and the real nourishment for his own spirit be gathered. Krishna says in the *Bhagavad Gita* (7:23–25), 'These are men of little wisdom, and the good they want has an end. Those who love the powers go to the powers, but those who love me come unto me. The unwise think that I am that form of my lower nature which is seen by mortal eyes; they know not my higher nature, imperishable and supreme. For my glory is not seen by all, I am veiled by my magical power; and in its delusion the world knows me not – the Unborn and Changeless.'

CHAPTER

—— 5 ——

The Struggle between the Self and the Ego

Later on Jesus went up to Jerusalem for one of the Jewish festivals. Now at the sheep gate in Jerusalem there is a pool with five colonnades with the Hebrew name Bethesda. In these colonnades there lay a crowd of sick people, blind, lame and paralysed, waiting for the disturbance of the water; for from time to time an angel came down into the pool and troubled the water. The first to plunge in after this disturbance recovered from whatever disease had afflicted him. Among the sick was a man who had been crippled for thirty-eight years. When Jesus saw him lying there and was aware that he had been ill a long time, he asked him, 'Do you want to be healed?' 'Sir,' he replied, 'I have no one to put me in the pool when the water is troubled, and while I am on the way someone else gets in before me.' Jesus said, 'Rise, pick up your bed and walk.' And immediately the man was cured, picked up his bed and walked (5:1–9).

Here is a man who becomes aware of the terrible spiritual situation he has been in for much of his life: he has been sick with both an inner and an outer paralysis, trying to walk and live only from, and for, his ego. Now, past 38, he finds himself lost in the darkness of the world. He is by the sheep gate with others who are also sick and hope for healing. But among them all he is the only one who seems to have some understanding that the real sheep to be sacrificed to the Deity is oneself. It is one's own ego that needs to be dethroned from the central place it always occupies, so that it could listen and obey the real Self within, which alone participates in the Divine being. Every spiritual tradition recognises and attempts to reconcile a deep-seated duality in human nature. There is the lower self, the separated and all self-important ego, arrogating to itself the total identity of the person, in conflict with the Spirit. As long as a person is under its sway, he is estranged from God, and in sorrow. It is, however, possible for a human being to be radically reorientated and come to his right mind and to be led by the Spirit. Only then an inner reconciliation, a true healing, can take place. Jesus Christ said, 'He who would follow me must leave self behind' (Matthew 16:24).

The man by the healing waters of the pool recognises that he is sick of himself, and that by himself he is unable to do anything. He knows that he needs help, but his ego is too strong for him and he has not been disciplined enough to be able to obey his higher self. Even when the great truth is available nearby, because the waters have been stirred by the angelic energies from Above, he is unable to be healed because he cannot place himself in the right relationship with regard to the Truth. He does not have a developed inner unity with enough strength to plunge into the stirred water; someone else, his own little self, always interferes.

> I came out alone on my way to my tryst. But
> who is this who follows me in the silent dark?
> I move aside to avoid his presence
> but I escape him not.
> He makes the dust rise from the earth with
> his swagger; he adds his loud voice to every
> word that I utter.
> He is my own little self, my lord, he
> knows no shame; but I am ashamed to come to
> thy door in his company.
>
> (Rabindranath Tagore in *Gitanjali*)

Jesus Christ sees this man's plight and takes the initiative without any pleading on the part of the sick man, for always is he occupied in doing his Father's work, the only thing that sustains him. He sees this man's real dilemma: his higher self knows the right way but is too weak; the lower self is much stronger but too self-willed and has no interest in submitting to the higher will of heaven. The Divine messenger, in the house of mercy (which is what Bethesda literally means), has compassion for him and places the weight of his own will on the side of the higher self of the sick man, who is immediately rightly aligned and healed, and is able to walk, not even knowing who it is who helped him.

Action and Rest from Action

That day was a Sabbath. So the Jews said to the man who had been cured, 'It is the Sabbath. You are not allowed to carry your bed on the Sabbath.' He answered, 'The man who cured me said, "Take up your bed and walk."' They asked him, 'Who is the man who told you to take up your bed and walk?' But the cripple who had been cured did not know; for the place was crowded and Jesus had disappeared. A little later Jesus found him in the temple and said to him, 'Now that you are well again, leave your sinful ways, or you may suffer something worse.' The man went away and told the Jews that it was Jesus who had cured him (5:10–15).

It was works of this kind done on the Sabbath that stirred the Jews to persecute Jesus. He defended himself by saying, 'My Father has never yet ceased his work, and I am working too' (5:16–17).

In the story of the paralytic, even at the most external level, the crowds and their leaders forget the miraculous cure they have just witnessed, and are instead occupied with the minutiae of the Sabbath regulations! What we do have here is a reminder that Jesus Christ kept an eye on the progress of those who he intentionally helped. He sought out the cured man, whom he found in the temple, to give him the sound advice to follow a disciplined path, so that he would not be constantly off the true aim and mark of his existence, which is the literal meaning of the Greek word for sin, *amartia*, otherwise he would suffer more and more as the gap between his real wish and his ability widened. His telling the Jews about the fact that Jesus is the one who cured him seems to be an innocent act of reporting, and not any act of betrayal; after all, Jesus is not hiding himself from anybody.

'What is action, and what is actionlessness? About this even the wise are perplexed,' says Krishna in the *Bhagavad Gita* (4:16). Owing to the centrifugal orientation of the energy of Prakriti

(Nature), inside human beings as well as outside, we are constantly drawn into this or that activity, asserting ourselves, initiating ever new causal chains of action, reaction and further action, moving further and further away from our own centre and from the Source of all energy. In physical sleep we renew ourselves but only minimally at the level of the physical body, and in any case unconsciously. In all spiritual traditions it has been recognised that unless one repeatedly renews one's contact with the centre, in meditation, prayer or quiet contemplation, one is depleted and lost. Therefore, we need to place ourselves in the mode of receptivity with respect to the energies from above.

In general, a person in motion cannot maintain contact with the centre and cannot remain internally rightly ordered. That is why it is so much emphasised in the Indian tradition that human beings are constantly in the bondage of reactive actions (karma). Of course, motion is not associated with bodily activities alone. There is a story of the Buddha asking one of his disciples to report what he saw. The disciple reported a *flag* in motion. Asked to look again, he reported the *wind* in motion. Only when asked to look still deeper, the disciple realised that the *mind* was in motion. That is why we find the following in the *Bhàgavad Gita* (3:4–9):

Not by leaving works undone does a person gain freedom from the bondage of karma; nor by renunciation alone does one attain supreme perfection. For not for a moment can a person stand still without any activity, for everyone is helplessly driven to activity by the forces of Nature. Whoso controls his limbs through which he acts but sits thinking of sense-objects deludes himself, and is a false follower of the path. But great is he who with the mind controls the senses, and remaining detached undertakes the yoga of karma through the limbs with which he acts. To work is better than to do no work at all; perform therefore your task in life. Even the life of the body could not be maintained if there were no action at all. This world is bound in the bondage of karma except when the work is done as sacrifice. Work to this end, Arjuna, freed from the bonds of desire.

Since no one can be without some sort of external or internal activity, the practical question is how to act rather than whether to act. Only that action is recommended by Krishna which is done as a sacrifice to God; then it is not only not depleting but also deeply nourishing, a real food for our growth. There can hardly be much question that the real meaning behind keeping the Sabbath day is to make for oneself, as a helpful ritual, time that is for meditation and prayer for the sake of renewing one's contact with the Most High from whom comes all healing. Since most human beings cannot easily surrender the fruits of their actions to God and engage in action as a service to Him, they cannot be outwardly active and still maintain some connection with the centre. The practice of external stillness and quiet is necessary so that one can be internally actively related with the Source of energy. Ideally, at any time one should undertake only those actions which are of service and sacrifice to God, which are not egoistic and which do not contribute to the strength of the centrifugal tendencies inherent in all creation. Since man is destined to labour, he engages in the work of creation for six days, and for at least one day in seven he should do the work of God and for God, thus, as is said in Leviticus 23:32, keeping a sabbath of complete rest and self-mortification. With the passage of time, all teachings degenerate and have to be constantly renewed by great teachers. The same, of course, happened with the teaching dealing with the Sabbath, so much so that Jesus Christ had to bring the reminder that 'The Sabbath was made for the sake of man and not man for the Sabbath' (Mark 2:27).

Of course, he who is freed of himself, and of all his personal projects and concerns, he who is one with God, such as Jesus Christ, does only God's work in every action, and is therefore completely free of the bondage of karma. For such a one, the Sabbath has no particular importance. Although he may observe it to honour the tradition, he is not bound by it, for truly being the master of yoga he goes beyond the law (*torah, dharma*). Such a being does not act out of compulsion, but out of love and compassion for mankind, in order to offer human beings a way of freedom from their own inner slavery to their egos. Such are the bodhisattvas and Krishna; or as Christ reminded his hearers, such is God Himself who works ceaselessly for the maintenance of the cosmic order. Similarly, Krishna says in the *Bhagavad Gita* (3:22,24), 'In the three worlds there is nothing that I need do, nor anything unattained that I need to gain. Yet I work. If I were to cease working, these worlds would perish, confusion would reign everywhere and this would be the destruction of all beings.'

Only He can be Just who Does Nothing by Himself

This made the Jews still more determined to kill him, because he was not only breaking the Sabbath, but, by calling God his own Father, he claimed equality with God (5:18).

To this charge Jesus replied, 'In truth, in very truth I tell you, the Son can do nothing by himself; he does only what he sees the Father doing: what the Father does, the Son does. For the Father loves the Son and shows him all His works, and will show him greater works yet, much to your surprise. As the Father raises the dead and gives them life, so the Son gives life to men, as he determines. And again, the Father does not judge anyone, but has given full jurisdiction to the Son; it is His will that all should pay the same honour to the Son as to the Father. To deny honour to the Son is to deny it to the Father who sent him. In very truth, anyone who gives heed to what I say and puts his trust in Him who sent me has hold of Eternal Life, and does not come up for judgement, but has already passed from death to Life' (5:19–24).

'In truth, in very truth, I tell you, a time is coming, indeed it is already here, when the dead shall hear the voice of the Son of God, and all who hear shall come to Life. For as the Father has the life-giving power in Himself, so has he given it to the Son. And He has turned over to him the power to pass judgement because he is Son of Man. Do not wonder at this, because the time is coming when all who are in the tomb shall hear his voice and come out: those who have lived good lives will resurrect into Life, and those whose lives were evil, will rise to be damned. I can do nothing of my own accord. I judge as I am bidden, and my judgement is just because I follow, not my own will, but the will of Him that sent me' (5:25–30).

On the face of it, it may seem strange that the Jews would wish to kill Jesus because he called God his Father; after all, the Jewish tradition is not without references to God as Father, for example Deuteronomy 32:6; I Chronicles 29:10; Isaiah 63:16, 64:8. However, in all these contexts God is Father in a general way, the progenitor and creator of all beings. What is radically new with Jesus Christ is his sense of an intimate and direct paternity from God. He addressed God with the intimate word *Abba*. This Aramaic word is rightly translated as 'Father', except that it does not convey quite the sense of intimacy in English; it may almost be better to render it as 'Daddy', but for the childish association of that word. It is clear, however, that at least St Paul and one of the gospel writers wished to preserve the special sense of the word *Abba* enough so that they retained the original Aramaic word even when writing in Greek (Romans 8:15; Galatians 4:6; Mark 14:36).

This intimate sonship with God was not reserved by Jesus Christ exclusively for himself, but for every human being who will accept the Logos (John 1:12,13). God gives to every human being the possibility of becoming a part and parcel of Himself, his own very Son, by accepting in the deepest part of himself the Light He sends. The Word became flesh so that every human being may have the possibility of becoming the Son of God. As St Paul put it, 'All who are led by the Spirit of God are sons of God. You did not receive a spirit of slavery leading you back into fear, but a spirit of adoption through which we cry out, 'Abba!' (that is, 'Father'). The Spirit himself gives witness with our spirit that we are children of God. But if we are children, we are heirs as well: heirs of God, heirs with Christ, if only we suffer with him so as to be glorified with him' (Romans 8:14-17).

To be sure, Jesus Christ himself said that the real intent of what Moses and the other prophets in the tradition had taught was in fact an inner and intimate kinship with God; but the official keepers of tradition had clearly lost this real essence. This has also happened in subsequent centuries in official Christianity so that anyone, Jesus Christ himself being the sole exception, who has expressed an intimate oneness with God has been declared a heretic and has been dealt with severely. This is bound to happen when the keepers of the tradition are themselves bereft of such subtle experiences. If they do not have the necessary humility to acknowledge their own limitations they cannot tolerate anyone else who speaks with the authority of direct knowledge. In the present instance, we find that the leaders were unable to comprehend the sort of intimacy with God that Jesus Christ spoke about and therefore wished to kill him, for according to their understanding of their tradition his words were blasphemous.

It is absolutely clear, however, that Jesus Christ is not arrogating to himself any special power or honour, in any egoistic sense. He repeatedly says words to the effect that 'without the Father the Son cannot do anything.' Unless the Son remains in connection with the Father, constantly being renewed by His energy from Above, he can do nothing by himself. 'The teaching that I give is not my own; it is the teaching of him who sent me. Anyone whose teaching is only his own is bent on self-glorification' (John 7:16,17). That is the total meaning of *right order*, namely that one gives only what one receives from above, without any distortion. As the great German mystic Meister Eckhart said, 'What we receive in contemplation, we give out in love.' Because the Son is rightly ordered internally, his judgement is just. The Father, however transcendent, has a part of himself, his very Son, right here in this world, as the Son of Man; who, furthermore, can prepare each one of us, if we follow the way he shows, to receive a part of God, the Spirit of Truth, deep within ourselves. There is no need to wait for any judgement after death or in some other realm; the judge is right here: the Son of God in the Son of Man, the *Atman*, our deepest Self. In the mirror of our own impartial and clear conscience, we shall judge ourselves fit for Eternal Life or for damnation. To deny honour to that kin of God is to deny honour to God, for no one can have any experience of God except through that being who has come into man from God.

The Esoteric Message of the Tradition

'If I testify on my own behalf, that testimony does not hold good. There is another who bears witness for me, and I know that what He says of me is true. You have sent to John, and he has testified to the truth. Not that I rely on human testimony, but I remind you of it for your own salvation. John was a lamp burning brightly, and for a time you were ready to exult in his light. But I rely on a testimony higher than John's. The work that the Father gave me to accomplish, the very work I am doing now, declares that it was He who sent me here. And the Father who has sent me has Himself given testimony on my behalf, although you never heard His voice or saw His form. And His Word you do not have abiding in your hearts because you do not believe the one He sent' (5:31–38).

'You search the scriptures, thinking to find Eternal Life in them. They also point to me, yet you will not come to me in order to possess yourselves of Life. I do not look to men for honour. But then I know you – I know that the love of God finds no place in your hearts. I have come in my Father's name and you reject me. Yet if another comes in no name but his own you will accept him. How can such as you believe, content as you are with praise from one another, and not seeking the glory which is from the One? Do not imagine that I shall be your accuser before the Father; the one to accuse you is Moses on whom you have based your hopes. For if you believed Moses you would believe me, because it was of me that he wrote. But if you do not believe what he wrote, how can you believe what I say?' (5:39–47).

The greatest witness of Christ is the revelation by God within the human heart. But if His word finds no responsive place, as seems to be the case of the people whom Jesus Christ was addressing, then an appeal can be made to the entire tradition, by referring both to the Scriptures as well as the prophets from the ancient Moses to the recent John. Here Jesus Christ discloses the inner, or the esoteric, meaning of the whole tradition. The Scriptures and the prophets, he says, are all pointing to him, that is to the presence of the Word in the flesh, the presence of God within the human being. The Buddha said, 'I declare to you that within the body . . . you can find the world, and the origin of the world, and the end of the world, and the path . . . to all the goals.' Whoever would open up to the light of this eternal presence within himself will have a spiritual birth, begotten by the Spirit, and will become a child of God.

The exoteric interpreters of the Christian tradition have often taken the Christ (Messiah) quite as externally defined and particularised as the exoteric interpreters of the Jewish tradition did. The only difference is in the two sets of external specifications. This is why one always needs a spiritual path, which is

not the same as having a religious dogma or belief, in order to
cleanse one's organs of perception and discernment so that one
can hear and understand the inner and subtler vibrations still
resonant within the traditions. But as Jesus well knew this can
never be possible for the masses: what is needed for the vision of
the depth is a letting go of the hold of the surface, but the crowd
clings to the surface of things. As Krishna says in the *Bhagavad
Gita* (7:3), 'Maybe one among thousands seeks self-perfection.
And among those who seek and attain perfection, perhaps one
will come to know me as I truly am.' Jesus Christ intentionally
excluded the crowds from his teaching by speaking in parables,
so that they would not understand him. He was convinced that
if they heard the truth without the proper preparation, they
would misuse it for egotistic purposes, and some general evil
or calamity would come about.

> Having spoken this parable, he added, 'Let him who has
> ears to hear me, hear.' Now when he was away from
> the crowd, those present with the Twelve questioned him
> about the parables. He told them, 'To you the mystery of the
> kingdom of God has been confided. To the others outside it
> is all presented in parables, so that they will look intently
> and not see, listen carefully and not understand, lest per-
> haps they repent and be forgiven' (Mark 4:9–12).

Ordinary mankind must follow the natural law, and the
corresponding justice is meted out to everyone. Christ has
no intention of interfering with it; such interference would be
a denial of the orderliness of the cosmos, with appropriate laws
and justice. Interference is possible only if a person is willing to
follow a spiritual discipline so that he is gradually placed under
the sway of higher laws. Those who wish to be forgiven their
sins without the payment of the sacrifice of their sinful egos
have no advocate in Jesus Christ. It is only by becoming a
different being that one can be placed under different laws, and
be freed of the lower ones. His love and mercy do not manifest
themselves in interfering with the laws of the cosmos, but more
in his undertaking to teach us, at whatever cost and suffering
to himself, the way towards a new birth. Only those who have
a little spark of this new being in them will seek its proper
nourishment and growth, as is expressed in the old alchemical

principle that only he who has some gold can make some more. The new being can be born only in the one who is willing to die to his old self, full of egoistic cravings and fears, and turn around radically so that he may be healed. As Jesus said,

> To the man who has, more will be given until he grows rich; the man who has not, will lose what little he has. I use parables when I speak to them [the crowd] because they look but do not see, they listen but do not hear or understand. Isaiah's prophecy is fulfilled in them which says, 'Listen as you will, you shall not understand, look intently as you will, you shall not see. Sluggish indeed is this people's heart. They have scarcely heard with their ears, they have firmly closed their eyes; otherwise they might see with their eyes, and hear with their ears, and understand with their hearts, and turn back to me and I should heal them' (Matthew 13:13–15).

CHAPTER

— 6 —

The Bread from a Simple Heart

Later on Jesus crossed the Sea of Galilee (or Tiberias), but a large crowd kept following him because they saw the signs he was performing in healing the sick. So Jesus went up the mountain and sat down there with his disciples. It was near the Passover, the great Jewish festival.

When Jesus looked up he saw a large crowd coming toward him; so he said to Philip, 'Where are we to buy bread to feed these people?' He said this to test Philip, knowing well enough himself what he was going to do. He replied, 'Two hundred denarii would not buy enough loaves for every one of them to have a little' (6:1–7).

One of his disciples, Andrew, the brother of Simon Peter, said to him, 'There is a boy here who has five barley loaves and two dried fish. But what is that among so many?' Jesus said, 'Get the people to recline.' Even though the men numbered about five thousand, there was plenty of grass for them to find a place on the ground. Jesus then took the loaves of bread, gave thanks, and passed them around to those reclining there; he did the same with the dried fish, as much as they wanted. When everyone had had enough, he told his disciples, 'Gather up the fragments that are left over so that nothing will perish.' This they did, twelve baskets of fragments left over by those who had been fed by the five barley loaves (6:8–13).

Jesus Christ was not interested in the crowd which was following him, impressed by his miraculous powers. His work lay primarily with his own chosen disciples who, having already abandoned all outer projects of wordly commerce, as well as all concerns with family ties, were learning to follow his path in spirit. Christ demanded a great deal from anyone who would be his follower:

He said to his disciples, 'Whoever wishes to be my follower must deny his very self, take up his cross each day, and follow in my steps.' . . . As they were making their way along, someone said to him, 'I will be your follower wherever you go.' Jesus said to him, 'The foxes have lairs, the birds of the sky have nests, but the Son of Man has nowhere to lay his head.' To another he said, 'Come after me.' The man replied, 'Let me bury my father first.' Jesus said to him, 'Let the dead bury their dead; come away and proclaim the kingdom of God.' Yet another said to him, 'I will be your follower, Lord, but first let me take leave of my people at home.' Jesus answered him, 'Whoever put his hand to the plough but keeps looking back is unfit for the kingdom of God.' (Luke 9:23, 57–62).

There is no use imagining that without a real hunger for the truth of the Spirit and a great deal of prior preparation anyone could follow the path of Jesus Christ. The masses were and are much more interested in making use of the powers of Christ for their own personal welfare and advantage or that of their immediate family. Jesus tried to escape into the hills where he could teach his disciples in peace. However, the crowd followed him there as well. We should also remember the inner multitude which is a part and parcel of each seeker of truth, including the disciples. The inner crowd, just like the outer one, has no unity, no single goal, each member of it being self-occupied with his own comfort and success. The crowd does not understand much, except what is at the surface, is easily swayed and wishes for very little other than bread and circuses.

The Gospel writer must have had, essentially, an inner crowd in mind, because for an outer crowd to come to Jesus Christ up in the hills expecting to be given external bread seems odd, particularly in relation to the fact that pilgrims on their way to Jerusalem for the Passover festival would have carried food with them. Even up in the hills, that is to say even at the higher level of understanding of the disciples, there was an inner multitude, asserting itself, wanting its needs to be met. They might have been hungry and unable to listen to the teachings of their master, thinking of something to eat. In any case, the hungry crowd burst upon the awareness of Jesus Christ who wondered what sort of nourishment was needed

and from where this was to be obtained. Philip's reply shows
what occupied his mind: quantity – of money, loaves, people.

On one occasion Jesus spoke thus (Matthew 11:25): 'Father,
Lord of heaven and earth, to you I offer praise; for what you
have hidden from the learned and the clever you have revealed
to the merest children.' Now, in this crowd which came up the
hill was a child, or someone who had a childlike innocence
and freedom from ambition. As we know from the gospel
accounts, the disciples themselves had to struggle against
personal ambition and a competitive spirit in themselves.

> A discussion arose among them as to which of them was
> the greatest. Jesus, who knew their thoughts, took a little
> child and placed it beside him. After which he said to them,
> 'Whoever welcomes this little child on my account welcomes
> me, and whoever welcomes me welcomes Him who sent me;
> for the least one among you is the greatest.' . . . 'Trust me
> when I tell you that whoever does not accept the kingdom
> of God as a child will not enter into it' (Luke 9:46–48; 18:17).

The young boy in the crowd seems to have been the only one with
some real bread, which as the later part of this very chapter (6:51)
attests must be understood as participation in the life and being
of the Christ himself. Andrew, although the one who notices
the boy with the loaves, perhaps in his competitiveness, tries
to belittle the spiritual attainment of the young boy or of the
child-like simple man.

Jesus Christ, ever the teacher, seized this opportunity to teach an
important lesson to his disciples and showed them the spiritual
superiority of a simple and trusting heart over all the calcula-
tions and schemes of the mind. He multiplied the loaves and
the fishes, and expanded upon the understanding of the child,
until all those assembled there, with their varied intelligence
and levels, could have their fill, leaving enough even for all the
disciples, whom he instructed not to waste even the crumbs of
the bread of this child's wisdom. Even the crumbs were sufficient to fill a whole basket for each ot the twelve disciples.

The Fear and Temptation of Becoming King

When the people saw the sign that Jesus had performed, they began to say, 'Surely, this must be the Prophet that was to come into the world.' With that Jesus realised that they were about to come and seize him so that they might make him king, so he fled back to the mountain alone (6:14–15).

What interested the crowd, however, was not the teaching or the way shown by Jesus Christ. They are always captured by signs and wonders and see only the surface of things. Regarding him as the Prophet who was to come, which in this instance seems to be the same as the Messiah who was to come, they wish him to conform to their own pre-formed idea of such a person. Even though the whole life and teachings of Jesus Christ are concerned with the inner spiritual birth, for as he said, 'My kingdom is not of this world' (John 18:36), he was constantly being understood only externally by almost everyone, and certainly by the multitude. It is possible that even some of his close disciples might have still wished him to be an external king; certainly the crowd did. Fearing that they would come and carry him off, against everything that he stood for, to make him the king, he left even his disciples behind and fled back to the mountain.

Since all fear is connected with a certain kind of wishing and temptation, one may wonder if Jesus Christ was tempted to become the king, and he had to flee away from the crowd into a higher part of himself to regain his equilibrium and to continue the work he came to do:

Once again, the devil took him to a very high mountain, and showed him all the kingdoms of the world in their glory. 'All these', he said, 'I will give you, if you will only fall down and do me homage.' But Jesus said, 'Begone, Satan! Scripture says, "You shall do homage to the Lord your God and worship Him alone."' Then the devils left him; and angels appeared and waited on him (Matthew 4:8–11).

The Power of I AM

> At nightfall his disciples went down to the sea, got into their boat and pushed off to cross the water to Capernaum. Darkness had already fallen and Jesus had not yet joined them. By now a strong wind was blowing and the sea grew rough. When they had rowed about three or four miles they saw Jesus walking on the sea and approaching the boat. They were terrified, but he told them, 'I AM! Do not be afraid.' So they wanted to take him into the boat, and suddenly the boat reached the shore towards which they were heading (6:16–21).

It is clear that unless there are some people prepared enough to recognise the real nature of the Word and bear witness to it, it cannot come down, become flesh and dwell inside human beings and among them. Therefore, a preparation and education of the disciples is a necessary part of the activities of Jesus Christ. Even with them, however select a band they already are, it is not easy. Every time there is something miraculous or mysterious, unexpected by them according to their understanding of the ordinary natural laws, the disciples display disbelief and fear: 'He got into the boat with them and the wind died down. They were taken aback by these happenings, for they had not understood about the loaves. On the contrary, their minds were completely closed to the meaning of events' (Mark 6:51–52).

However, in that very state of shock, there is an opening for the disciples, and Christ displayed to them for the first time the power and the majesty of the sacred name of God, I AM. To know the real name of someone, or to do something in his name, means both in the Old Testament and the New, as it does in many ancient traditions, to be able to participate in that person's being and to share in his power. This is true even in present-day English usage: if someone speaks in the name of someone else, for example if the Secretary of State speaks in the name of the President of the United States of America, he does so with the other person's authorisation and authority, with the backing of his power. If a disciple believed in the name of Christ, it meant that he understood the real nature of Christ and was able to participate in his being and power, and could act on his authority. In the Greek original, the word for 'name' is *onome*, which also has the connotations of 'power' and 'being'. It may also be remarked here, somewhat parenthetically, that for the Jewish philospher Philo, name was equivalent to *Logos*.

A radical change of being of a person was often acknowledged by the giving of a new name to him; thus Abram was called Abraham, Jacob was called Israel, Simon was renamed Peter, and Saul was named Paul – in each case, after a momentous encounter with a higher level, an encounter which left the person essentially transformed. It may be remarked here that the name *Jesus* is the English version of *Joshua*, which in its turn comes from the Hebrew *Yehoshua*. This literally means "Yahweh saves". Although it is not completely clear what precisely *Yahweh*, or the more traditional form without the vowels, *YHWH*, means, it may well signify *I AM* – as the very name of God. The name *Jesus* would then literally mean "I AM saves":

> Moses said to God, 'Who am I that I should go to Pharaoh and lead the Israelites out of Egypt?' He answered, 'I will be with you; and this shall be your proof that it is I who have sent you: when you bring my people out of Egypt, you will worship God on this very mountain.' 'But', said Moses to God, 'when I go to the Israelites and say to them, "The God of your fathers has sent me to you," if they ask me, "What is His name?" what am I to tell them?' God replied, 'I AM WHO I AM.' Then he added, 'This is what you shall tell the Israelites: I AM sent me to you' (Exodus 3:11–14).

I AM itself has been declared by God to be his most mysterious and sacred name; and the real power of this name seems to have been shown and given to only two great persons in the entire biblical literature; namely, Moses and Jesus Christ, to the former only temporarily whereas to the latter permanently. Since Jesus Christ was one with the Father, and only because of that and certainly not in isolation from God, he could speak with the authority and the power of the secret name of God. The Greek expression for I AM is *ego eimi*, which is used in John's Gospel as well as in the Septuagint, the oldest extant Greek translation of the Old Testament, dating from 250 BC and familiar to the Greek-speaking Christians, including St Paul and the authors of the Gospels. There is evidence to believe (see Raymond Brown's *The Gospel According to John I-XII*, in the Anchor Bible, vol.29,

appendix iv) that for the users of the Septuagint the expression
ego eimi (I AM) had come to mean a divine name. The relevant
verses from Isaiah in the Septuagint, for example 43:25, 51:12,
and 52:6, could be translated as 'I am "I AM" who blots out
transgressions', 'I am "I AM" who comforts you', and 'My people
shall know my name; in that day [they shall know] that "I AM"
is speaking to them.' In these examples one can see that I AM
functions as a proper name of God, with His power and being in
it. It is in this mode that Christ uses I AM, to indicate his identity
with God and his participation in His power and being, and not
as an identification of his own particularity or specialness.

I AM as the Bread of Eternal Life

Next morning the crowd was standing on the opposite
shore. They had seen only one boat there, and Jesus, they
knew, had not embarked with his disciples, who had gone
away without him. Then some boats came out from Tiberias
near the place where they had eaten the bread. So, once the
crowd saw that neither Jesus nor his disciples were there,
they too embarked and went to Capernaum looking for Jesus
(6:22–24).

And when they found him on the other side of the sea,
they said to him, 'Rabbi, when did you come here?' Jesus
answered, 'In very truth I know that you have not come
looking for me because you saw signs, but because you ate
the bread and your hunger was satisfied. You must work,
not for this perishable food, but for the food that lasts, the
food of Eternal Life. This food the Son of Man will give you
for it is on him that God the Father has set His seal.' 'Then
what must we do', they asked him, 'if we are to work as God
would have us work?' Jesus replied, 'This is the work of God:
believe in the one whom He has sent' (6:25–29).

They said, 'What sign can you give us to see, so that we
may believe you? What is the work you do? Our ancestors
had manna to eat in the desert; as Scripture says, "He gave
them bread from Heaven to eat." Jesus said, 'I tell you this:
the truth is, not that Moses gave you bread from heaven,
but that my Father gives you the real bread from heaven.
God's bread comes down from heaven and brings Life to

the world.' They said to him, 'Sir, give us this bread now and always' (6:30–34).

As the crowd catches up with Jesus Christ, he is aware that they are not following after him out of any understanding that his miraculous activities are a sign of some deeper truth and teaching, but only out of the satisfaction they have derived for their surface hunger. Still, they are drawn to him, and regard him as a teacher, a rabbi. He advises them not to be occupied wholly with the food for their physical bodies but to search for nourishment for their souls, which alone can give them Eternal Life. This spiritual nourishment for the soul is what the Son of God, now and always incarnated as the Son of Man in every man, brings to anyone who would receive him, and this is all that he is concerned with. Of course, everybody wants Eternal Life; it sounds like a good idea. Part of oneself is willing to do the right thing, the good work, God's work, but always according to one's own crowd-level and surface ideas, for the sake of one's own personal self, made up of fears and desires. One wishes to invoke all the saints and prophets, even God, for calming the fear of judgement or for fulfilling the desire for self-continuity and personal salvation.

So, the crowd asks how can they do God's work? The answer is given by Christ that they will do God's work if they would understand and accept and follow the spiritual being which has been sent by God, and dwells within the very flesh of each one of them. One would love this being if one saw clearly and deeply, and one would obey it. As he said to his close disciples, 'If you love me, you will keep my commandments. I will ask the Father and He will send you another guide to be with you forever; the Spirit of Truth which the world cannot accept, because it does not see it or know it, but you do recognise him because it remains with you and is within you' (John 14:15–17).

But the crowd takes the remarks of Jesus Christ completely externally, as if he is pointing to himself as the particular carpenter's son, born at such and such a place! And they ask for an external sign or a miracle so that they could accept what he has to say. Can he compete with Moses, the great prophet, whose works have already been completely externalised in the exoteric tradition, and produce wonders like him? Why should they believe him? What proof can he give of his occult powers? Can he, like Moses, call forth manna from heaven? Jesus speaks to them solemnly and tells them that all power comes from God: it is not Moses, nor Jesus himself (as he repeatedly says), who is the source of power and the corresponding astonishing works. The real bread from heaven is sent by God, and that is the only nourishment which can lead to Eternal Life. It is nothing specially to do with a particular incarnation of the eternal Christ as historical Jesus. St Paul is explicitly clear about it, in 1 Corinthians 10:3–4: 'And [the ancestors] all ate the same supernatural food and all drank the same supernatural drink. For they drank from the supernatural Rock which followed them; and the Rock was Christ.' The Christ who said 'Before Abraham was, I AM' (John 8:58), is always there, if one would be sensitive to the I AM and open one's heart. Without understanding what Christ is attempting to say, and without the least willingness to undertake the corresponding dying to one's egoistic self, the crowd demands what none of the close disciples has yet dared imagine himself prepared for: 'give us this bread now and always.'

> Jesus said to them, 'I AM the bread of Life. Whoever comes to me shall never be hungry, and whoever believes in me shall never be thirsty. But you, as I have said, do not believe although you have seen. All that the Father gives me will come to me, and the man who comes to me I will never turn away. I have come down from heaven, not to do my own will, but the will of Him who sent me. It is His will that I should not lose even one of all that he has given me, but raise them all up on the last day. For it is my Father's will that everyone who looks upon the Son and believes in him should have Eternal Life. And I shall raise him up on the last day' (6:35–40).
>
> At this the Jews started to murmur in protest because he claimed: 'I am the bread who came down from heaven.' And they kept saying, 'Isn't this Jesus, the son of Joseph? Don't we know his father and mother? How can he claim to have come down from heaven?' (6:41–42).

Although there are no parables in this gospel, unlike in the synoptic gospels, the teaching here is most enigmatic of all. John's Gospel is certainly the most spiritual and inner, and in that sense the most esoteric of all the gospels. It is not esoteric in the sense of hiding anything or making a secret of something, although as has already been remarked (see comments on John 5:31–47 in Chapter 5) that Jesus went out of his way to speak to the crowd in a manner designed to keep the real truths from them lest they misuse what they heard, rather it is esoteric in the sense of being on the other side of the natural veil that exists between the way things are and the clouded perception and understanding of humanity. This is precisely where the need of any spiritual teaching and the corresponding discipline actually reside, so that with their aid one's perceptions are cleansed more and more as one's ego is progressively displaced from the central role its occupies in one's life. Only then something which is not from the level of one's own little ego may in fact be heard.

The ego says 'I am this' or 'I am that', stressing the pride of particularity, of being special, exclusively important. This is what is termed *asmita* in the *Yoga Sutras* of Patanjali, and is said to be one of the most fundamental impediments to inner freedom. This exclusivity is the cause of the destruction of Babylon (Isaiah 47:8–10), who said, 'I am, and there is none beside me.' On the other hand, one who is liberated from his own ego, one who does not proclaim himself, knows that 'by myself, I am nothing.' Only by the sacrifice of himself is he made sacred. Such a one, when he is included in All There Is, when he knows of God that *He Is*, or of *Brahman* that *It Is*, can say *I AM*. [This is *Aham asmi* in Sanskrit; *Ego eimi* in Greek, and perhaps *YHWH (Yahweh)* in Hebrew.] In the removal of the particular and limiting centre in the ego, he is not dissolved and dispersed, but is centred in God. Whenever Jesus Christ invokes I AM as the nourishment for or the way to Eternal Life, he is always intensely aware of his Father, and knows that without Him he can do nothing. What he says is not said from himself, nor from his own will, but on the authority of and in the name of God; only then can he bring, in fact *be*, truth and the bread from heaven. His Father and he are one; he is the very *Atman* who is one with *Brahman*, as is expressed in one of the great utterances of the Upanishads.

To be able to be called by Jesus Christ is already a gift from God; only those already somewhat blessed can come to him. The people in the crowd, of course, do not *believe*; that is, they do not understand him, nor do they recognise his true nature. They are not at all prepared for his esoteric teaching, even though they have seen some of his miraculous works. They do not see the Christ in him, but only Jesus, the son of Joseph and his earthly mother: 'Isn't this the son of the carpenter and Mary, the brother of James, Joses, Jude and Simon? Aren't his sisters here among us?' (Mark 6:3).

'Stop your murmuring,' Jesus told them. 'No one can come to me unless the Father who sent me draws him. And I shall raise him up on the last day. It is written in the prophets: "And they shall all be taught by God." Everyone who has heard the Father and learned from Him comes to me' (6:43–45).

'Not that anyone has seen the Father: only the one who is from God has seen the Father. In truth, in very truth, I tell you, the believer possesses Eternal Life. I AM the bread of Life. Your ancestors ate manna in the desert, but they died. I am speaking of the bread that comes down from heaven, which a man may eat, and never die. I AM the living bread that came down from heaven. If anyone eats this bread, he will live forever. And the bread that I shall give, to bring the world to Life, is my own flesh' (6:46–51).

At this the Jews started to quarrel among themselves, saying, 'How can he give us his flesh to eat?' (6:52).

Jesus replied, 'In truth, in very truth I tell you, unless you eat the flesh of the Son of Man and drink his blood you can have no Life in you. Whoever eats my flesh and drinks my blood possesses Eternal Life, and I will raise him up on the last day. My flesh is real food; my blood is real drink. Whoever eats my flesh and drinks my blood dwells continually in me and I dwell in him. As the living Father sent me, and I live because of the Father, so he who eats me shall live because of me. This is the bread that came down from heaven. Unlike those ancestors who ate and yet died, the man who feeds on this bread will live forever' (6:53–58).

Whenever one hears anything that one does not understand, because it comes from a level higher than oneself, one makes noises and creates associations with this idea or that fact. The monkey in the mind ceaselessly chatters: it cannot stop murmuring and come to a stillness where one could be drawn by the Father. Only a silent mind can come to understand Christ. Furthermore, everyone who hears the call from God will recognise the true nature of Christ. There is nothing sectarian here about believing or understanding Christ, any more than there is about Christ himself or about God. Ultimately, the real teacher is God, and all true teaching comes from Him alone, and not from any human agency, however exalted.

This, however, does not mean that God is a person like everyone else and can thus be *seen* in the usual manner, by the ordinary eyes. That is not how anyone has ever seen God; one sees Him only through the spiritual being who is directly linked with God and comes from Him, and who alone can say 'I AM'. Only those who understand this can possess Eternal Life. The real bread of Life is the I AM; this is what is connected with the Spirit and gives the true spiritual nourishment, which alone can lead to Eternal Life. This I AM has to be understood internally as dwelling within oneself, corresponding to that representative of divinity within each person who can receive the Word and be begotten by God, and in whom the Word takes flesh.

The real nourishment for one's soul is gained only by eating the flesh of Christ, and by drinking his blood. This is not a statement which needs to cause alarm to a vegetarian's heart! One is not being asked to carve up the physical body of a person called Jesus, son of the carpenter Joseph and his wife Mary, and to eat it. The statement is not about a physical body, as the assembled crowd thought. The flesh here, as well as elsewhere in this gospel where the flesh of Christ is mentioned, specifically (in 1:14) where it is said that 'The Word became flesh', refers to the subtle body, as distinguished from the gross physical body, also mentioned in this very chapter (6:63), which is said by comparison to be useless. Ordinary flesh is needed for ordinary life, whereas the flesh of Christ is needed for Eternal Life, for which the ordinary body is of no use. As St Paul says

There are heavenly bodies and there are earthly bodies. The splendour of the heavenly bodies is one thing, that of the earthly another . . . So it is with the resurrection of the dead. What is sown in the earth is subject to decay, what rises is incorruptible. What is sown is ignoble, what rises is glorious. Weakness is sown, strength rises up. A natural body is put down and a spiritual body comes up. If there is a natural body, be sure there is also a spiritual body. Scripture has it that Adam, the first man, became a living soul; the last Adam has become a life-giving spirit. Take note, the spiritual was not first; first came the natural and after that the spiritual. The first man was of earth, formed from dust, the second is from heaven. Earthly men are like the man of earth, heavenly men are like the man of heaven. Just as we resemble the man from earth, so shall we bear the likeness of the man from heaven (1 Corinthians 15:40–49).

It has been said repeatedly that Christ is from heaven; he is from Above, he is the Son of God. This man of heaven has a heavenly body; his flesh and blood are not of the same gross kind as of ordinary humanity. This does not make them immaterial, only subtler, just as the matter constituting light is subtler than that constituting a rock. Indeed, they are real substances, although of a different order of materiality than the ordinary body. It is by accepting the sustenance and energy from the subtle body, which is the flesh and blood of Christ, that one's own spiritual body is formed. That is how a person can become of one substance with him and participate in his being. Without this participation, that is without the subtle spiritual body, all one has is the natural physical body which will return to dust after the physical death, and one can have no share in the resurrection and Eternal Life. He who imbibes the substance of Christ dwells in him, just as Christ dwells in God.

This movement of energy, and of indwelling, works both ways, simply because there is an essential unity, even though there are differences in forms. Not only Christ dwells in God, but also God dwells in Christ. Similarly, he who would follow Christ would dwell in him; but Christ would also dwell in the disciple. What in some other traditions, particularly in Tantra, is conveyed by the symbolism of erotic love, is being conveyed here by the symbolism of food and eating: participation and indwelling of two levels of being. 'I live,' said St Paul, 'yet no longer I, but Christ liveth in me' (Galatians 2:20).

The possibility of the indwelling of Christ in the soul of a human being is continually and directly being conveyed in this gospel by the repeated reference by Jesus Christ to the *Son of Man*. We are told that unless we eat the flesh of the Son of Man and drink his blood we can have no Life in us. The Son of Man is close to us in a way that the Son of God is not. And Jesus Christ is both the Son of God as well as the Son of Man, precisely why he is the the link between man and God, and the way from here to There.

The spiritual hierarchy in the Gospel may be represented in the following schema:

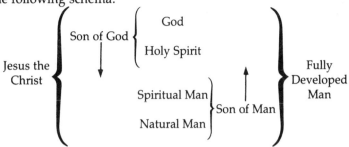

There is a movement of energies from above downwards, as well as from below upwards. Christ descends from Above so that we may, in the words of St Paul, 'all at last attain to the unity inherent in our faith and our knowledge of the Son of God – to mature manhood, measured by nothing less than the full stature of Christ' (Ephesians 4:13).

Levels of Struggle

This was spoken in the synagogue when Jesus was teaching in Capernaum. After hearing his words, many of his disciples remarked, 'This sort of talk is hard to bear. How can anyone accept this?' (6:59–60).

Jesus was quite aware that his disciples were murmuring in protest at this, and asked them, 'Does this scandalise you? What if you see the Son of Man ascending to the place where he came from? The Spirit alone gives Life; the flesh is useless. The words I have spoken to you are both Spirit and Life. But among you there are some who do not believe.' (Jesus knew from the start those who refused to believe, as well as the one who would hand him over.) He went on to say, 'This is why I have told you that no one can come to me unless it is granted to him by the Father' (6:61–65).

At this many of his disciples broke away and would not accompany him any more. So Jesus asked the Twelve, 'Do you also want to leave me?' Simon Peter answered, 'Lord, to whom shall we go? It is you who have the words of Eternal

Life; and we have come to believe and are convinced that you are God's Holy One.' Jesus said to them, 'Did I not choose the twelve of you myself? Yet one of you is a devil.' He was talking about Judas, son of Simon the Iscariot; for, though the first of the Twelve, he was going to hand Jesus over (6:66–71).

The crowd had already abandoned Jesus Christ because they could not follow what he was saying. Now many of the disciples were also having difficulty understanding or accepting his words. 'The natural man does not accept what is taught by the Spirit of God. For him, that is absurdity. He cannot come to know such teaching because it must be appraised in a spiritual way' (1 Corinthians 2:14). A spiritual man is one who already has a particle of divinity in him, placed there by God, and that particle seeks to grow in the Spirit and Life, and is therefore naturally drawn to the teaching of Christ. Now only a few of his close disciples remain with him, given to him by the Father, and chosen by him himself from the world. It is important to stress, as is done in the Gospel text here, that we may have the impression or the illusion that we are the ones to choose the right teaching and the teacher for ourselves; but in fact, as is said in many traditions, the choice is from Above. We are called from Above, tested and then either rejected to go on the way of the world, or accepted for instruction and guidance along the way of Truth and Spirit, if we are willing to die to our egoistic self to earn the right for a spiritual birth.

In view of the fact that the choice of the disciples is from Above, it is clear that Judas has been chosen by Jesus Christ himself, and that the later action by Judas came as no surprise to Jesus. In any case, it is evident throughout the Gospels that Jesus Christ had an amazing insight into character; it should thus be surprising if the activities of Judas were not foreseen by Jesus. The question then arises as to why Judas was chosen, not only to be one of the close disciples in the inner circle, but also to be given the first position among the Twelve. Judas was the keeper of the treasury for the family of Jesus, that is, himself and his close disciples, and he was given the important place of honour at the last supper. One must search for an intentional reason for the choice of Judas on the part of Jesus Christ. One possibility is suggested by the remark in the text above: Considering a symbolic parallel, often suggested in this gospel, between the old creation and the new, one might wonder if the first among the disciples of Christ is parallel to the first among the angels created by God. It is possible that in both cases their struggle is with their forgetting of their proper place, and a prideful assertion to be equal to their masters:

> How have you fallen from the heavens, O Lucifer, son of the dawn! How are you cut down to the ground, you who mowed down the nations. You said in your heart: 'I will scale the heavens; above the stars of God I will set up my throne; I will take my seat on the mountains where the gods meet, in the recesses of the north. I will ascend above the tops of the clouds; I will be like the Most High!' (Isaiah 14:12–14).

However, whatever the reason for the later behaviour of Judas, which will be discussed in some detail in Chapter 13, one wonders why Jesus Christ would have allowed him the important place in the sacred circle of his disciples. A similar question naturally arises in the case of the continued existence of Lucifer as a force of resistance to the omnipotent God who could, if He so wished, get rid of the adversary. We must conclude that the continued existence and the corresponding opposing activity of the adversary is necessary for the unfolding of creation as well as the spiritual drama of Jesus Christ. Perhaps it is only by an endless struggle between the forces of consciousness and forgetfulness that the play of the forces, which is the cosmos, continues. A complete destruction of one side or the other will bring this play to a halt, which is possible only for the end of days when time shall be no more. Otherwise, as Krishna says in the *Mahabharata*, the choice is not between struggle and absence of it, but only between one kind of struggle or another. The real question then is at what level of existence and consciousness one is going to struggle. As St Paul says, 'Finally then, find your strength in the Lord, in His mighty power . . . For our fight is not against human foes, but against cosmic powers, against the authorities and potentates of this dark world, against the superhuman forces of evil in the heavens' (Ephesians 6:10–12).

CHAPTER

— 7 —

Conflict between the Spirit and the World

Afterwards Jesus went about in Galilee; he wished to avoid Judaea because the Jews were looking for a chance to kill him. As the Jewish Feast of Tabernacles was close at hand, his brothers said to him, 'You should leave this district and go into Judaea, so that your disciples there may see the great things you are doing. For no one keeps his actions hidden and still expects to be in the public eye. If you really are doing such things as these, show yourself to the world.' In fact, even his brothers did not believe in him. Jesus said to them, 'The right time for me has not yet come, but any time is right for you. The world cannot hate you; but it hates me for exposing the wickedness of its ways. Go to the festival yourselves. I am not yet going to this festival because the time is not yet ripe for me.' With this answer he stayed behind in Galilee (7:1–9).

However, once his brothers had gone up to the festival, then he too went up, but as if in secret and not for all to see. The Jews were looking for him at the festival and asking, 'Where is that man?', and there was much whispering about him in the crowds. 'He is a good man,' said some. 'No,' said others, 'he is leading the people astray.' However, no one talked about him openly, for fear of the Jews (7:10–13).

Four other sons of Mary, and thus brothers of Jesus, are mentioned by name in Matthew 13:55, as well as in Mark 6:3, namely, James, Joses, Simon and Jude. They, unlike some of his close disciples, did not yet understand the true nature of Jesus Christ; only after the resurrection did they believe in him, which is the same as becoming his disciples and accepting his discipline. In spite of the great works they themselves saw Jesus Christ perform, they wanted an external confirmation and approval from the social and religious authorities in Jerusalem. Therefore they wanted him to show himself and his works, even though they were aware that the religious hierarchy was not very kindly disposed to Jesus Christ, who had exposed their misunderstanding of the real meaning of the tradition which they claimed to follow and represent. Such an exposure of an inner emptiness is always resented by the hollow men, especially by those among them, like the clergy and the teachers, whose profession depends on maintaining authority derived from an appearance of subtle understanding of the Scriptures and the tradition, but who are not dead to their egoistic selves. Clearly, it is the *leaders* who are meant in the last sentence of the text above for it to make sense that the very Jewish crowd are afraid of the *Jews*. This is how Jesus Christ addressed the people and his disciples, according to Matthew 23:2–28, in which we can make appropriate contemporary substitutions in order to maintain the spirit and the universality of the message of Jesus Christ:

> The doctors of law and the Pharisees have succeeded Moses as teachers; therefore do everything and observe everything they tell you. But do not follow their example. Their words are bold but their deeds are few. They bind up heavy loads, hard to carry, to lay on other men's shoulders, while they themselves will not lift a finger to budge them. Whatever they do is done for show. . . . Do not call any man on earth father; for you have one Father and He is in heaven. . . . Woe to you scribes and Pharisees, you hypocrites! You shut the door of the kingdom of Heaven in men's faces; you do not enter yourselves, and when others are entering, you stop them. Alas for you, lawyers and Pharisees, you hypocrites! You travel over land and sea to win one convert, but once he is converted you make a devil of him twice as wicked as yourselves. Alas for you, blind guides! . . . You strain out the gnat and swallow the camel! . . . You cleanse the outside of cup and dish and leave the inside filled with loot and self-indulgence. Blind Pharisee! Clean the inside of the cup first; then the outside will be clean also. . . . You are like whitewashed tombs, beautiful to look at on the outside but inside filled with filth and dead men's bones. Thus you present to view a holy exterior while hypocrisy and evil fill you within.

It is not clear what had changed for Jesus Christ now to decide to go to Jerusalem. Why was the time now right, three or four days later, when the feast was already half over? Was he waiting for a certain religious pitch to have developed in the crowd before he appeared to them in the temple? Was he determining the right time according to astrological considerations? Or did he simply wish to go by himself and not associate on that occasion with his brothers, who did not understand him and could not therefore be expected to be of any real help? He was not in any case interested in the sort of considerations which motivated his brothers and he had his own internal reasons for doing what he did. This is not to say that he did what he personally liked to do; on the contrary, he completely disregarded his own convenience and pleasure, or likes and dislikes, and did what he had to, in obedience to the will and dictates of the only reality that mattered to him, namely God. Everything else, and everyone else, including himself, was secondary. 'Anyone that comes to me and does not hate his father, mother, wife, children, brothers, sisters, and not only them but his own self (psyche), can be no disciple of mine. The man who does not bear his cross and follow in my steps can be no disciple of mine' (Luke 14:26–27). What is at issue here are the relative priorities of the seeker: compared with God, oneself is nothing, and all these relations are nothing, for 'none is good but God alone' (Luke 18:19).

The fundamental question is that of authority. Everyone is constantly seeking some external authority which will approve of what he does, thinks, feels, is drawn to or considers worthy. If it is not adulation of the masses, then people hanker for approval from their parents, or concurrence of scholars, or blessings of the priests, or quotations from scriptures, or sanctions from tradition, or acceptance by some external God. Almost all of the self-valuation of human beings is based on what others say or think, or rather what one imagines they say or think, about oneself. Of course, one can be in reaction to these sources of authority and engage in contrary action. That itself is no freedom from them. True freedom is not possible either in seeking approval or courting disapproval; freedom cannot in fact be sought. It is not an achievement of any kind; it arises naturally when a person is engaged in what he must do, in response to an inner call, corresponding to an authority from deep within himself, without fear and without self-importance. In the depth of one's soul resides Divinity which alone provides the authority which does not need the approval of further authority. If anyone speaks from that depth, as did Jesus Christ when he was one with the Father, in the state of the I AM, then he is not merely personal; he is at the source of the Logos and speaks and acts with true authority.

My Teaching is not My Own

The feast was half over by the time Jesus went into the temple area and began to teach. The Jews were astonished: 'How is it', they said, 'that this untrained man has such learning?' Jesus replied, 'The teaching I give is not my own; it is the teaching of Him who sent me. Whoever chooses to do the will of God will know about the doctrine – namely, whether it comes from God or is merely my own. Anyone whose teaching is merely his own, aims at self-glorification. The man who seeks glory for him who sent him, is truthful; there is no dishonesty in his heart' (7:14–18).

'Moses has given you the law, has he not? Yet not one of you keeps it. Why are you trying to kill me?' The crowd answered, 'You are possessed! Who wants to kill you?' Jesus replied, 'I have performed just one deed, and you are all taken aback by it. But consider: Moses gave you the law of circumcision (not that it originated with Moses but with the patriarchs) and you circumcise on the Sabbath. Well then, if a child is circumcised on the Sabbath to avoid breaking the law of Moses, why are you angry with me for curing a whole man on the Sabbath? Don't judge by appearances, and make a just judgement'(7:19–24).

This led some of the people of Jerusalem to remark: 'Is this not the man they want to kill? Here he is speaking in public and they don't say a word to him. Can it be that even the authorities have decided that this is the Messiah? And yet we know where this man comes from, but when the Messiah appears no one is to know where he comes from.' Thereupon Jesus cried aloud as he taught in the temple, 'So you know me and you know where I am from? Yet I have not come on my own. No, there is truly One who sent me and Him you do not know. I know Him because it is from

Him that I come and He sent me' (7:25–29).

Then they tried to arrest him, but no one laid a finger on him for his hour had not come. Many in the crowd came to believe in him. They kept saying, 'When the Messiah comes can he be expected to perform more signs than this man does?' The Pharisees overheard this debate about him among the crowd, and the chief priests and the Pharisees together sent temple guards to arrest him (7:30–32).

Again and again it can be seen that Jesus Christ was not speaking from his own personal authority, or with his own personal power, but with the power and the authority of God; not in his own name but in the name of the Father. He was not seeking his own self-advancement or glory, but the glory of Him who sent him, whose apostle he was. He was not speaking from *asmita* ('I am this' of the *Yoga Sutras*), but rather from *I AM*. In that sense, he was truly a prophet (which literally means an instrument) of God. This is the fundamental difference between self-glorification and Self-glorification, whether one is working from one's own energy for one's own sake, or whether one is working for the sake of God and on His energy acting through oneself. As has already been said, without God it cannot be done; without man it will not be done. Just as Krishna needs Arjuna to carry out His will, so God needs Jesus Christ to carry out His work. He in turn sacrificed himself to the will of God, mindful of the suffering involved as well as of the absolute necessity for disciplined obedience: 'My Father, if it is possible, let this cup pass me by. Nevertheless, not as I will, but as thou wilt' (Matthew 26:39).

The vision that Jesus Christ had was that of a great Yogi: he could easily see into the real character and intentions of the people, as well as into the past and the future, for the *whole sequence of time*, as the *Yoga Sutras* says, is present to an enlightened person all at once. He foresaw that he would be formally charged with a violation of the Mosaic Law, which was being continually violated by his listeners, in spirit if not in letter. In fact, the leaders wanted to destroy what they did not understand but what they could not easily dismiss, because even in them, in some dark recesses of their hearts, a voice was dimly heard which nudged their conscience. Even in the Sanhedrin, the very citadel of entrenched authority and orthodoxy, at least two members were secret admirers and followers of Christ, namely Nicodemus and Joseph of Arimathea, who buried Jesus after his death when his own close disciples were disheartened and had hidden themselves. Nevertheless, what was at issue concerns the perpetual warfare between the spiritual truth, which is ever fresh and cannot be encapsulated in any formulation or laws, speaking on its own authority and recognisable by those who are inwardly prepared, and what is merely conventional truth, constantly appealing to external authority and tending to rigid formulations and laws. It is the struggle between the truth of eternity and the truth of time, between the Self and the ego, or in the language of the Gospels between Spirit *(Pneuma)* and self (psyche, also translated as 'soul' and as 'life'). Peace between the two is possible only when the lower is contained in the higher, and the higher is received by the lower and given its due place. But those who judge by appearances only cannot appreciate the words of depth, and cannot make room for them, for that involves a dying to oneself. If one cannot die to oneself, or at least understand the need for leaving oneself behind, one cannot follow Christ or any other spiritual teacher; then one attempts to eliminate the gnawing call of the spirit. As Christ said, 'You are trying to kill me because my word finds no place in you' (John 8:37).

Jesus Christ did not fit the expectations of the people who had a particular image and idea of what the Messiah should be like, what his origins would be and what functions he would perform. All this had been buttressed by scriptural and priestly authority. These images, ideas and expectations constitute the idols which men worship, and which block them from seeing the plain truth staring them in the face. This idolatory is what prevents a vision of the unexpected; it stops a radically fresh insight into the unknown, and places a mental straightjacket on what one sees and knows. Precisely here is the need for an emptying of oneself, for becoming poor in spirit, for the state of active unknowing, so that what is usually unhearable can be heard, what is customarily unseen may be seen. This is why a man prays to God, as did Meister Eckhart, to rid him of the idea of God, because anyone who takes hold of God in any form takes hold of a creation of his own mind and not of God who is ultimately beyond any idea or image that we can make of Him.

There is a story of a man with a deep faith in God. In one of the periodic turnings of the wheel of fortune, his village was ravaged by a great flood, and his house was washed away. While clinging to a tree branch in the middle of the torrent, he held fast to his faith and prayed to God, and was certain that God would listen to him and save him. A boat came by and the person in the boat asked him to get aboard. He refused and said he would wait because he had no doubt that God would save him. Twice again someone in a boat offered to help; but he refused and waited for God to save him. Slowly the flood waters rose and he drowned. When he appeared in heaven he demanded to know why his faith was not heeded, and why God had not come to save him from the flood. God replied, 'You fool! Thrice I came with a rescue boat but you refused to be saved!'

The people around Jesus Christ continued to wait for the Messiah to come because he did not fit their image of the Messiah. They knew his origins: he was the son of Mary and the carpenter Joseph; they knew his brothers and sisters; they knew that when the Messiah comes no one is supposed to know his origins; and they knew that the Messiah could not come from Galilee. With all this *knowledge*, they *understood* very little, and *saw* even less. They could not believe because they could not see. And they could not see because they kept clinging to what they knew and made no room for any surprise or wonder which is so often an accompaniment of real insight. They saw only the surface of things and judged by appearance alone; if their judgement had been just, they would have judged the Spirit with the spirit, and not the Spirit with the body or the mind. As Plotinus writes, 'To any vision must be brought an eye adapted to what is to be seen, and having some likeness to it. Never did eye see the sun unless it had first become sun-like, and never can the soul have vision of the First Beauty unless itself be beautiful' (Enneads I.6.9)

Where I Am, No One Can Come

Jesus then said to them: 'Only a little while longer am I to be with you; then I am going away to Him who sent me. You will look for me and not find; where I AM, you cannot come.' So the Jews said to one another, 'Where does he intend to go, that we should not be able to find him? Will he go to the Diaspora among the Greeks and teach the Greeks? What is this he is talking about: "You will look for me and not find," and "Where I AM, you cannot come"?' (7:33–36).

Only he who chooses to do the will of God, that is whose self-will has been yoked to Self-will, he who subjects himself to the *yoga* (related to the English word *yoke* in its root meaning) of Jesus Christ, can understand his teaching, and know his true origins. No teaching worth its salt can be understood only by the mind, for the simple reason that a *teaching*, a *yoga*, is not simply a set of propositions for the mind to assent to or to argue over; nor is it a matter of emotional exultation. To be sure, a teaching has ideas, and a whole field of feelings connected with it, but these arise from a higher mind and can be understood only when one is oneself transformed enough to be in touch with the higher mind. Above all, what a teaching demands is that one engage in practice, that a wayfarer actually tread the path by which alone his body, mind and emotions are brought into submission to the higher mind and feelings. Thus disciplined, the disciple can begin to hear behind the words of the master, and participate with him in the divine mind, so that he leaves behind his mind which thinks about God, and lets God think in and through his mind. 'Not I, the I that I am, know these things,' says Jacob Boehme, 'but God knows them in me.' 'I live, yet no longer I, but Christ liveth in me,' says St Paul (Galatians 2:20). And the great teacher himself said (John 14:10), 'I am not myself the source of the words I speak to you: it is the Father who dwells in me doing His own work.'

As was said (John 1:11), 'To his own he came, yet his own did not accept him.' The majority did not, and could not, recognise the true being of Jesus Christ, and the indwelling Logos to which he constantly attempted to draw their attention. Even when he was right there in front of them, the very lighthouse of palpitating spiritual energy, their untrained eyes could not perceive his real nature. They were too occupied with their religious observances, traditional ideas, scriptural authority and the approval of the leaders. After his departure, when the present would have become the past, and the Presence only a memory, they would search for him and not find. Where he is, in the eternal present, in the state of the I AM, they could not, and cannot, come because they were, as we are all, bewitched by time and by the things of time, and had not died to themselves in love.

> Man's curiosity searches past and future
> And clings to that dimension. But to apprehend
> The point of intersection of the timeless
> With time, is an occupation for the saint—
> No occupation either, but something given
> And taken, in a lifetime's death in love,
> Ardour and selflessness and self-surrender.
> (T. S. Eliot, 'The Dry Salvages' in *Four Quartets*)

Here, in the words 'where I AM, you cannot come', is the terrible secret and the haunting call of the Devouring Flame and the Source of Life, the Sword that cuts and the Elixir which heals. Where I AM, the very source of All Being, no one who is any one, separate from It can come. In the presence of the Almighty, all else is false and unreal, even the Son of God. 'A certain ruler asked him, "Good teacher, what shall I do to inherit Eternal Life?" And Jesus said unto him, "Why call me good? None is good but God alone"' (Luke 18:18–19). God wants nothing less than the total human sacrifice, for in man's end is his beginning. 'The man who loves his self (psyche) loses it, while the man who hates his life in this world preserves it to Life eternal' (John 12:25).

What is true etymologically is evident throughout the teaching of the Gospels: in order to be *sacred* we must *sacrifice* ourselves. Jesus Christ issues a call and an invitation, and sets a model: to suffer with him his baptism, to die to ourselves in denying our self-will; to take up our cross as he did his, so that our old self may be crucified, and we may do the will of Him who sent him and us.

Rivers of Living Water from the Belly

On the last and greatest day of the festival Jesus stood and cried aloud: 'If anyone thirsts, let him come; let him drink who believes in me. As Scripture says, "From his belly rivers of living water shall flow"' (7:37–38).

(Here he was referring to the Spirit which those who came

92

to believe in him were to receive. For there was as yet no Spirit, since Jesus had not been glorified.) Some of the crowd who heard began to say, 'This is undoubtedly the Prophet.' Others were claiming, 'This is the Messiah.' Others again, 'Surely the Messiah is not to come from Galilee? Does not the Scripture say that the Messiah is to be of the family of David, from David's village of Bethlehem?' Thus the crowd was sharply divided because of him. Some were for seizing him, but no one laid hands on him (7:39–44).

When the temple guards came back, the chief priests and Pharisees asked them, 'Why did you not bring him in?' 'No man ever spoke like that before,' the guards replied. 'Do not tell us you too have been taken in!' the Pharisees retorted. 'You do not see any of the Sanhedrin believing in him, do you? Or the Pharisees? Only this mob, that knows nothing about the law – and they are lost anyway!' One of their own members, Nicodemus (the man who had come to him), spoke up to say, 'Since when does our law condemn any man without first hearing him and knowing the facts?' 'Do not tell us you are a Galilean too,' they taunted him. 'Look it up; you will not find the Prophet arising in Galilee' (7:45–52).

He who seeks the Spirit, and is thirsty for it, is invited by Jesus Christ to come to him. And if one recognises his true nature, which is to say if one is able to follow him and be his disciple, and thus believe in him, he is invited to drink from the source, and become one with the Spirit, as is Christ, the Son of God, who is one with the Father. As he himself said, 'Yet an hour is coming, and is already here, when those who are real worshippers will worship the Father in Spirit and truth. Indeed, it is just such worshippers the Father seeks. God is Spirit, and those who worship Him must worship in Spirit and truth' (John 4:23–24). At the centre, the pilgrim himself becomes the source of the Spirit which flows out in life-giving streams from his belly. Rabbi Aqiba, in the century after Jesus Christ, said, 'The disciple who is beginning is like a well who can give only the water it has received; the more advanced disciple is a spring giving living water.'

The seat of the spirit here is identified with the belly (Greek *koilia*), in keeping with many spiritual traditions, including the Hebraic. One finds in Proverbs 20:27, 'The breath of man is the lamp of the Lord, searching all the inner parts of his belly.' The breath, of course, in practically all traditions is intimately related with the Spirit. In Japan, the centre of the body and the soul in a person is called *hara*; this centre is given a particular emphasis in many spiritual disciplines of Japan, and especially in Zen Buddhism, where it is maintained that he who is not centred in his *hara* is not centred at all. This centre is in the belly, below the solar plexus, which designation itself is suggestive of the great importance attached to it, for the spirit is very often and in many traditions symbolised by the sun. The centre is near the navel, which physically is the place for the inflow of the life-sustaining energies in the womb through the umbilical cord. In the theory of yoga, one of the very important *chakras* (centres of energy) located near the navel is the *manipura chakra* which literally means the centre which fills with jewels.

The parenthetical remark in the text above quite rightly identifies the 'living water' with the Spirit, and reminds us that the crucifixion of the man Jesus was necessary for the Christ to rise. And similarly, by a complete analogy, for any person to become one with the Source so that the life-giving water will flow from his belly, his old self must be crucified for him to enter into the path towards Eternal Life. St Paul asks

> Have you forgotten that we who were baptised into Jesus Christ were baptised into his death? Through baptism into his death we were buried with him, so that, just as Christ was raised from the dead by the glory of the Father, we too might live a new life. If we have been united with him through likeness to his death, so shall we be through a like resurrection. This we know: our old self was crucified with him so that the sinful body might be destroyed and we might be slaves to sin no longer. A man who is dead has been freed from sin. If we have died with Christ, we believe that we are also to live with him' (Romans 6:3–8).

However, we must guard against a literal interpretation of dying to ourselves, or of crucifixion necessary for a new life, or of being baptised into the death of Jesus Christ. Clearly, there is no suggestion of an actual killing of oneself by committing suicide; it is the question of being crucified to the world, that is to the egoistic fears and desires which keep one from seeing reality clearly and impartially, so that one can do what needs to be done whether one likes it or not. There is a constant danger of an external interpretation in which interior spiritual and mythic truths and events are viewed only externally and historically, without sensitivity to their inner significance. This tendency is inherent in the crowd in us, which is easily swayed this way or that, without any permanent centre from which to discern subtle truths.

The temple guards, who had been sent four days earlier to arrest Jesus, are more open in their non-learned simplicity than the priests and the scholars to the extraordinary force and authority of Jesus Christ. 'No man ever spoke like that before'; they could hear something fresh and sense a different level of being of the source of these words than those who were professionally committed to pigeon-holing into different scriptural categories all that they heard. 'He taught as one with authority and not as the scribes' (Matthew 7:29); perhaps understandably, the scribes had the greatest difficulty in sensing this authority. Even when one of their own, namely Nicodemus, objected to the disregard of proper procedures in condemning Jesus Christ, they hurled scriptures at him, using the sacred words as weapons in the defence of the status quo of their positions rather than as a means for transformation of their being. This is always true: the mind which is not yoked to the service of the Spirit cannot accept any higher authority; it serves itself as the highest good, in this hubris becoming the perfect instrument of the Devil. This may well be the meaning of the saying of Jesus Christ, Luke 11:23, 'He who is not with me is against me, and he who does not gather with me scatters.'

CHAPTER
— 8 —

Adultery: Mixing of Levels

They went each to his home, and Jesus to the Mount of Olives. At dawn he appeared once more in the temple; and when all the people started coming to him, he sat down and started to teach them. The doctors of the law and the Pharisees now brought in a woman caught committing adultery. Making her stand out in the middle they said to him, 'Master, this woman was caught in the very act of adultery. Moses laid it down for us in the Law that such a woman should be stoned. What do you say about it?' (7:53 – 8:5).

They put the question to trap him, hoping to frame a charge against him. Jesus bent down and wrote with his finger on the ground. When they continued to press their question he sat up straight and said, 'Let the man among you who is without sin be the first to cast a stone at her.' Then once again he bent down and wrote on the ground. When they heard what he said, one by one they went away, beginning with the elders; and Jesus was alone with the woman still standing there. Jesus raised his head and said, 'Woman, where are they? Has no one condemned you?' 'No one, sir,' she answered. Jesus said, 'Nor do I condemn you. Go now, and sin no more' (8:6–11).

In order for us to hear and understand the words and actions of Jesus Christ subtly rather than literally, and not to judge by appearances, we cannot be satisfied simply with the surface and moralistic interpretation of the story told here. That level of morality, which clearly has its place, is not the main concern of Jesus Christ or of the Gospel writer; it would be completely out of place anywhere in the entire Gospel, and more particularly in relation to what has preceded this incident and what follows. Even at that level of morality, it would seem strange to find sentimental forgiving on the part of Jesus Christ who elsewhere makes very stern demands on people. The necessary qualifications, recommended here by Jesus Christ, of any person charged with dealing out punishment prescribed by law, would mitigate against all social justice, for who but God is good and without sin? These, and other considerations such as the fact that this story is not mentioned in the oldest manuscripts, have led scholars to a near unanimous conclusion that these verses don't belong to the Gospel at all. However, if one does not judge only according to the flesh, a caution recommended later in this very chapter (8:15), but by the spirit, the inclusion of this part of the teaching here is not out of place.

Recalling that the 'Word became flesh and dwelt in us', and recalling the fact that the temple is at least sometimes the body, and bearing in mind that the Christ is one with the Father who is Spirit (John 1:14, 2:21, 4:24), we are justified in attempting to understand the incident recounted here in an internal manner. Christ, the Spirit (*Atman*), has again descended into the body of the seeker hard at work in prayer and meditation, at the spiritually auspicious time of dawn. The analytical and legalistic mind is here and throughout the Gospel represented by the scribes and the Pharisees or the leaders of the Jews, often simply called 'the Jews'. The rational mind is always uneasy about the Spirit which displaces it from the centre of being, and therefore wants to analyse it, question its existence and right, and wants to trap the Spirit by trying to force it into some system or some category of thought. Above all, the mind wants to have only mental conclusions about everything, even about how to come to the Spirit or worship God.

Here, the mind brings to the Christ the very interesting puzzle of a soul (psyche) without the appropriate inner unity, as in the case of the Samaritan woman, who was without a strong connection with the real master within to husband her properly and to keep her yoked to the Spirit. She wanders off in search of this or that satisfaction, forgetting her true calling, and adulterating (a word which has the same etymological root as *adultery*) her understanding of the Spirit with phantoms and imaginings. One may be reminded here also of the fact that in the Old Testament reference to the sin of fornication often signifies the worship of false gods. Speaking innerly, adultery is a mixing of levels, and thus a mixing of the true with the false, of the real with the imaginary. This is a *sin* in the original Greek sense of *amartia* which means 'missing the mark'; and every soul commits adultery, to a greater or a lesser degree, until it finally finds oneness with God. Only he who is one with the Father unconditionally is without sin. Now the mental question to the Spirit is whether such a soul which deviates from the true Spirit should be killed and altogether eliminated. The mind can thus even pretend to be self-righteous and especially zealous in the service of God, as every learned priest is professionally required to be before the simple folk.

It is possible to understand the teaching of Christ, about leaving one's soul (psyche) behind if one wishes to follow him, at a literal level. One may thus imagine that the advice to 'die to oneself' is an advice to kill oneself, just as the admonition to be free of the world can be interpreted to mean a monastic retirement from the world. Especially when a man is struck by the fact that the world is too much with him, or that his soul is too adulterous, chasing phantoms rather than seeking God, a seeker can be disheartened and brought to the brink of suicide. Others in their self-righteousness, and with the mental assurance of their own salvation, owing to their place in some conventional system and adherence to the letter of the scriptural law, are all too quick to condemn such a soul. From the perspective of Christ, however, not a single person is without sin, without deviation from the true mark, for 'none is good but God alone' (Luke 18:19). In his awareness of the human fallibility, he is less concerned with condemnation of their sins; he has not come to judge, as he often said – certainly not a judgement by any external standards, or by appearances. He is much more interested in drawing human beings to the One, the ultimate reality, the only good. This he does not by a condemnation of wrong-doing, nor with a fear of the devil or of punishment, nor even with many promises of rewards in Heaven, but by his own example of self-sacrifice, unity of mind, body and soul in one single purpose, obedience to the will of the Father, and above all by his love of God. Love and compassion, exercised without sentimentality, are far more potent instruments of human transformation than fear and coercion, or reward and punishment. In the sight and presence of one's own highest possibility, all of one's lower and erring parts can be rightly aligned; one is justified in imagining that the advice of Jesus Christ not to sin any more went straight to the very core of the adulterous woman, making her whole-hearted and chaste again. The doctors of the law and the Pharisees, representatives of the mind, are also chastened, convicted by their conscience, and are able to submit to the force of the manifestly superior being and listen for a while.

The Highest Person as the Witness Within

Then Jesus spoke to them again: 'I AM the Light of the world. No follower of mine shall wander in the dark; he shall have the Light of Life' (8:12).

The Pharisees said to him, 'You are witness in your cause; your testimony is not valid.' Jesus replied, 'My testimony is valid, even though I do bear witness about myself, because I know where I come from, and where I am going. You do not know either where I come from or where I am going. You judge according to the flesh, but I pass judgement on no man. Yet even if I do judge, that judgement of mine is true because I am not alone: I have at my side the One who sent me. It is laid down in your law that evidence given by two persons is valid. I AM a witness in my own cause, and the Father who sent me gives testimony on my behalf.' They asked, 'Where is your father?' Jesus replied, 'You know neither me nor my Father; if you recognised me you would recognise my Father as well' (8:13–19).

These words were spoken by Jesus in the treasury as he taught in the temple. Yet no one arrested him, because his hour had not yet come (8:20).

I AM, the divine *ego eimi*, is the true Light shining in the darkness of the world; and a follower of this I AM, who can be a follower only if he dwells in the Logos as the Logos dwells in him (John 8:31, 14:23), naturally participates in the Light. Here again, as in the previous chapter, a question arises about the authority on the basis of which the statement of Jesus Christ can be accepted. Jesus Christ always appeals to the inner authority, the testimony of quality and spiritual sensitivity, and not to the judgement of the flesh, of appearances or of quantity. His testimony is true because, unlike others, he knows where he comes from and where he is going. Furthermore, he is not proclaiming himself and trying to impress others with his personal greatness. In all his words and deeds, the one being he proclaims is God: he is transparent to Him and is seen by Him, and therefore can be witnessed by Him.

It is a useful reminder, in the words of Jesus Christ himself, that he did not always speak from the highest vantage point of his complete oneness with God, as he does in John 10:30, where he says, 'My Father and I are one.' Here, a clear distinction is made between God as one of the two witnesses, and His name and power, I AM, as the other. Furthermore, both of these are witnessing on behalf of yet another, namely Jesus who is speaking. These are different levels of spiritual reality, accessible in different states of consciousness. Clearly, Jesus Christ is able to be so completely impartial to himself, and stand apart from himself, that he can simultaneously operate at the whole scale of being: from God, the Most High, to the flesh.

In many teachings in India, these various levels are understood as distinct bodies (*kayas*) or coverings (*koshas*) or persons (*purushas*), the subtlest and the innermost being the highest. Krishna teaches in the *Bhagavad Gita* (15:15–20):

> I am lodged in the heart of all. From Me stem recollection, wisdom and removal of doubt. Through all knowledge (Veda) it is I who should be known, the knower of all knowledge and the maker of the purpose of knowledge. There are two persons (*purushas*) in this world: the mutable and the immutable; the mutable is all these existences, the high-seated self is immutable. But other than these two is the highest spirit called the Supreme Self, who enters the three worlds and sustains them, the imperishable Lord. Since I transcend the mutable, and am higher than the immutable even, I am proclaimed the Highest Person (*purushottama*) in the world and the Veda. He who undeluded thus knows me as the Highest Person, knows all and dwells in me with all his being, all his love. Thus by Me has been revealed the most esoteric teaching, O sinless one. He who understands it is perfected in wisdom; his work is done.

Thus mindful of the three persons (*purushas*) simultaneously present in him, taking his stand in the subtlest and the most esoteric understanding of the human being, that of the *Mahapurusha* (the great person), Jesus Christ could speak as the phenomenal and mutable self (Jesus), calling as his two witnesses the immutable I AM and his Father, the Highest Person, lodged in his heart. His listeners, who judged according to the flesh, could hardly be expected to understand these subtle words about the inner presences. He spoke from a deep and guarded place in himself, symbolised by the treasury in the temple, and they asked him about his father in the external sense only. The difference in the levels of Jesus Christ and his audience is immense, as it is between our highest Self and our ordinary mind. Not only do they not understand him, but also they seem unaware of their lack of true being and their need for an inner transformation. There is a particular sadness in the words of Jesus Christ, about our human incomprehension, when he says that we neither recognise *him* nor his Father. His real suffering is because of our inability to be related with the necessary level of understanding; owing to this he is constantly crucified in us and by us. He speaks in the sight of God and His name, I AM; he is therefore true and right, and we judge him with the eyes of the flesh, denying him and remaining in the prison of our own ego.

Without Knowing I AM, One Dies Missing the Mark

Then he said to them again, 'I am going away and you will look for me but you will die in your sin. Where I am going you cannot come.' At this some of the Jews began to ask, 'Does he mean to kill himself when he says "Where I am going you cannot come"?' But he went on to say, 'You are of what is below; I AM of what is Above. You are of this world: I AM not. That is why I said you would die in your sins. Unless you come to believe I AM, you shall die in your sins' (8:21–24).

'Who are you, then?' they asked him. Jesus answered: 'What I have told you in the Beginning. I could say much about you in condemnation; but the only things I say to this world are what I have heard from Him, the truthful One who sent me.' They did not understand that he was speaking to them about the Father (8:25–27).

101

Jesus continued, 'When you lift up the Son of Man, you will come to realise I AM, and that I do nothing by myself. I say only what the Father has taught me. And the One who sent me is with me; He has not deserted me since I always do what pleases Him.' While he was speaking this way, many came to believe in him (8:28–30).

Within a human being, I AM is what constitutes the bridge between this world and the world of the Father, between what is below and what is Above. Without such a possibility of a link between the flesh and the Spirit, human existence would be completely condemned to this world without any hope for spiritual salvation. It is for the sake of those in whom this higher aspiration to live in the Light of the Spirit is active that the Word became flesh. Jesus Christ said towards the end of his life on the earth, 'Father, the hour has come! . . . I have given you glory on earth by completing the work you gave me to do . . . I have made your name known to those you gave me out of the world. These men you gave me were yours; they have kept your Word' (John 17:1–6). His whole mission was to reveal to the disciples, who were disciples by his or God's choosing and by their keeping the commands, the true and mysterious name of God, I AM (*ego eimi*), with all the *power* and *being* inherent in it. How do disciples come to know and realise I AM, except by discovering its echoes deep within their own soul? Situated there alone, in the 'centre of the soul', as St Teresa of Avila expressed it, or the 'spirit of the soul', as Eckhart said, without egoism, mindful of I AM, can one speak in the name of God. 'One that seeks to penetrate the nature of the Divine Mind', according to Plotinus (*Enneads* V.3.9), 'must see deeply into the nature of his own soul, into the Divinest part of himself.'

When a person lifts up the Son of Man, that is to say when a person realises the highest possibilities of the human being, he comes to realise I AM. Traversing this bridge of being and consciousness, he will become the Son of God. I AM is the way for a son of man, when he has been lifted up above the density of the flesh, to become a son of God, of one family with the Son of God, 'for all who are moved by the Spirit of God are sons of God' (Romans 8:14). This begetting of the inner being by the Spirit is the virgin birth, having nothing to do with any gender, as much a possibility for males as for females, as long

102

as their heart and soul are opened and they let themselves be fecundated by the Spirit. 'The virgin will conceive and bear a son, and he shall be called Emmanuel, a name which means "God is with us"' (Matthew 1:23). Meister Eckhart understood the inner significance of this verse as indicating that *Emmanuel* is said of each of us as a son of man become a son of God.

The schema given earlier (see Chapter 6), of the spiritual hierarchy in the Gospel According to St John, can now be filled out a little as follows:

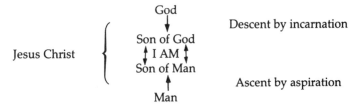

Unless a person comes to understand and love I AM, and dwell in it, his human birth will be in vain, in the literal sense that he will live from vanity, from his own ego, and not from the Divine Ego. He would thus miss the true mark, the purpose of his human incarnation, and die in sin, not realising that by oneself one can do nothing; that, in fact, one *is* nothing. Unless related with the Father, by himself even Jesus Christ is nothing; he can *do* nothing or *say* nothing of real value. He is the great teacher precisely because the teaching he brings is not his own, but of the One who sent him. The less his own self enters into it, the greater is the master. His importance does not lie in the fact that he is any specific or particular one – from a special place or lineage, or of a specific colour, form or shape. Having become no one in particular, having sacrificed and emptied himself completely, he has been made worthy to open the scroll of hidden wisdom and to break its seven seals, so that he can behold that which no vision of ego can see. Having become nothing himself, he becomes one with the All. He then does not speak from *I am this* or *I am that*, but from *I AM*. 'He has no father, no mother, no lineage; his years have no beginning, his life no end. He is like the Son of God: he remains a priest for all time' (Hebrews 7:3).

The teaching about I AM is a specific instruction to seek God within oneself; it parallels the injunction in another tradition, namely 'Look within: you are the Buddha!' 'The Kingdom of heaven is within you,' said Jesus Christ in one of the non-canonical sayings, found on the papyri discovered in Oxyrhynchus (Egypt), 'and whosoever knoweth himself shall find it. And having found it, ye shall know yourselves that ye are the sons and heirs of the Father, the Almighty, and shall know yourselves that ye are in God, and God in you. And ye are the City of God.'

When Jesus Christ speaks of dying to himself, the crowd around wonders if he is going to kill himself. When he says 'I AM, from the Beginning,' that is *timelessly*, they ask 'What are you specifically, in time?' With such a vast gulf between Jesus Christ and his audience, it is no surprise that they do not comprehend him. The surprise is that he continues to teach them. Why? Is he trying to teach his own disciples, who must have been around although they have not been mentioned for some time now, something about the nature of the outer and inner crowd? Is he undergoing all this for the sake of a few scattered seekers who might hear and be called? Is he testing his own understanding and resolve and preparing himself for a greater baptism to come? Meanwhile, we are told, that some among those who heard him did understand and recognise his nature, and thus believed in him. To deepen their insight, so that it may become integrated with their whole being, he continued his teaching.

A Disciple is He who Lives the Teaching

Then Jesus went on to say to those Jews who had believed in him, 'If you abide in my word, you are truly my disciples; and you will know the truth and the truth will set you free.' 'We are descendants of Abraham,' they retorted, 'and never have we been slaves to anyone. What do you mean by saying, "You will be free"?' Jesus answered them, 'In very truth I tell you that everyone who lives in sin is a slave. The slave has no permanent standing in a household, but the son belongs to it for ever. If then the son sets you free, you will indeed be free. I know that you are descended from Abraham, but you are trying to kill me because my word finds no place in you. I tell what I have seen in the Father's presence; therefore, you should do what you heard from the Father' (8:31–38).

'Our father is Abraham,' they answered him. Jesus replied, 'If you really are Abraham's children, you would be doing works worthy of Abraham. But actually you are looking to kill me, just because I am a man who told you the truth which I heard from God. Abraham did nothing like that. Indeed you are doing your own father's works!' They protested, 'We were not born illegitimate. We have but one father, God Himself' (8:39–41).

Jesus told them, 'If God were your father, you would love me, for God is the source of my being, and from him I come. Why do you not understand my language? It is because you cannot bear to hear my word. Your father is the devil, and you willingly carry out your father's desires. He was a murderer from the beginning and never based himself on truth, for there is no truth in him. When he tells a lie, he speaks his native language, for he is a liar and the father of lying. But I speak the truth and therefore you do not believe me. Can any one of you convict me of sin? If I am telling the truth, why do you not believe? The man who belongs to God hears the words of God. The reason why you do not hear is that you do not belong to God' (8:42–47).

There is a great deal of difference in believing out of some mental conviction or from scriptural authority, or from some enthusiastic response to an overwhelming situation or charismatic person, and the *seeing* which results in a radical transformation of the whole of one's being. Some of the people around Jesus partially understood him and were touched by his words. Immediately, Jesus Christ goes on to stress the necessity of his teachings actually being put into practice by those who would follow him. A real believer is one, as we are told in John 5:38, in whom the word of God abides. Furthermore, 'one who does not abide in the teaching of Christ does not have God' (2 John 9). Until the words of Christ enter the whole mass and structure of a person, he is not a real disciple of him; his belief can easily turn into disbelief and he is ready to stone the very person to whom he was willing to hand his soul:

Not everyone who calls me 'Lord, Lord' will enter the kingdom of Heaven, but only those who do the will of my heavenly Father. When that day comes, many will say to me, 'Lord, Lord, did we not prophesy in your name, cast out devils in your name, and in your name perform many miracles?' Then will I tell them to their face, 'I never knew you; out of my sight, you and your wicked ways!' What then of the man who hears these words of mine and acts upon them? He is like a man who had the sense to build his house on rock. The rain came down, the floods rose, the wind blew, and beat upon that house; but it did not fall, because its foundations were on rock. But what of the man who hears these words of mine and does not act upon them? He is like a man who was foolish enough to build his house on sand. The rain came down, the floods rose, the wind blew, and beat upon that house; down it fell with a great crash (Matthew 7:21–27).

It is only by trying to live according to the words of Jesus Christ that one can hope to find their truth and meaning, and not merely by scriptural learning or a logical and rational analysis of the teachings.

The way we can be sure of our knowledge of him is to keep his commandments. The man who claims 'I have known him,' without keeping his commandments, is a liar; in such a one there is no truth. But whoever keeps his word, truly has the love of God been made perfect in him. The way we can be sure we are in union with him is for the man who claims to abide in him to conduct himself just as he did (1 John 2:3–6).

Analysis and learning can, of course, be useful in leading one towards a holy life; but, above all, the words need to be embodied, just as the Word needs to be incarnated, for them to have any action and lasting influence on the wayfarer.

The sort of action which is required is the one that will transform the aspirant, to start with, from being a slave of sin to being a slave of God. This latter slavery is the necessary prerequisite for a real freedom of the soul, which needs to undergo a radical reorientation (*metanoia* in Greek, usually translated as 'repentance') and to begin obeying God's commandments against its own self-will. 'Have you never learned', asks the scripture (James 4:4), 'that love of the world is enmity to God?

Whoever chooses to be the world's friend makes himself God's enemy.' More and more, as the soul understands the need for this turning of the mind and the heart, it willingly accepts the yoke of Christ, thus becoming a servant of God rather rather than a slave. Still further, as a person does what he is commanded by God and comes to know all the things of God, that is, when the Son of Man is lifted up in him, he becomes a *friend*, as the disciples were called by Christ (John 15:14–15) at the end of their training under him.

After the struggle within oneself between the Son of Man and the son of man, between the parts which wish to love God and the parts which love the world, after obedience, service and training, as and if one is begotten by the Spirit, one becomes a son of God, finally, as St Paul says (Ephesians 4:13), coming 'to mature manhood, measured by nothing less than the full stature of Christ', and becoming one with God. The soul is then at the end of the journey; the wayfarer is then no longer a Christian but *Christ*.

Full freedom is only then; however, the way to it begins from turning away from one's slavery to the world – that is the world of fear and desire – towards a discipleship and the spiritual discipline, the yoke and the yoga of Jesus Christ. The progressive liberation from one's slavery to fear and desire, from one's own little ego, is the purpose of any transformational teaching or spiritual path. The more one progresses along a spiritual path, more and more as one sees the necessity and the rightness of the way, the easier it becomes to accept it. As one knows it and loves it more and more, the discipline loses its heaviness: it becomes natural, good and light. From being a slave, a spiritual labourer becomes a lover of the way and of God: for him every demand of the Beloved is welcome and easy. 'Come unto me, all you that labour and are heavy laden, and I will give you rest. Take my yoke upon you, and learn of me; for I am gentle and humble of heart: and you shall find rest unto your souls, for my yoke is easy and my burden is light' (Matthew 11:28–30).

The audience of Jesus Christ did not understand; full of themselves and their traditions and expectations, they had not much room in their hearts where his words could find a place. Still, since they were somewhat touched by him and could not ignore him completely, they wished to eliminate his troubling presence. The more vigorously and unsentimentally he exposed their nakedness, their misunderstanding of the real meaning of the Abrahamic tradition, their lack of spiritual sensitivity and relationship with God, their slavery and kinship with the devil, the more outraged they were. The edifice of their belief in him clearly had no firm foundation; it was simply an enthusiastic reaction to his personality and words without the necessary practice; and when he let loose on them the force of the gale of the Spirit the whole structure collapsed. The man they had believed in as the saviour of their souls, and as one able to lead them into Eternal Life, was now a ready target of their stones!

Losing One's Mind Rightly

The Jews answered, 'Are we not right after all in saying that you are a Samaritan, and that you are demented?' Jesus replied, 'I am not demented, but I do honour my Father, while you insult me. However, I am not seeking glory for myself; there is One who does seek it and He passes judgement. In very truth I tell you, if a man keeps my word, he shall never see death.' 'Now we are sure you are demented,' the Jews retorted. 'Abraham died; so did the prophets. Yet, you claim, "A man shall never taste death if he keeps my word." Are you greater than our Father Abraham, who is dead? The prophets are dead too. What do you claim to be?' (8:48–53).

Jesus replied, 'If I glorify myself, my glory amounts to nothing. The One who glorifies me is the Father whom you claim as "our God", even though you do not know Him. But I do know Him; and if I say I do not know Him, I will be just like you, a liar! Yes, I do know Him and I keep His word. Your father Abraham rejoiced to see my day; he saw it and was glad' (8:54–56).

This caused the Jews to object, 'You are not yet fifty years old. How can you have seen Abraham?' Jesus said, 'In very truth I tell you, before Abraham came to be, I AM.' Then they picked up stones to throw at Jesus, but he hid himself and slipped out of the temple precincts (8:57–59).

Here one finds the classical reaction of the authorities to any-one who meddles in the established order and challenges conventional wisdom. He is either an outsider or crazy, either a Samaritan or demented, or perhaps both!

There is the constant difficulty, encountered by practitioners of all transformational teachings, of understanding something that is higher than oneself. A person naturally wishes to understand everything according to his own lights and on his own terms; he has nothing else of his own to rely upon. On the other hand, the very *raison d'être* of every teaching depends on the truth of the assertion that as a person ordinarily is he lives in sin or in illusion or in ignorance, and that it is possible for him to be transformed and to live differently, in grace, reality and truth. In this transformation, it is the very heart and mind, and even the body, of the person which undergo subtle but thorough change, so that all his perceptions and understanding will be different. Essentially, the pilgrim responds to a mysterious prompting in his heart, without being able to say clearly and rationally what he seeks, and what its characteristics are. Of course the traditions can help here and the Scriptures and other texts can provide some sort of a map of the territory fundamentally unknown to the traveller. But as he progresses along the way, he comes to a different level of being within himself, different from the one he started with.

As he comes to a new being, or as a new being is born in him, he also has a new mind, the right mind, whereas until now he was in a wrong mind. Letting go of one's anchor in the wrong mind, the ordinary mind, is therefore essential to come to truth. The question largely is this: how to lose one's mind rightly? A person can, of course, be out of one's mind in a subnormal direction. But a sage or a messenger from God is out of his mind in a supernormal direction, even though from our ordinary point of view he may behave as if he is dead to the world. But those who, like St Paul, 'possess the mind of Christ', declare: 'Make no mistake about this: if there is anyone among you who fancies himself wise – wise, I mean, by the standards of this passing age – he must become a fool to gain true wisdom. For the wisdom of this world is folly in God's sight' (1 Corinthians 2:16; 3:18–19). A person has to be out of his worldly mind in order to be raised from the dead and made new in mind and spirit (Ephesians 4:22–24; 5:14). Through the yoga of Jesus Christ, through his cross, the world is crucified to him who would follow him, and he is crucified to the world (Galatians 6:14).

As Jesus Christ had so completely moulded himself to the will of his Father, he had no mind of his own, separated from that of God. Since the people around him, except the ones who were his disciples and were actively attempting to live by his teachings, could not understand the mind of God, nor therefore the mind of Christ when he spoke from that level, he appeared to them to be demented. They were not even aware of the limitations of their own mind; that is the real slavery, blindness and sin in which they lived. Not to realise that one is blind and needs to be healed is the greatest impediment to gaining sight; one is not even prepared to accept help when it is offered.

Being freed of his egoistic self, and of any particularity of being this or that, in this place or that time, he was one with the Father, one with the All, freed of all constraints of time and space. Thus he could view all temporal phenomena from the vantage point of eternity, which must not be understood as an endless duration of time but altogether a different mode of consciousness and being in which all time can be simultaneously present. It is in such a state, a moment in the eternal now of I AM, that Christ *is* before Abraham came to be. Those who heard him did not understand, and asked him the expected question, as Arjuna had asked Krishna in the *Bhagavad Gita* (4:1–4), not realising that the limitation imposed by time sequence is binding only on those at a level of consciousness inferior to that of Christ or Krishna.

The Gospel writer is a master of style and irony: the chapter opens with the doctors of the law asking Jesus if the woman caught in adultery should be stoned; by the end of the chapter, they are about to stone Christ himself for blasphemy, a form of spiritual adultery! As the hostility of the ignorant level of being became manifest, and since his hour had not yet come, he exercised one of the many powers of accomplished yogis described in the yoga literature (for example in the *Yoga Sutra* 3:21): he made himself invisible and walked away!

110

CHAPTER

—— 9 ——

Spiritual Blindness is Natural

As he walked along, Jesus saw a man who had been blind from birth. His disciples asked him, 'Rabbi, was it his sin or that of his parents that caused him to be born blind?' 'Neither,' answered Jesus. 'It was no sin, either of this man or of his parents. Rather, it was to let God's work be revealed in him. We must do the works of Him who sent me while it is day. Night is coming when no one can work. As long as I AM in the world, I AM the Light of the world' (9:1–5).

With that he spat on the ground, made a paste with the spittle, and anointed the man's eyes with it. Then Jesus told him, 'Go and wash in the pool of Siloam.' (This name means 'one who has been sent'.) The man went away and washed, and when he returned he could see (9:6–7).

The spiritual blindness of every man is placed on the largest cosmological scale: it does not arise out of a person's subjectivity, nor from his heredity, but from natural laws. Spiritual blindness is an objective consequence of universal laws, and everyone, without regard to his particular genetic constitution or his own moral behaviour, is born spiritually blind. It is not a matter of personal fault, but it is inherent in the very laws by which one becomes a creature. In that sense, the blindness to truth and reality, turning away from the Light, is a part of the original and universal sin: it is not a personal failing of this man or his parents, but something in which everyone participates by the mere fact of being human. Yet by that very fact of being born human, each one inherits the specifically human potentiality of being able to turn to the Light, and to live in the presence of truth. Thus we are faced with not only the *terror* of our human

111

situation, our general sleep and proclivity for living in illusion, but also with the *wonder* of it all and with the possibility of waking up. We are in the midst of this play of forces taking place not only in the cosmos as an outer whole but also in the interior cosmos of our soul.

In the Christian tradition, the forces competing for the possession of our souls are usually personified, owing to a preference for the theological rather than the metaphysical mode of expression: the evil ones as demonic, originating from and controlled by the Devil, and the good ones as divine, sent by God, even though, strictly speaking, the Devil also comes from God. What is important to emphasise here is the large scale of the forces, of sin as well as of virtue, which are involved, a scale much larger than any individual's fault or credit. St Paul is clear about it: 'Finally then, find your strength in the Lord, in his mighty power. Put on all the armour which God provides, so that you may be able to stand firm against the devices of the devil. Our fight is not against human foes, but against cosmic powers, against the authorities and potentates of this dark world, against the superhuman forces of evil in the heavens' (Ephesians 6:10–12).

A distinction needs to be made between what is actual and what is real. According to the spiritual traditions of India, an ordinary human being is born *prakrita*, which is to say, natural, common, vulgar, unrefined, unspiritual. But with proper education, by yoga, he can become *samskrita*, that is to say well-made, sculpted, refined. St Paul also says (in 1 Corinthians 15:46–49):

> Take note, the spiritual was not first; first came the natural and after that the spiritual. The first man of earth, formed from dust, the second is from heaven. Earthly men are like the man of earth, heavenly men are like the man of heaven. Just as we resemble the man from earth, so shall we bear the likeness of the man from heaven.

This movement from the natural self to the spiritual Self is the second birth, but it is the birth of a being which was already deep within oneself. At the end of the journey, the pilgrim in fact arrives home, becoming in actuality what he has really been all along, a reality which to start with was only an ideal but which can now be said to be actual in him.

The method of any spiritual tradition corresponds to the procedure inherent in the etymology of the word 'education', which is derived from the Latin *educare*, meaning 'to draw out'. It is from deep within the aspirant that the real is drawn out, almost always with the external help of teachers and teachings. A search for reality is, therefore, a struggle against the natural tendencies inherent in all creation; all spiritual teachings are thus fundamentally in opposition to the common, outward current of human nature, the current of illusion, ignorance and sleep. This battle, waged for the possession of his soul and primarily within the psyche of a person, is the battle between God and the Devil or between the *Word* and the *world*, or between the Spirit and the flesh. 'Have you never learned that love of the world is enmity to God? Whoever chooses to be the world's friend makes himself God's enemy' (James 4:4).

So what is at issue is not the personal sin of the blind man, but the fact that blindness is natural, and that he must undertake a spiritual journey to gain sight, to wake up, to be spiritual and become a son of God, 'to let God's work be revealed in him' and not only the work of the flesh. This man is already a seeker very well advanced. He knows that he is blind and ignorant and needs to be transformed into a new being; he has already disciplined his natural self and has humbled his ego, for 'isn't this the fellow who used to sit and beg?' (John 9:8). He is almost ready, his opportune time has come, it is now his day, and God's work must be done before it is too late for him and his organism fails or his attention flags, and night descends over him and sleep overtakes him again.

In the struggle between sleep and wakefulness, taking place in the soul of the aspirant, the Master did what he must do in order to carry out the work of the One who sent him: he saw the ripeness of the blind man and his near oneness with the Son of God in the state of I AM, the Light of the world, and chose him unpetitioned. He anointed him with a substance of himself, and reminded him of his true nature, that in reality he does not exist by himself but is 'one who has been sent' from God; in truth he is a son of God just as is the Son of God. After he realised this in his being, he returned to his ordinary ego consciousness, but now a transformed man, bathed in the source of light, a *seer*, one who sees not only what is grossly apparent, but also what is subtle. How marvellously well this is expressed here as *washing in the pool of Siloam*! For scripture shares with all art the question of making perceptible what is ordinarily imperceptible – in paint or stone or musical notes or symbols or legends. If there is no external and portable support for the major insights of a culture, in the form of symbols, metaphors or stories, the transmission of these insights across generations is likely to suffer. If, on the other hand, there is not a periodic renewal of the inner significance of these symbols and metaphors, one would be left largely with the gross chaff without the subtle kernel which by its very nature can be visible only to transformed spiritual eyes.

Sight as New Birth

His neighbours and the people who had been accustomed to see him begging began to ask, 'Isn't this the fellow who used to sit and beg?' Some were claiming it was he; others maintained it was not, but someone who looked like him. He himself said, 'I AM'. So they said to him, 'How were your eyes opened?' He answered, 'That man they call Jesus made a paste and anointed my eyes, telling me to go to Siloam and wash. When I did go and wash, I was able to see.' 'Where is he?' they asked. 'I have no idea,' he replied (9:8–12).

Next, they took the man who had been blind to the Pharisees. Note that it was on a Sabbath day that Jesus had made the paste and opened his eyes. The Pharisees now asked him by what means he had gained his sight. He told them, 'He anointed my eyes with paste; and I washed and now I can see.' Some of the Pharisees said, 'This man cannot be from God because he does not keep the Sabbath.' Others objected, 'If a man is a sinner, how can he perform signs like these?' They were sharply divided over him. Then they questioned the blind man again: 'Since it was your eyes he opened, what do you have to say about him?' 'He is a prophet,' he replied (9:13–17).

'If anyone is in Christ, he is a new creation' (2 Corinthians 5:17). The man who had gained sight, insight and new being, had been so transformed even externally that people who knew him

114

did not recognise him easily. He had died to his old self and had been resurrected anew, encountering the same sort of difficulty in being recognised as Jesus Christ had after his resurrection (John 20:11–18). He shared another aspect with Jesus Christ: he is the only person in this gospel, other than Christ himself, who uttered the divine name I AM (*ego eimi*). Not even one of the closest disciples of Jesus Christ had come to such ripening of the soul as this blind man who had woken up. He had washed in the pool of the one who has been sent, he had seen and recognised the Son of Man, he dwelt in Christ and Christ in him; at least for a while they shared in a common divinity, which, of course, is not their own, and does not belong to them or to anyone, but to which anyone could belong who is not exclusively possessed by his own selfhood.

There is a directness and simplicity in the responses of this transformed man which vouch for the authenticity of his deep experience. He knows that the man Jesus had something to do with his awakening, but he refused to philosophise about the mystery of the Christ, about his real identification or dwelling-place. He took his stand only on direct perception; 'I have no idea' conveys the same clarity of self-awareness as his recognition and acknowledgement of his blindness. Asked directly about his own judgement, in the middle of contending learned theologians and at considerable risk to himself, he had no doubt that Jesus Christ is a prophet.

As was said above, spiritual development is against the current of the outward and expansive natural tendencies inherent in all creation. All outward assertion stems from 'I am this' or 'I am that'; whereas the inward journey is an undertaking to bring all such predicates of 'I am' to rest in the divine I AM. True spirituality is a ceaseless practice of dying to the enchantment of the ego and of the world, and turning to God. Only as the creational urge, with its centrifugal thrust, is quietened, one's attention can be turned inwards, from the sons of men to the Son of Man, from procreation to the virgin birth in the heart. Sabbath day, with all its pregnant symbolism derived from the archetype *in divinis*, is given to man as a day of rest from outward labours which of necessity disperse one, for turning inward, and to God for recuperation and healing. This is the day when one can attempt to set one's own little self aside and come to the Self. It is a holy day for healing and wholeness. Whenever real healing takes place, it is Sabbath, as we saw in Chapter 5 as well. But the eyes of flesh cannot see and discern the works of the Spirit; for not keeping some outward convention the holiest of men is judged to be a sinner. 'Why are you angry with me for curing a whole man on the Sabbath?' asked Jesus Christ, and taught, 'Don't judge by appearances, and make a just judgement' (John 7:23–24).

Insight or More Sights?

But the Jews refused to believe that he had really been born blind and had begun to see, until they summoned the parents of this man who now could see. 'Is this your son?' they asked, 'and if so, do you attest that he was born blind?' The parents answered: 'We know this is our son, and we know he was blind at birth. But we do not know how he can see now, nor do we know who opened his eyes. He is old enough. He will speak for himself.' (His parents gave this answer because they were afraid of the Jews, who had already agreed among themselves that any-one who acknowledged Jesus as the Messiah would be put out of the synagogue. That is why the parents said, 'He is of age; ask him') (9:18–23).

A second time they summoned the man who had been born blind and said to him, 'Give glory to God! First of all, we know this man is a sinner.' 'I do not know whether he is a sinner or not,' he answered. 'I know this much: I was blind before, now I can see.' They persisted, 'Just what did he do to you? How did he open your eyes?' 'I told you once and you did not listen,' he answered them. 'Why do you want to hear it again? Do not tell me you want to become his disciples too?' They retorted scornfully, 'You are the one who is that man's disciple. We are disciples of Moses. We know that God spoke to Moses, but we have no idea where this man comes from' (9:24–29).

The man replied, 'What an extraordinary thing! Here is a man who has opened my eyes, yet you do not know where he comes from! We know that God pays no attention to sinners, but He does listen to someone who is devout and obeys His will. It is unheard of that anyone ever opened the eyes of a man born blind. If this man were not from God, he could have done nothing.' 'What!' they exclaimed. 'You were born steeped in sin, and now you are lecturing us?' Then they threw him out (9:30–34).

Once again we have the question of *authority* and the *authorities*. A new order is being created, a new vision, and the custodians of the old order are uneasy. They do not know how to understand it and what to make of it. In the presence of a higher truth what is called for is a deepening of the look, a new set of eyes with a new insight, rather than more information and data seen with the same eyes. It is a cleansing of the perceptions which is necessary rather than more perceptions; a different *quality* rather than additional *quantity*. But the authorities, who ought to know, as the previously blind man reminded them because for him the great surprise is the discovery that they, the learned leaders, do not know the sort of mysteries to which even he has been initiated, are blinded to higher levels of quality. They try to gather more data – from the parents and from the cured blind man again. The parents say only what they are certain of, without further speculation, acknowledging that their son is mature in body and soul and is capable of seeing and speaking the truth. The man himself repeats what he told them earlier, even in the face of their prejudgement about Jesus as a sinner. And he is puzzled at the density of the leaders in spiritual matters, for in his judgement they ought to know better.

As always, the leaders appeal to the tradition and conventions, and they truly have no idea where the power of Jesus Christ comes from; they do not know the place of his real dwelling – which is in the heart of the disciple who believes in him, and lives according to his commands. Nor do they understand his mission, which is to do the will of his Father who sent him, and to reveal His true name to the disciples. They realise that there is something quite extraordinary about the works and teachings of Christ; they could not but come from God. But what he says and does is unusual and unconventional, not according to their understanding of the tradition and their expectations and image of a prophet. In this dual pull, they finally settle for the security of their own limited understanding, rather than open themselves to a vaster vision beyond their control. And anybody who would remind them of a choice made against their own higher conscience could not be tolerated. In throwing out the awakened man who had been asleep, the blind man who could now see, on a smaller scale they pre-enact the crucifixion of Jesus Christ himself.

The Sighted and the Sightless

When Jesus heard of his expulsion, he sought him out and asked him, 'Do you believe in the Son of Man?' He answered, 'Who is he, sir, that I may believe in him?' 'You have seen him,' Jesus replied, 'for it is he who is speaking to you now.' 'I do believe, Lord,' he said, and bowed down to worship him. Then Jesus said: 'I came into this world to divide it, to make the sightless see and the seeing blind' (9:35–39)

Some of the Pharisees who were there with him overheard this and said, 'Do you mean that we are blind?' To which Jesus replied, 'If you were blind there would be no sin in that. But because you say, "We see," your sin remains' (9:40–41).

The expulsion of the wakeful man from the halls of acceptability seems to have pushed him closer to Jesus Christ who sought him out, as if something in him had providentially brought about his emergence from the circles of darkness into the circle of light. He might have himself hoped for a little acknowledgement and respect from the social and religious authorities, perhaps as a prized witness to the work of God. If he had been accorded some recognition, he might have been satisfied with his spiritual progress and ceased searching further. His separation, even though not voluntary on his part, from the domain of approval and disapproval, reward and punishment, seems to have been a necessary preparation for him for a still deeper insight which is brought to him by Jesus Christ as the Son of Man.

Seeing and understanding the Christ as the Son of Man, or as the Son of God, or as I AM, are intimately related with each other, as shown in the schema in Chapter 8. Furthermore, to understand the true nature of Christ means to see him within oneself, to let him dwell in oneself, to become of one substance with him by taking in his very flesh and blood into one's own being. Believing in him means not only knowing him and loving him, but participating in his being. Krishna says:

Within all beings, yet without them; unmoved, It yet moves indeed; so subtle is It one cannot comprehend It; far off It stands, and yet how near It is! Undivided in beings It abides seeming divided: this is That which should be known – the one who generates, sustains and devours all beings. Light of lights . . . It is true knowledge and the object of knowledge. It is seated in the hearts of all . . . knowing this, the person who loves me and worships me participates in my own mode of being' (*Bhagavad Gita* 13:15–18).

There is a constant judgement on the part of Jesus Christ – that is to say, discernment, discrimination, division and separation – between lower and higher levels of being. Within the realm of general humanity, prior to the birth of a new and spiritual being in man, that is to say prior to his obtaining spiritual vision, three levels are distinguished. There are people who see with ordinary eyes, but begin to be aware of a lack in themselves. Such people make progress when they are made 'blind' by Christ, aware of their blindness, as well as blind to the world which no longer bewitches them with its fascinations. Those who are in anguish because of the limitation on their vision and attempt to come to light are made whole and given sight. In being blind and knowing that one is blind, there is no sin. But sin remains for the third group: being in fact blind and asleep and yet pretending to see because they know the right scriptural reference or the rule of conduct, exalting themselves as they are and protecting their blindness.

It is less the distance from God but more the pretension of nearness to Him that leads a person in the wrong direction. He who knows he is far away from truth can aspire and be shown the way; but he who takes falsehood to be truth and justifies himself in remaining the way he is cannot be helped, for he who is full of himself has no room for God. There is a parable told by Jesus Christ:

Two men went up to the temple to pray; one was a Pharisee, the other a tax collector. The Pharisee with head unbowed prayed in this fashion: 'I give you thanks, O God, that I am not like the rest of men – greedy, dishonest, adulterous – or even like this tax collector. I fast twice a week; I pay tithes on all that I get.' But the other man kept his distance, not even daring to raise his eyes to heaven. All he did was to beat his breast and say, 'O God, be merciful to me, a sinner.' Believe me, this man went home from the temple acquitted of his sins, but the other did not. For everyone who exalts himself shall be humbled while he who humbles himself shall be exalted' (Luke 18:10–14).

CHAPTER

— 10 —

Many Sheep and One Shepherd

In truth I tell you, in very truth, the man who does not enter
the sheepfold through the gate, but climbs in some other way,
is a thief and a bandit. The one who enters through the gate is
shepherd of the sheep; for him the keeper opens the gate. And
the sheep recognise his voice as he calls the sheep that belong
to him and leads them out. When he has driven all his own
sheep out, he walks in front of them; and the sheep follow
him because they know his voice. But they will not follow a
stranger; they will run away from him because they do not
recognise the voice of strangers. This was a parable spoken
by Jesus to them, but they did not understand what he meant
by it (10:1–6).

So Jesus said, 'In truth, in very truth I tell you, I AM the
sheepgate. All who came (before me) are thieves and bandits,
and the sheep did not heed them. I AM the gate. Whoever
enters through me will be saved; and he will go in and out
and find pasture. A thief comes only to steal, slaughter and
destroy. I came that they may have life and have it abundantly.
I AM the model shepherd; the proper shepherd lays down his
life for the sheep. The hireling, when he sees the wolf coming,
abandons the sheep and runs away, because he is no shepherd
and the sheep are not his. I AM the right shepherd: I know my
sheep and mine know me, just as the Father knows me and I
know the Father. And for these sheep I give my life. I have
other sheep, too, that do not belong to this fold. These also
must I lead, and they will listen to my voice. Then there will
be one flock and one shepherd. This is why the Father loves
me: because I lay down my life in order to take it up again. No
one takes it from me; rather, I lay it down of my own accord. I
have power to lay it down and I have power to take it up again.
This command I received from my Father' (10:7–18).

121

Because of these words the Jews were again sharply divided. Many of them said, 'He is possessed, he is raving. Why listen to him?' Others said, 'No one possessed by an evil spirit could speak like this. Could an evil spirit open a blind man's eyes?' (10:19–21).

A sheep of nature, as everyone inevitably is, can also become a sheep of the Spirit. Each one must die, that is so according to the law of the flesh. But if a person dies intentionally to his lower self, he can rise as his higher Self and find Eternal Life.

The beginning as well as the end of the text above indicates its continuity with the previous chapter. The parable spoken by Jesus begins with *Amen, Amen,* translated here as 'In truth, in very truth,' indicating an enhanced emphasis and a change in the intensity and the level of what was being said; this mode is rarely used in the Gospel to begin a new discourse. And at the end of the text, the audience is again reminded of the miracle of the blind man being given eyesight. Thus it is fruitful to look at the text here in the light of what was said before, in John 9:39–41.

Jesus Christ, himself the Lamb of God, made a division between those who yearn for more and more light and are suffering in their blindness, and those who are satisfied with their level of being and make no effort to come closer to truth. The former are *his* sheep whom he knows, just as the Father knows him; the latter are not his sheep because they are unable to recognise him and thus refuse to believe (John 10:26). On their part, his sheep are aware of their being lost, without a true guide, and are seeking help. And these sheep have enough discernment to be able to recognise the difference between a guide from above, the right guide, and those who are unable to guide, and, worse still, pretend to be the true guides but are themselves blind.

These others, even when they pretend to be shepherds and guides, are really thieves and bandits interested only in taking advantage of the sheep; they are strangers and hirelings who abandon the sheep in the face of danger. It is said in the *Bhagavad Gita* (3:10–12) that of old the Lord of Being brought forth creatures with sacrifice (*yajna*) and instructed them that 'it is with sacrifice that you shall sustain the gods so that the gods may sustain you; by this reciprocal sustenance you shall attain the highest good. Sustained by sacrifice the gods will give you the food of your aspiration. He who enjoys their gifts yet gives the gods nothing in return is verily a thief.' The greatest sacrifice is that of the self, which must be left behind in order to follow Christ. Only through this sacrifice can an exchange of energies take place between levels of being; otherwise, one makes oneself into a black hole of greed, stealing and hoarding every good for one's own egoistic purposes. The sheep, viewed internally as a person's own unconscious parts and externally as those who are in his care, rely upon the guidance of the more conscious and the more learned members, and can be misled if the guide himself be blind.

But the sheep of Jesus Christ know their true shepherd as he knows the Father, his Shepherd. I AM is the right shepherd. The adjective that is used three times for the shepherd is *kalos* in Greek, which has connotations of beautiful, good, noble, model, proper, true, useful and right. As has been remarked several times earlier (and see also the schema in Chapter 8), I AM is the divine name, *ego eimi*, which when used without the egoism of 'I am this' allows the speaker to participate in the being and power of God. Throughout this Gospel, whenever Jesus Christ proclaims the divine name I AM, he does so in the sight of God, invariably invoking the Father, and reminding the hearers that he does not speak in his own name but in the name of the One who sent him. Having completely sacrificed his self, he has become a perfect instrument and mouthpiece of God. Without this self-abnegation, ceaselessly practised by Jesus Christ and consummately symbolised by the cross, his use of I AM would be a self-proclamation and a Luciferian boast.

I AM is not only the true shepherd, but is also the gate through which the sheep must pass to find pasture. Proper spiritual nourishment comes from Above, and must be sought there. The son of man, having become the Son of Man, knocks at the door I AM from below. The Son of God, who already is I AM, opens the door from Above, welcoming the prodigal son returned home.

It was for the sake of such sheep who seek to return home that the Son of God came, descended from Above – in that sense, laid down his life – to give them true life, his life. It is the same sort of descent (*avatara*) one finds in the story associated with the *Bhagavad Gita* where Krishna (who in a different geographical and cultural context is the cowherd, gathering and guarding his cows, the human souls, as Jesus Christ is the shepherd) lowered himself to the status of a charioteer for the sake of guiding the chariot of his beloved disciple and friend Arjuna. According to the celebrated simile, found in many traditional sources, such as Plato (*Phaedo* 24–28) and the *Katha Upanishad* (1.3:3–9), the charioteer is the higher intelligence integrating and guiding the various parts of a human being which are otherwise scattered and dispersed, disabling him from coming to the necessary inner unity for the sake of the Spirit.

Similarly, in the metaphor used here, the shepherd is the one who descends in the heart of a human being in order to gather all the dispersed and lost sheep, all the various scattered energies of the person, to enable him to be lifted up to the Son of Man. The descent of the Son of God and the ascent of the son of man are two parts of the same rhythm of energy, a breathing out and a breathing in, incarnation and ascension.

Meanwhile, in the festival of life, in Jerusalem at the centre of the universe, to return to the symbolic language of the Gospel, the Feast of Tabernacles is yielding to the Feast of Dedication. The Word had become flesh and pitched his tent (etymologically related with *tabernacle*) in us and among us, and strengthened his presence, in an outward arc. Now, the inward arc begins; and he who came down from heaven prepares to return home, in a total dedication of his life, even unto crucifixion.

No seeker needs to imagine that he alone is the one who seeks God or whom God calls. There are different seekers, of different folds, following different ways. These would all be led, each according to his own need and capacity, by the Spirit, by I AM; and each will discover that he belongs to one herd, the herd of God, and the only Shepherd, the one Cowherd, the sole Charioteer, He who Alone is Good, namely God.

The Father and You are One

It was winter, and the time came for the feast of Dedication at Jerusalem. Jesus was walking in the temple precincts, in Solomon's arcade, when the Jews gathered around him and demanded, 'How long are you going to keep us in suspense? If you are really the Christ, tell us so in plain words.' Jesus answered, 'I did tell you, but you do not believe. The works I do in my Father's name give witness for me, but you refuse to believe because you are not my sheep. My sheep hear my voice; I know them, and they follow me. I give them Eternal Life, and they shall never perish; no one shall snatch them from my hand. My Father, who has given them to me, is greater than all, and from the Father's hand no one can snatch away. The Father and I are one' (10:22–30).

When some of the Jews again reached for rocks to stone him, Jesus protested to them, 'Many a great deed I have shown you, done by my Father's power, for which of these would you stone me?' The Jews replied, 'It is not for any "great deed" that we are stoning you, but for blasphemy, because you who are only a man make yourself God' (10:31–33).

Jesus answered, 'Is it not written in your Law, "I have said, 'You are gods'"? If it calls those men gods to whom God's word was addressed – and the Scripture cannot lose its force – then why do you charge me with blasphemy when I, as the one whom the Father consecrated and sent into the world, said, 'I am God's son'? If I do not perform my Father's works, put no faith in me. But if I do perform them, accept the evidence of my deeds, even if you do not believe me, so that you may recognise and know that the Father is in me and I am in the Father' (10:34–38).

At these words they again tried to arrest him, but he eluded their grasp. Then he went back across the Jordan to the place where John had been baptising earlier; and while he stayed there, many people came to him. 'John may never have performed a sign,' they commented, 'but whatever John said about this man was true.' And there many came to believe in him (10:39–42).

The leaders of the crowd are blaming Jesus for not talking plainly, rather than realising that the difficulty lies in their limited understanding and vision. They want him to speak in their language, and at their level, and to say whether he is or is not the Christ according to their own notions and expectations. As far as Christ himself is concerned, he has been speaking to them precisely about this from the very beginning of his teaching, and from the Beginning. But they do not comprehend, for they are not called by God; they are not his sheep. Elsewhere (see John 8:44), he had told them they were sons of the Devil;

otherwise they would hear his call, and understand his words. If they cannot follow him internally, at least they could see the external works he has been doing among them and realise that he comes from God, as one of their own, Nicodemus, did even though he could not follow him as a disciple.

In the face of their incomprehension he becomes increasingly exasperated with them, and they with him. He cannot understand their limitation: why don't they see that he is not doing anything with his own power, in his own name, and that he really is, in the depths of himself, one with the Father, just as they themselves, in their depths, could be one with Him? On their part, they do not understand why he is so unmindful of the tradition, with its insistence on the unbridgeable gap between the Creator and the creature. How can he, a mere man, make himself God?

Herein lies the greatest subtlety, and therefore the possibility of the largest misunderstanding. Jesus Christ appeals to the works he has done in the name of the Father, as well as to the tradition and their own Law and Scripture, to make one point again and again: *no man can make himself God*, but a man can empty himself so that he will be filled with God; if a person is worthy, if he has denied himself, he can be chosen by God and be begotten by Him. Jesus was anointed by God, and was the Chosen One. He himself anointed the blind man and was instrumental in his awakening, as he was in the awakening of his chosen disciples who to be sure, ripened only after his own crucifixion. There is nothing exclusive either about the Divine sonship of Jesus, as is shown by many traditional references, including the Scripture which he himself quoted (Psalm 82:6), or about his essential oneness with God, and their mutual indwelling.

The important distinction is between 'I am, and there is none beside me' (Isaiah 47:8–10), and 'I AM, but I do nothing by myself, I do what my Father tells me to do'; between 'I am equal to and as good as God' and 'Why call me "good"? None is good but God alone' (Luke 18:19). Between the two attitudes lies the whole difference between hell and heaven, between self-will and the Will of the Father, between blasphemy and consecration.

Every high priest is taken from among men and appointed

their representative before God, to offer gifts and sacrifices for sins. He is able to bear patiently with the ignorant and erring, since he too is beset by weakness; and because of this he is bound to make sin-offerings for himself as well as for the people. And nobody arrogates the honour to himself: he is called by God, as indeed Aaron was. So it is with Christ: he did not confer upon himself the glory of becoming high priest; it was granted by God, who said to him, 'Thou art my Son; today I have begotten thee'; as also in another place he says, 'Thou art a priest for ever, in the succession of Melchizedek.' In the days of his earthly life he offered up prayers and petitions, with loud cries and tears, to God who was able to deliver him from the grave. Because of his humble submission his prayer was heard: son though he was, he learned obedience in the school of suffering, and, once perfected, became the source of eternal salvation for all who obey him, named by God high priest in the succession of Melchizedek' (Hebrews 5:1–10).

The audience of Jesus Christ did not understand what he was saying, and understood him as 'making himself God' and thus expressing a blasphemy. By their reactions to his words and actions, the people around Jesus Christ clearly divided themselves into two groups: the sheep that belonged to him, and the sheep that did not. This separation of the two groups was a preliminary part of his mission. When that is completed, at the end of this discourse and the subsequent attempt of the authorities to arrest him, he turned away from the crowd and their leaders altogether, and confined his activities and teachings exclusively to an inner and more prepared circle of disciples and friends. Still, the disturbing news of his teachings and works kept coming to the notice of the social and religious hierarchy; finally, after the raising of Lazarus from the dead, they launched a concerted effort to eliminate him (John 11:46–53).

It is clear, however, that Jesus Christ was not 'making himself God', but rather that he was expressing the fact that 'God finds place in him and dwells in him,' and furthermore that his own individual being is included in the Vastness that is God. Thus God and the Son of God are *one* in the subtlest aspect of their being. It is worth remarking that the 'one' in the great enunciation "The Father and I are one" (10:30) is neuter and not masculine. We are not encountering any gender-limited person here, but One who is beyond gender, and One who is not limited by any personality. Of course, we may choose, as we have to for the sake of communication, to speak of the One as the 'Highest Person' or as 'The Father' or as 'Absolute', and many other names. Each of the great traditions has found one or more designations especially appealing to its sensibilities and expressive of its aspirations. But the great teachers in each tradition have also insisted that the Truth is beyond any of these designations, and these names and descriptions serve the Highest only if with their aid a human being is able to be transformed and opens his heart upwards to a reality which he does not know and possess, but by which he could be known and possessed.

What in some traditions is described in terms of the most intimate union of lovers (as in the Song of Songs or of Krishna and Radha in the *Gita Govinda*), and what is elsewhere expressed metaphysically as the supreme identity of *Atman* and *Brahman* (as in the *Upanishads*), is exquisitely expressed here in the Gospel in terms of a kinship relationship: 'The Father and Son are one.' Each expression carries its own vibration, calling into resonance different modalities of our being. It is music of the subtlest level, however, which can call us to the highest silence in which different melodies find their proper place.

The One, the Highest Person, dwells in the deepest part of each human being. To any one who is able to come to rest in that profoundly silent part of himself, in the soul of his soul, Jesus Christ could have said not only that 'The Father and I are one,' but also that 'The Father and you are one.' On the eve of his death, when his work was completed, he prayed to God not only for his close disciples but also for those who may come to understand through their instruction, 'that they all may be one, just as you, Father, are in me and I in you, so that they also may be in us in order that the world may believe that you sent me. And I have given them the glory that you gave me, that they may be one as we are one, I in them and you in me, so that they may be perfected into one' (John 17:21–23).

CHAPTER

— 11 —

He whom Christ Loves, Dies to Himself

There was a certain man named Lazarus who was sick. He was from Bethany, the village of Mary and her sister Martha. (This Mary whose brother was sick was the one who anointed the Lord with perfume and dried his feet with her hair.) The sisters sent word to inform him, 'Lord, the one you love is sick.' Upon hearing this, Jesus said, 'This sickness is not to end in death, rather it is for God's glory, that the Son may be glorified through it.' Now Jesus loved Martha and her sister and Lazarus. So when he heard that he was ill, he stayed two days longer in the place where he was (11:1–6).

Then after this he said to his disciples, 'Let us go back to Judaea.' 'Rabbi,' protested the disciples, 'with the Jews only recently trying to stone you, you are going back up there again?' Jesus answered, 'Are there not twelve hours of daylight? If a man goes walking by day, he does not stumble because he sees the world bathed in light. But if he goes walking at night he will stumble since there is no light in him' (11:7–10).

After saying this he added, 'Our beloved Lazarus has fallen asleep, but I am going there to wake him.' The disciples said, 'Master, if he has fallen asleep, he will recover.' (Jesus had been speaking about his death, but they thought he meant sleep in the sense of slumber.) Then Jesus spoke out plainly: 'Lazarus is dead. For your sakes I am glad I was not there, that you may come to believe. In any event, let us go to him.' Then Thomas (the name means 'Twin') said to his fellow disciples, 'Let us also go, that we may die with him' (11:11–16).

The teaching here is very similar to that in the previous two chapters, except that the metaphor there was from blindness to sight, whereas here the metaphor is from death to life. There is a Vedic prayer which says:

> From the unreal lead me to the Real;
> From darkness lead me to Light;
> From death lead me to Life.

The *Brihadaranyaka Upanishad* (I.3:28), which quotes this prayer, goes on to add that 'darkness means death, of course, and Light means Life.' The same understanding is echoed in the Prologue of the Gospel where the Logos is both Light and Life, without which there is darkness and death.

Both situations, that of the blind man and of the dying man, are diagnosed on a similar large scale of cosmic laws, in quite similar words. This world is under the sway of the Prince of Darkness, and the Father's will is not done here; human beings naturally prefer darkness over Light. And spiritual awakening is against the current of natural tendencies of mankind. To wish for Light and Life, for an embodiment of the Logos, is undoubtedly *real* – it corresponds to the deepest and the most sacred part of man – but it is not *actual* in his usual existence. In other words, a human being lives in the denial of his own profoundest part; he lives in sin. But this is not a sin of his personal making: what governs him, after his own individual failings are accounted for, is *original* sin, on the scale of cosmic illusion and universal ignorance, inherent in the human condition. When a person becomes aware of his limitations, of being in sin, realising that he is not alive as he might be in the sight of God, he knows that he is like 'a widow who has given herself up to selfish indulgence, dead while she lives' (1 Timothy 5:6).

> I am dead because I lack desire;
> I lack desire because I think I possess;
> I think I possess because I do not try to give.
> In trying to give, you see that you have nothing;
> Seeing you have nothing, you try to give of yourself;
> Trying to give of yourself, you see that you are nothing;
> Seeing that you are nothing, you desire to become;
> In desiring to become, you begin to live.
>
> (René Daumal in *Mount Analogue*)

The awareness of being dead is a mark of spiritual progress; only those who love Christ and are called by him and try to follow him can come to that realisation. That awareness is a partial awakening to one's actual situation, and to wake up to one's deadness is the first major step towards the plenitude of real Life. 'How long, O Lord, wilt thou forget me? How long wilt thou hide thy face from me?' asks the Psalmist (Psalm 13:2,4): 'Look on me and answer, O Lord my God. Give light to my eyes or I will sleep in death.' This awakening can give oneself the courage to let go of the tenacious servility one has to the surface existence we call life, a life of 'I like this' or 'I don't like this', a life almost wholly governed by the expectation of reward or the fear of punishment, by others' approval or disapproval.

Lazarus appears to have been the closest pupil of Jesus Christ. He was the one whom Jesus loved, and this special relationship is acknowledged by Jesus himself, by the sisters of Lazarus, by the Gospel writer, and by the Jews who had come to condole Mary. This is an astoundingly unanimous testimony, from all levels of consciousness, about the love of Jesus Christ for Lazarus. Furthermore, since there is no reason or evidence for expecting any sentimental love on the part of Christ whose life was totally dedicated to the work of God, one may conclude with some justification that Lazarus was not only the closest disciple but also very advanced.

It is relevant to remark that Lazarus is not mentioned in any of the other gospels. To be sure, there is another Lazarus, in Luke (16:20–25), who was a leper and a beggar longing to eat the scraps fallen from a rich man's table. He was taken to Abraham's bosom after his death, whereas the rich man went to the abode of the dead where he suffered torment. From there he had cried out to father Abraham to let Lazarus go from the dead to warn the rich man's brothers to repent before it was too late. Abraham said to him, 'If they do not listen to Moses and the prophets, they will not be convinced even if one should rise from the dead.'

It is unlikely that this Lazarus is the same who was raised from the dead, although the possibility cannot be entirely ruled out. In any case, the omission of this specific miracle from the other gospels is even more puzzling since this is the greatest of all miracles performed by Jesus Christ, if the resurrection of Lazarus is taken literally and externally as the bringing of a clinically dead man back to life. In John this incident is the turning-point after which the Sanhedrin decided to kill Jesus, since 'the crowd that was present when he called Lazarus out of the tomb and raised him from the dead kept testifying to it' in public (John 12:17).

It is possible that the whole episode is inner and symbolic, enacted in an intimate circle of love and thus not recounted in the more exoteric synoptic gospels. Whatever Jesus might have taught the crowds, his call to his own close disciples always was to practise *dying* – dying to one's life, dying to personal human relationships, dying to the whole world, dying to everything that did not pertain directly to the will of God. This was his baptism of Spirit and fire. Not only for the crowds, but even for most of his disciples, his teaching was hard to bear. As has been said earlier, one needs to be prepared not only to *understand* truth but also in order to *withstand* it.

When the raising from the dead is mentioned, as here in John's Gospel, it has to fit into the logic and demands of the literary form and the dramatic narrative, which in their turn can seduce a reader's attention away from the real substance, unless he is on guard and keeps an ear open for the subtle vibration behind the words, behind the seemingly historical details, and behind the requirements of the medium being used by the author of the Gospel. 'The face of Truth is covered with a golden vase. Uncover it, O Lord, that I who love the Truth may see' (*Isha Upanishad* 15).

The name *Lazarus* literally means 'God helps', suggesting rich symbolic possibilities. Also, to recall what was said earlier, the name *Jesus* (*Joshua*, from *Yehoshua*) means 'Yahweh saves'. The two are close to each other in the meaning of their names, and they were close to each other in love; they should be expected to be close in their work for God: both in their dying as well as in rising. Lazarus, of all the pupils of Christ, should be expected to be more aware of himself, and thus more cognizant of his being estranged from God, and asleep in death, especially in the light of the fullness of life displayed by his master, the Christ himself.

The very awakening to the fact of being spiritually dead is itself the first major step towards freeing oneself from the clutches of this death. As clinging to one's wordly life, with its domination by fear and desire, is what constitutes spiritual death, longing for Life and disgust with the superficial existence

of sin constitute the two-pronged goad for a radical reorientation, *metanoia*, and dying to this clinging. Thus, awareness of
spiritual death gives a man understanding, strength and courage to die to the egoistic self that keeps him in the realm of
darkness and sorrow. Dying to this self means to die to self-will,
and to all the habits that bind a man like vast serpents to the very
self from which he needs to be free. Liberation or salvation is not
freedom *for* myself; rather it is freedom *from* myself.

Only those who can die to this self can wake up to the eternal
Self, the *Atman* and the *Christ*. The Son of God came specifically
to invite those who would hear, to participate in his being, to
share his baptism, and to die to their self-will, as Jesus did, so
that they can also share in the resurrection. 'In truth, in very
truth I tell you, unless a grain of wheat falls to the earth and
dies, it remains just a grain of wheat. But if it dies, it produces
much fruit. The man who loves his self (*psyche*, soul, life) loses it
while the man who hates his self in this world preserves it to Life
Eternal. If anyone would serve me, let him follow me; where I am
there will my servant be' (John 12:24–26). Without dying to the
old level of one's existence, there is no new birth; without being
born again, there is no entry into the kingdom of heaven.

Mary, who is identified by an action yet to be recounted in
the next chapter in the future, and her sister Martha and their
brother Lazarus were all loved by Jesus Christ. On hearing the
news that Lazarus was sick, he stayed two days longer where he
was. Callousness? Hardly; that is not the level at which one can
understand Jesus Christ. It was precisely because he loved them
that he delayed. Anyone who has ever been seriously engaged in
inner work, in meditation and prayer, knows the extreme fragility of the higher states of consciousness, and the importance of
guarding the aspirant against any interference or excitement.
The sisters knew this: they had simply informed Christ about
the progress of the spiritual birth of Lazarus, as a nurse may
inform a doctor about the progress of a physical birth. Having
immediately known that the sickness was not of a bodily kind
that would lead to physical death, but a sign that God's work
in Lazarus was nearing fruition, Jesus tarried to let the process
continue until full ripeness, so that his beloved Lazarus could be
completely emptied of himself and die to his egoistic life totally.
Then he could be filled with the Logos, made anew, begotten by
the Spirit.

Like a master physician, Christ knows how long it would be before the necessary death was completed, setting the stage for the emergence of the new being, born by virgin birth. He then tells the disciples that he is going back to Judaea. They are understandably concerned about his physical safety. He himself gives no weight to such considerations, for 'doing the will of him who sent me and bringing his work to completion is my food' (John 4:34).

As far as Christ is concerned, the important matter is that the crucial hour of Lazarus has now come, as it soon would for Jesus himself. This is Lazarus' day; now is the time for him to walk without stumbling, for he sees the world bathed in light. Soon it may be too late; night may overtake him, leaving him without light and he may miss the mark. Now is the moment for Christ to help him from Above, to open the door of I AM for him. Until now, Lazarus needed to exert himself, with all his strength, even until death, to come and knock at the sun-door of resurrection; now he must wait, with nothing anymore of himself.

If Jesus Christ had been there with Lazarus earlier, his other disciples might have misunderstood the respective parts played from Above and from below, by God and by man. They might have attributed the entire spiritual process to the Son of God, ignoring their individual responsibility, that of the Son of Man, in their own transformation, and would have come to wrong belief. As it is, they did not quite understand the relationship between sleep and death, nor between death and Life. It is noteworthy that the one exception was Thomas, who according to an ancient tradition (for example in Acts of Thomas 1:31), was a twin brother of Jesus: born together with Jesus of the same earthly mother, although not yet born of their common Heavenly Mother. He expressed a clear understanding of the need for dying to oneself when he invited his fellow disciples to go together to die with Lazarus.

Awake, O Sleeper, Arise from the Dead

When Jesus arrived, he found that Lazarus had been four days in the tomb. Now Bethany was not far from Jerusalem, just under two miles, and many of the Jews had come out to condole with Martha and Mary on their brother's death.

134

When Martha heard that Jesus was coming, she went to meet him, while Mary sat quietly at home. Martha said to Jesus, 'Lord, if you had been here, my brother would not have died. Even now, I know that whatever you ask of God, God will grant you.' Jesus said, 'Your brother will rise again.' 'I know he will rise again,' Martha replied, 'in the resurrection on the last day.' Jesus told her, 'I AM the resurrection and I AM Life: whoever believes in me, though he should die, will come to Life; and whoever is alive and believes in me will never die. Do you believe this?' 'Yes, Lord,' she replied. 'I have come to believe that you are the Christ, the Son of God: he who is coming into the world' (11:17–27).

When she had said this she went back and called her sister Mary. 'The Teacher is here, asking for you,' she whispered. As soon as Mary heard this, she got up and started out in his direction. (Actually Jesus had not yet come into the village but was at the spot where Martha had met him.) The Jews who were in the house with Mary, consoling her, saw her get up quickly and go out; and so they followed her, thinking she was going to the tomb to weep there. When Mary came to the place where Jesus was and saw him, she fell at his feet and said to him, 'Lord, if you had been here my brother would not have died.' Now when Jesus saw her weeping, and the Jews who had accompanied her also weeping, he was deeply troubled in the spirit and trembled. 'Where have you laid him?' he asked. 'Lord, come and see,' they said. Jesus began to weep, which caused the Jews to remark, 'See how much he loved him!' But some said, 'He opened the eyes of that blind man. Could not he also have done something to stop this man from dying?' Once again troubled in spirit, Jesus approached the tomb (11:28–38).

It was a cave with a stone laid across it. 'Take away the stone,' Jesus directed. Martha, the dead man's sister, said to him, 'Lord, it has been four days now; surely there will be a stench!' Jesus replied, 'Did I not assure you that if you believed you would see the glory of God?' So they took away the stone. Then Jesus looked upward and said, 'Father, I thank you for having heard me. I know that you always hear me but I have said this for the sake of the crowd, that they may believe that you sent me.' Having said this, he called loudly, 'Lazarus, come out!' The dead man came out, bound head and foot with linen strips, his face wrapped in a cloth. 'Untie him,' Jesus told them, 'and let him go'(11:39–44).

Christ came to make the living dead and the dead alive, the seeing blind and the sightless sighted. Himself being awake (literally in Sanskrit, *buddha*), he came to awaken those who sleep. St Paul quoted an anonymous source, in Ephesians 5:14:

> Awake, O sleeper,
> arise from the dead,
> and Christ will give you light.

Both Martha and Mary have a sisterly concern over the extreme state of their brother, exhausted from his spiritual exertions. They are relieved to see Jesus Christ, who reassures them that all is as it has to be, and that their brother will rise again. But, as the Pharisees and the scribes constantly looked back in time to be reassured by the authority of the tradition and the Scriptures, the disciples and followers of Christ looked to the future, in the hope of resurrection yet to come. In either case, everybody around Christ was trapped in the linear dimension of time, past or future, rarely able to be free of it to come to the eternal present, the living moment of I AM.

Jesus Christ, however, was free both of the authority of the past as well as of the hope of the future; and of their psychological correlates, tyranny and fear. He always tried to recall his hearers from the imaginings and lesser realities of time back to the present moment, where one can be present to I AM. In that presence alone is the resurrection and the Life. 'His disciples said to him, "When will the repose of the dead come about, and when will the new world come?" He said to them, "What you look forward to has already come, but you do not recognise it. . . . Take heed of the Living One while you are alive, lest you die and seek to see Him and be unable to do so"' (Gospel of Thomas II, 2:51, 59).

Martha herself must have been highly prepared, as one would expect from the fact that Christ loved her. Although she too had, until then, thought of the resurrection only in terms of the future, but directly confronted with the divine manifestation in the state of I AM, she could make the leap and *see*, and in that sense *believe*, that she was in the presence of the Christ, the Son of God: he who is coming in to the world, the Son of Man, the I AM. However, the fragility of the state of this realisation is evident from the fact that very soon Martha forgets, that is to say she falls asleep again into her ordinary consciousness, and has to be reminded by Christ. Her inability to stay awake and keep watch with her brother Lazarus is reminiscent of the inability of the disciples to watch with Jesus in the Garden of Gethsemane (Matthew 26:38–43): 'My soul is exceeding sorrowful, even unto death: tarry ye here and watch with me,' Jesus said to the disciples. When he came back, he found them sleeping. 'What, could ye not watch with me one hour? Watch and pray, that ye enter not into temptation: the spirit indeed is willing, but the flesh is weak.' And he came and found them asleep again.

In order to raise Lazarus from the dead, to assist in him the birth of the Spirit, Jesus Christ himself has to be fully awake and present, summoning all his spiritual energy. On all such momentous occasions, when the Spirit descends, there is a trembling of the body, and the soul is troubled, as the water in the pool of Bethesda was troubled by an angel before it could heal the sick. This troubling is mentioned twice when the hour of Lazarus is here; similarly, when the hour of Jesus himself comes, his soul is troubled. According to the Gospel of Thomas (II, 2:2), Jesus said, 'Let him who seeks continue seeking until he finds. When he finds, he will become troubled. When he becomes troubled, he will be astonished, and he will rule over the All.'

'In truth, in very truth, I tell you, a time is coming, indeed it is already here, when the dead shall hear the voice of the Son of God, and all who hear shall come to Life' (John 5:25). The stage is finally set, the hour of Lazarus is here, and the Son of God, in the name of the Father, opens the door of I AM to the Son of Man. God calls, 'Come!' This man, who has died to himself and is now nobody, is able to respond: 'I AM here.'

There is feasting in heaven:

The father said to his servants: 'Quick! bring out the finest robe and put it on him; put a ring on his finger and shoes on his feet. Take the fatted calf and kill it. Let us eat and

137

celebrate because this son of man was dead and has come back to life. He was lost and is found' (Luke 15:22–24).

It is possible to look at the various stages of development in the different metaphors encountered so far as follows:

FROM ABOVE

Life	Sight/Light	Shepherd	Health	Son of God
I AM	Anointing	Sheepgate	Touch	New Birth
Dying to self	Blindness to world	Sheep of Christ	Sick of flesh	Son of Man
Awake to living death	Awareness of darkness	Oneself known as sheep	Cognizance of sickness	Aspirant
Living death	Blindness, darkness	Sheep of Nature	Paralysis	son of man

FROM BELOW

Alien People Clutching their Gods

This caused many of the Jews who had come to visit Mary to believe in him. But some of them went to the Pharisees and reported what he had done. The result was that the chief priests and the Pharisees called a meeting of the Sanhedrin. 'What are we to do,' they said, 'with this man performing all sorts of signs? If we let him go on like this, the whole world will believe in him. Then the Romans will come and take away our holy place and our nation.' One of their number named Caiaphas, who was high priest that year, addressed them: 'You have no sense at all! Can you not see that it is better for you to have one man die for the people than to have the whole nation destroyed?' (It was not on his own that he said this; but, as high priest that year, he could prophesy that Jesus was to die for the nation – and not for the nation alone, but to gather into one all the dispersed children of God.) So from that day on they planned to kill him (11:45–53).

For this reason Jesus no longer moved about openly

among the Jews, but withdrew to a town called Ephraim in the region near the desert, where he stayed with his disciples (11:54)

Now the Jewish Passover was near; and many people from the country went up to Jerusalem to purify themselves for Passover. They were on the lookout for Jesus; and the people around the Temple were saying to one another, 'What do you think? Is he likely to come for the feast?' The chief priests and the Pharisees had given orders that anyone who knew where Jesus was should report it so that they could arrest him (11:55–57).

As always, the revelation by Jesus Christ of the power and purpose of his Father caused a dissension among those who heard him or saw him. Some really saw and understood; they became his disciples, abandoned everything else – family, profession, social and religious conventions, comforts – and tried to put into practice what he taught – dying to 'I am this', and waking up to I AM. Others, like Nicodemus, were quite clear that Jesus Christ was the Son of God and that his teaching was true, but they were unable in practice to overcome their worldly attachments completely in order to follow him as radically as he demanded. These two groups were very small in numbers and posed no threat to any established authority. But there was a much larger number of people impressed by his miraculous powers, who 'believed' in him, as long as he made no demands on them, hoping to get some rewards in the afterlife. There was also a group of people, in general strong supporters of religious conventions and rules, and often constituting the established authority, who disapproved of him, and of his cavalier disregard of traditional conduct. They were not so certain that his powers originated from a divine source, a source with which he seemed to be on very intimate terms, and which he said was one with him, and could be discovered by every man within himself if he would not remain clinging to his surface self constituted by heredity, society, tradition and history.

This last group gradually became more and more hostile to Jesus Christ, as their authority was threatened by his appeal to every man to drink at the spring of the living water flowing from his own belly. Furthermore, he preached that this was the true meaning of scripture when rightly understood. In truth his teaching was radically subversive, and potentially destructive of all external authority, thus also of society, which is basically founded on the principles of reward and punishment, the very principles for which he had no regard. He could neither be bribed nor threatened.

Then the devil took him up higher and showed him all the kingdoms of the world in a single instant. He said to him, 'I will give you all this power and the glory of these kingdoms; the power has been given to me and I give it to whomever I wish. Prostrate yourself in homage before me, and it shall all be yours.' In reply Jesus said to him, 'Scripture has it, "You shall do homage to the Lord your God; Him alone shall you adore."' Then the devil led him to Jerusalem, set him on the parapet of the temple, and said to him, 'If you are the Son of God, throw yourself down from here, for Scripture has it, "He will bid His angels watch over you"; and again, "With their hands they will support you, that you may never stumble on a stone."' Jesus said to him in reply, 'It also says, "You shall not put the Lord your God to the test."' When the devil had finished all the tempting he left him, to await another opportunity (Luke 4:5–13).

It is said that after his enlightenment the Buddha was almost tempted not to return to the world to set the Wheel of Dharma in motion, for he knew that his teaching was very difficult in practice and could not be understood by many. It seems, on the contrary, the Christ was tempted to preach to too many. He knew his teaching was very difficult; his baptism was with fire. He advised his disciples, 'Do not give what is holy to the dogs or toss your pearls before swine. They will trample them under foot, at best, and perhaps even tear you to shreds" (Matthew 7:6). Against his own advice, he seems to have been overcome by compassion for the suffering humanity, asleep in death. Or, perhaps he was tempted to accomplish the impossible: to bring the kingdom of heaven to everyone on earth, disregarding the enormous gulf between the two, and the absolute necessity of inner preparation for entering the kingdom. In any case, it was the teaching of the subtle and the esoteric doctrine to the masses, who more responded to his external miracles rather than to the marvellous possibility of human transformation, which finally got him into trouble with the authorities whose power was threatened. The authorities did not hear his call; they were not his sheep. They had their own gods, alien to the God of Christ, which they clutched fervently. And they had their own sheep whose safety and allegiance they wished to ensure. Since he could neither be seduced into becoming the king as the masses wished nor threatened with anything, all they could do, for the sake of preserving the social order, as they understood it at their own level, was to eliminate him.

All this was a long time ago, I remember,
And I would do it again, but set down
This set down
This: were we led all that way for
Birth or Death? There was a Birth, certainly,
We had evidence and no doubt. I had seen birth and death,
But had thought they were different; this Birth was
Hard and bitter agony for us, like Death, our death.
We returned to our places, these Kingdoms,
But no longer at ease here, in the old dispensation,
With an alien people clutching their gods.
I should be glad of another death.

(T. S. Eliot, *Journey of the Magi*)

Giving One's All to the Master

Six days before Passover Jesus came to Bethany where Lazarus was whom he had raised from the dead. There they gave him a banquet, at which Martha served. Lazarus was one of those at table with him. Mary brought a pound of costly perfume made from genuine aromatic nard, with which she anointed the feet of Jesus. Then she dried his feet with her hair, while the fragrance of the perfume filled the house. Judas Iscariot, one of his disciples (the one about to hand him over), protested: 'Why was not this perfume sold? It could have brought three hundred silver pieces, and the money have been given to the poor.' (He did not say this out of concern for the poor, but because he was a thief. He held the common purse, and used to help himself to what was deposited there.) To this Jesus replied, 'Leave her alone. The purpose was that she might keep it for the day of my embalming. The poor you will always have with you, but you will not always have me' (12:1–8).

The hour of Lazarus had already come, and he had been raised from the sleep of death to a state of awakening; now he is able to participate in the usual activities of the world, but from a different level of being. Martha had understood something, she had tasted a different state, but she could not stay with it for long. She is back in her usual role of worldly activity, though undertaking it with care and in a spirit of service. Now it is the time of Mary: she stakes her all for the sake of the master, without any concern for the world. By all accounts, she had bought an outrageously expensive perfume, costing almost a year's wages, and uses it to wash the feet of Jesus in a consummate gesture of humility and dedication. Furthermore, she is totally oblivious to

142

any conventions of the society according to which loosening her hair in public would have been considered extremely immodest. Mary did not let the worldly prudence whisper too loudly in her ears, for she knew it was the hour of the miraculous.

This Mary of Bethany, often identified with Mary Magdalene, may have been sinful according to the popular Christian tradition, but there can be no question about her overflowing love for Jesus Christ, eliciting an appropriate response from him. When Judas brings in the usual concern and caution, quite typical of everyone occupied with supplies and accounts, Jesus reminds him of the greater rightness of a higher scale of values. It is in that sense that he is a thief: wanting to divert the occasion from a high purpose to a lower one. Of course, money is important – otherwise, how would one give a banquet? Quite rightly, the poor need to be looked after. However, something else is more important: the sacred relationship of love between the master and the disciple, for nothing subtle can be taught or known except in a state of love. The fragility of moments of high feeling cannot be exaggerated, nor can the need for guarding them. Duties and obligations will always be there, but ecstasies of love do not last long.

The Kingdom of Christ is Not of This World

A great number of Jews heard that he was there and came out, not only because of Jesus, but also to see Lazarus whom he had raised from the dead. The chief priests, however, planned to kill Lazarus too, because on his account many of the Jews were going over to Jesus and believing in him (12:9–11).

The next day the large crowd that had come to the feast, having heard that Jesus was to enter Jerusalem, took palm branches and went out to meet him, shouting, 'Hosanna! Blessed is he who comes in the name of the Lord! Blessed is the King of Israel!' But Jesus found a young donkey and sat on it. As the Scripture has it: 'Fear not, O daughter of Zion! Your king approaches you on a donkey's colt.' At the time his disciples did not understand this, but after Jesus had been glorified they remembered that this had been written about him, and that this had happened to him (12:12–16).

The crowd that was present when he called Lazarus out of the tomb and raised him from the dead kept testifying to it. The crowd came out to meet him because they heard he had performed this sign. The Pharisees remarked to one another, 'See, there is nothing you can do! The whole world has run after him' (12:17–19).

Lazarus had now become a brother to Christ, having woken up from spiritual death. To those who remained blind and were hostile to Jesus Christ himself, because his teaching found no place in them, Lazarus also represented the other side. Contrary to his own advice elsewhere (Matthew 22:21) in another connection, to give to Caesar what is Caesar's, Jesus had not accorded the respect to the leaders of the established church which they thought was due to them, and they were determined to kill him, and anyone else who stood by his side. Lazarus was as much a marked man for the keepers of the tradition and law now as Jesus himself; they were both participants in the scandal of waking up in the midst of those who sleep.

The crowds, however, were neither *for* Jesus nor *against* him; they were more interested in spectacles and miracles. They could as easily hail him as the Messiah as throw stones at him. They came out to meet him because he was the wonder-working magician and to hail him as the King of Israel, which is what the Messiah was expected to be. Jesus, however, steadfastly refused to be drafted as the king. His concern was altogether different; as he said to Pilate later, 'My kingdom is not of this world' (John 18:36). He said the same thing to the crowd, but more in a language of gestures they could understand: he found a small ass and sat on it! He who could not be tempted by the Devil with the promise of all the kingdoms of the world, could hardly be made to deviate from his purpose by a fickle and motley crowd wanting to crown him the king!

Unless a Seed Dies it Bears No Fruit

Among those who had come up to worship at the feast were some Greeks. They approached Philip, who was from Bethsaida in Galilee, and put this request to him: 'Sir, we would like to see Jesus.' Philip went to tell Andrew; Philip and Andrew in turn came to inform Jesus. Jesus answered them: 'The hour has come for the Son of Man to be glorified. In truth, in very truth I tell you, unless a grain of wheat falls to the earth and dies, it remains just a grain of wheat. But if it dies, it produces much fruit. The man who loves his self loses it while the man who hates his self in this world preserves it to Life Eternal. If anyone would serve me, let him follow me; where I am there will my servant be. If anyone serves me, him the Father will honour. Now my soul is troubled. Yet, what should I say – "Father, save me from this hour"? No, this is just the reason why I came to this hour. Father, glorify your name' (12:20–28).

Then a voice came from the sky: 'I have glorified it and will glorify it again.' When the crowd that was there heard it, they said that it was thunder; but others maintained, 'An angel was speaking to him.' Jesus answered, 'That voice did not come for my sake, but for yours. Now is the judgement of this world. Now will the Prince of this world be driven out. And when I am lifted up from the earth, I shall draw all things to myself.' (This he said to indicate the kind of death he was to die.) To this the crowd objected, 'We have heard from the Law that the Messiah is to remain for ever. How can you claim that the Son of Man must be lifted up? Just who is this "Son of Man"?' (12:29–34).

Jesus answered, 'The Light is in you only a little while longer. Walk while you have the Light, or the darkness will overcome you. The man who walks in the dark does not know where he is going. While you have the Light, trust to the Light, and so become sons of Light.' After this utterance, Jesus left them and went into hiding (12:35–36).

Why does the arrival of the Greeks act as a signal for Jesus to say that his hour has now come? The way the details are recounted by the Gospel writer, one almost gets the impression of a pre-arranged code by which the falling of the curtain on the public teaching of Jesus Christ is initiated, which he has already tried to terminate several times earlier. This time, he does finally die to the world and is done with it; after this he goes into hiding with his disciples. The next time that we see him in public is when he has been arrested in order to be eliminated like a thorn in the flesh of the establishment. Of course, he could have gone away and escaped; but he was willing to face death for steadfastly holding on to principles which transcend any fear.

Reverting to the present chapter, however, we find here the classical expression of the doctrine discussed in the last chapter, namely the necessity of dying to oneself in the world, that is, dying to fear and desire, in order to be able to come to Eternal Life. This is how the Son of Man, the deepest Self in every son of man, is glorified, which is to say manifested, as we see later on when Jesus asks the Father to glorify His name. Only a few teachings are introduced by Jesus Christ with the expression 'In truth, in very truth I tell you' (which is *Amen, Amen* in the original), and these are always of the utmost importance. Here the significant teaching is about the necessity for the grain of wheat to die for it to yield much fruit. This is what Lazarus did, as must every other aspirant. This is what Jesus himself proceeds to do, for his hour has now come. And he sets an example for everyone who would follow him and serve God.

The teaching is not about physical death by crucifixion, lest anybody should be tempted to be literal-minded about this or any other portion of the Gospels. It is to do with struggling against one's own natural self and self-willing and yoking them to the way of the Spirit, as Jesus did himself. And let no one imagine that it is easy to die to oneself. No doubt, there are relative degrees of freedom from oneself, but ultimately, dying to oneself is salvation. It is in this very self that the struggle of the Buddha with Mara takes place, and it is in the wilderness of the soul that Jesus Christ is tempted by the Devil. If the self is completely emptied, the Devil can find no foothold there. However paradoxical it may sound, as long as there is a soul distinct from God it cannot be saved. This is why it is sometimes said in Eastern literature that no one who is anyone can be enlightened.

Jesus Christ is aware of the immense difficulty inherent in his hour, the hour of his inner trial, and his soul is troubled. Should he now ask to be saved from this hour? No, this is the very reason for which he came, and he submits himself completely to the will of the Father so that His name – His power and being – may be manifested. The account here is the same in feeling as that of the agony in the garden at Gethsemane told in Mark (14:33–36):

146

And he took with him Peter and James and John, and began to be sore amazed and to be very heavy; and said unto them, 'My soul is exceeding sorrowful unto death: tarry ye here and watch.' And he went forward a little, and fell on the ground, and prayed that, if it were possible, the hour might pass from him. And he said, 'Abba, Father, all things are possible unto thee; take away this cup from me: nevertheless not what I will, but what thou wilt.'

In the depths of his heart Jesus Christ knows that God has answered his cry and has reassured him that he is on the right path. There is a separation between two parts of himself, also mirrored externally in the world: one tending upward to Light, and the other wishing to stay in darkness. And the two struggle against each other. Only when the Son of Man is lifted up, that is when the son of man is purified to the core, everything in him will be saved, and the Prince of Darkness will be defeated. If one understands these sayings of Jesus Christ completely externally, that is to say materialistically, one would have to say that the Prince of this world has not been driven out in the two thousand years since his crucifixion. But the external interpretation is deeply rooted in the human psyche: we hope that someone else will save us, and we wish to imagine an external saviour, as did the crowd around Jesus Christ on every occasion. This sort of hope of external salvation, and its psychological correlate, a fear that we may not be chosen for salvation, are precisely the snares of the Prince of this world by which he keeps us bound to his domain; these are also the roots of exclusivism and bigotry on the one hand, and a need for some external authority – of the Scriptures, or tradition or the leaders – on the other.

The crowd takes externally what Jesus Christ says, and wonders how it fits in with their expectations about the Messiah, and what the tradition has to say about him. What is this 'Son of Man', and his being 'lifted up', that Jesus keeps talking about? Jesus ignores most of them, and speaks only to those few in the crowd who may still be able to hear him, in words reminiscent of the ones he used in connection with the blind man and the dead man, Lazarus, whom he assisted in coming to Light and Life. He exhorted them to walk while the Light was still *in* them. This is what the text literally says, even though it is almost always translated in keeping with an external understanding as the Light was *among* them. It is clearly stated by Jesus Christ that the Son of Man is the Light *within*, for which a son of man needs to make room by struggling against the darkness attempting to overcome it. And that if a man moves in this Light, keeping his trust in it, he will not be overcome by darkness; instead, he will become the Son of Light. 'What came to be in him was Life; and Life was the Light of mankind. And the Light shines on in Darkness, and the Darkness has not overcome it. . . . The Light was in being, Light absolute, enlightening every man born into the world. The Word was in the world, and through him the world was made, yet the world did not know who he was. To his own he came, yet his own did not accept him. But to all who did receive him, to those who have yielded him their allegiance, he gave the right to become children of God. . . . The Word became flesh and dwelt in us' (John 1:4–14).

Levels of Seeing

In spite of the many signs that Jesus had performed in their presence, they refused to believe in him. This was to fulfil the word of the prophet Isaiah: 'Lord, who has believed what we have heard? To whom has the might of the Lord been revealed?' The reason they could not believe was that, as Isaiah said elsewhere, 'He has blinded their eyes, and numbed their hearts, lest they should see with their eyes and comprehend with their hearts, and turn to me to heal them.' Isaiah said this because he saw God's glory, and it was of Him that he spoke (12:37–41).

There were many, even among the Sanhedrin, who believed in him; but they refused to admit it because of the Pharisees, for fear they may be ejected from the synagogue. They loved more the praise of men than the honour which comes from God (12:42–43).

It has already been remarked, in Chapters 9 and 11, that a blindness to reality and the state of spiritual death are quite natural and universal, according to God's own laws, in the sense that even the Devil cannot exist without God's consent and without ultimately serving His purpose. From that point of view, spiritual awakening is against the current of God's own law of nature; or, as it is sometimes said – for example by Krishna in the *Bhagavad Gita* or by Plotinus in the *Enneads* – that spiritual development is according to the higher nature of man and is contrary to his lower nature. So the power and glory of God is revealed only to a few, and what they hear is not heard or believed by the multitude, as the prophet Isaiah said. It is not that the masses do not wish to understand or believe, but that they *cannot*; or one may say that they understand only at the gross level and not very subtly. There is no question of any injustice here, any more than there is in remarking on the fact that a tiger can run faster than a man, but cannot think as well as an ordinary man. Within the general range of *homo sapiens* there are many levels of spiritual development; and every tradition is thoroughly cognizant of this obvious fact of spiritual hierarchy among men.

Sometimes, of course, a person may be very struck and sad-dened by the unrealised potential of human beings, and the general heaviness of humanity. Nevertheless, as is clear in the saying of Isaiah, it is God himself who has blinded the eyes of mankind and numbed their hearts so that they may not really see. The early Christians were so struck by the validity of this saying of Isaiah, that each of the four gospels reports it explicitly (John 12:40; Matthew 13:13–15) or implicitly (Mark 4:12; Luke 8:10); it is also to be found in St Paul's letter to the Romans (11:8), as well as in the Acts (28:26–27). It is clear that it was well understood that it is quite in accordance with God's will and intention that the general masses should not comprehend any subtle truths, and therefore they should not believe in Christ.

Furthermore, as was discussed in Chapter 5, it was consid-ered risky for the unprepared masses to be told higher truths, lest they misuse them for their egotistic purposes. Jesus Christ seems to have gone out of his way to ensure that even when the multitude heard him they would not really understand: 'To you the mystery of the kingdom of God has been confided. To the others outside it is all presented in parables, so that they will look intently and not see, listen carefully and not understand, lest perhaps they repent and be forgiven' (Mark 4:11–12); 'for many are called, but few are chosen' (Matthew 22:14). From all this, one is forced to conclude that even when he spoke to the large crowds, he did so only for the sake of the very few who were called by God to be able to hear him and see him with ears and eyes other than the gross ones. For the sake of these few, he suffered ridicule from the crowds, and bore their stones, and finally suffered crucifixion at the hands of the authorities who were afraid that he was inciting the crowds, whereas he himself had little interest in the crowds. In his last prayer to God, Jesus Christ said, 'I have given you glory on earth by completing the work you gave me to do . . . I have made your name known to those you gave me out of the world. These men you gave me were yours; they have kept your Word' (John 17:4–6).

The basic question is of the right inner preparation for understanding spiritual truth, which is the same as believing in Christ. Without the proper preparation of the recipient, truth can fall into the wrong hands and be misused, for as St Paul said, 'the Kingdom of God is not a matter of talk, but of power' (1 Corinthians 4:20). The higher forces and the great teachers, who are seldom sentimentally compassionate, are therefore as interested in imparting the higher knowledge to the well-prepared and rightly deserving people, as they are in hiding it and guarding it from the unprepared and the undeserving. This goes right back to the fall of man in Genesis (3:22–24):

> And the Lord God said, 'Behold, the man has become as one of us, knowing good and evil. He must not be allowed to put forth his hand and take also of the tree of life, and eat, and live for ever.' The Lord God therefore banished him from the garden of Eden, to till the ground from which he had been taken . . . and He stationed the cherubim and the fiery revolving sword, to guard the way to the tree of life.

Even when a person understands the truth, still more is needed for a whole-hearted commitment to it, of the kind shown by the close disciples of Jesus Christ, including Lazarus and Mary, so that one stakes one's all in order to follow it wherever it may lead. It is not easy to die to the overwhelming force of approval and disapproval of the others. We can have nothing but sympathy for those members of the Sanhedrin, Nicodemus and Joseph of Arimathea certainly, and perhaps others, who were able to recognise the quality of the being of Jesus Christ, even though the forces of human bondage were too strong for them to forsake all in order to follow Christ.

The Yoga of the Cross

Jesus proclaimed aloud: 'Whoever believes in me is actually believing not in me but in Him who sent me. And whoever sees me is seeing Him who sent me. As Light have I come into the world so that no one who believes in me need remain in darkness. If anyone hears my words and does not keep them, I am not the one to condemn him; for I did not come to condemn the world but to save it. Whoever rejects me and does not accept my words already has his judge, namely, the word that I have spoken – that is what will condemn him on the last day, because it was not on my own that I spoke. No, the Father who sent me has Himself commanded me what to say and how to speak, and I know that his commandment is Eternal Life. So when I speak, I speak just as the Father told me' (12:44–50).

As far as Jesus Christ is concerned, the right preparation consists in dying to one's self-will, and in denying oneself, so that one could obey the will of God. His yoga consists of this; and of this the cross is the supreme symbol. Whether or not it corresponds to any actual method of killing Jesus, the enormous psychological and spiritual significance of the cross cannot be exaggerated. Every moment, whenever a man is present to it, he is at a crossing; at this point of crossing he chooses whether to remain in the horizontal plane of the world or to be yoked to the way of the Christ and follow the vertical axis of being.

The way of the cross consists in surrendering oneself completely to the will of God, and emptying oneself of one's self-importance. Jesus Christ himself sets an example of this, as we have seen many times already. He has become so transparent to the Ground of Being that anyone who sees him sees God. He has nothing of his own; he does not speak in his own name, or on his own authority. To use an analogy given in the *Yoga Sutras* for a liberated person, his mind and being are like a perfectly polished clear diamond, without any blemish at all, so that he can reflect the glory of God as it is. The words and actions of the Father are transmitted by him without any distortions introduced by his own ego. Since his words are not his own, to hear them is to hear God; not to accept them is to reject God, who alone is the judge.

It is important to remember that Jesus was a *crucifer* before his arrest and trial, which eventually led to his death by crucifixion. The way of Christ is that of the cross. As he repeatedly told his disciples (see Matthew 10:38, 16:24; Mark 8:34; Luke 9:23, 14:27), no person is worthy and capable of being his disciple unless he takes up his own cross – not only as an idea but as a daily practice – and follows him. In the language of symbols, the only one appropriate to these realities, a fact not lost to the early Christians, crucifixion is the only just manner of death of the Crucifer. Naturally, he who is 'the Light of the world' (John 8:12) must be born on the darkest day of the year, just as 'the Lamb slain from the foundation of the world' (Revelation 13:8) should have been killed on the day appointed for sacrificing the paschal lamb. The actual historical facts follow from the mythic and symbolic necessity and truth of the Incarnation and the Crucifixion.

The way of the cross, like all authentic spiritual paths, demands human sacrifice. As the Gospel of Philip (II,3:63) says, 'God is a man-eater. For this reason men are sacrificed to Him.' When the man himself is ended, he can be filled with God and become one with the Source. Thus the end of man is the end of man. In the way of the cross, there is no place for man's own egoistic ambitions and projects; as a Hasidic saying has it, 'There is no room for God in him who is full of himself.'

CHAPTER

—— 13 ——

Washing Off the Surface Self

Before the feast of Passover, Jesus realised that the hour had come for him to pass from this world to the Father. He had loved his own in this world, and would show his love for them to the end. The Devil had already put into his heart that Judas, son of Simon Iscariot, should deliver him over; and so, during the supper, Jesus – fully aware that he had come from God and was going to God, the Father who had handed everything over to him – rose from the table and took off his garments and taking a towel tied it around him. Then he poured water into a basin and began to wash his disciples' feet and dry them with the towel. So he came to Simon Peter who said to him, 'Master, are you going to wash my feet?' Jesus replied, 'You may not realise now what I am doing, but later you will understand.' Peter replied, 'I will never let you wash my feet.' Jesus said, 'If I do not wash you, you have no part in me.' Simon Peter said to him: 'Lord, not only my feet, but also my hands and my head.' Jesus said to him, 'He who is bathed has no need to wash, but is clean all over. And you are clean: but not all of you.' (The reason he said, 'Not all of you are clean,' was that he knew his deliverer.) (13:1–11)

After he had washed their feet, put on his clothes and taken his place at supper, he said to them again, 'Do you understand what I have done for you? You call me "Teacher" and "Lord", and rightly so, for that is what I am. Now, if I washed your feet, even though I am Lord and Teacher, you too must wash one another's feet. For it was an example that I gave you: you are to do exactly as I have done for you. In truth, in very truth, I tell you, a servant is no greater than his master, nor a messenger than the one who sent him. If you know this, you are blessed if you practise it' (13:12–17).

Jesus is aware that his hour has come to cross over from here to There. Just as his incarnation was intentionally undertaken for the sake of love, so would he suffer crucifixion for love. His crucifixion was a conscious act on his part, just as his incarnation was, essentially in response to a demand from Above, and only secondarily and contingently according to the material conditions arranged below. The initiative for his death no more lies with Caiaphas or Pilate than does the initiative for his birth lie with Joseph and Mary. In the realm of the world, of course, there must be worldly causes and reasons for events to take place, all according to natural and social laws; but the purposes fulfilled by these events are all in a different dimension of the spirit, and have their beginnings elsewhere. The purpose of his death, as well as of his birth, centred on those few individuals who were in the world, were his own, and were given to him by God. These few were the ones he loved: for their sake was he born, and for their sake he died; or, perhaps more accurately, it was for their sake that he was sent into the world by the Father, and for their sake now the Father demands of Jesus Christ that he undergo the baptism of crucifixion. The work that Jesus Christ came to do on the earth is nearing its completion, the symphony of his sojourn in the world is approaching its finale.

As a part of the completion of his work, the disciples need to be prepared further for their transformation so that they can really understand the nature of the Christ and believe I AM. The major part of his teaching is self-abnegation, the setting aside of self-importance and pride. Only when a person has risen above the state of 'I am this' or 'I am that' can he come to be in the state of I AM. And in all his teaching, the master sets an example for the pupils from his personal behaviour, asking them to do as he does. Making oneself naked like a slave and washing the feet of the disciples is at the least an exquisite lesson in the practice of humility. Such lessons are always needed, for self-importance is the greatest instrument of the Devil: even at the close of Jesus' teaching to the disciples, and at the eve of his death, 'a dispute arose among them about who should be regarded as the greatest' (Luke 22:24). They, and everyman, will indeed be blessed if they understand this lesson and put it into practice.

However, something more is being conveyed by the laying down of his clothes before washing the disciples' feet. The external garments are always a symbol of an outer layer of personality covering the inner being. This inner being needs to be uncovered and acknowledged as it is; only then the right transformation of it can take place. According to the Gospel of Thomas (II, 2:37), his disciples asked Jesus: 'When will You become revealed to us and when shall we see You?' He said, 'When you disrobe without being ashamed and take up your garments and place them under your feet like little children and tread on them, then will you see the Son of the Living One, and you will not be afraid.' Only he who has taken his own covering off can help others to look into themselves deeply without being afraid. Only then can he help them cleanse themselves of the egoistic dust gathered on their feet. The disciples have been purified already, but not completely; not the whole of them is yet clean. They have not yet been fully 'saved by the bath of regeneration and renewal in the Holy Spirit', as St Paul puts it (Titus 3:5), and need more purification.

Peter does not understand the action of Jesus Christ, nor does he grasp the need for it. Even when he is told that without such washing he can have no part in Christ, a level of being in which only the inner self can participate, he takes it externally and wants his hands and head washed as well! If washing is necessary, then the more limbs washed the better, he seems to think in his impatience, forgetting that what Christ's teaching requires is for him to know himself to the core, which he does not as yet. He is the one who denied Christ three times during the night before the trial of Jesus, and also one of the disciples who could not keep watch with Jesus in his hour of agony in the garden of Gethsemane. Is Peter not as advanced a disciple as Judas?

The Trial of Judas

I am not speaking of all of you. I know the kind of men I chose. But so as to fulfil what is written: 'He who eats bread with me has raised his heel against me.' I tell you now before it happens, so that when it happens you will believe I AM. In truth, in very truth, I tell you, he who accepts anyone I send accepts me, and he who accepts me accepts him who sent me' (13:18–20).

After saying this Jesus was deeply troubled. He said, 'In truth, in very truth, I tell you, one of you will deliver me.' The disciples looked at one another in bewilderment: whom could he be speaking of? One of them, the disciple whom Jesus loved, was at the table close beside Jesus; so Simon Peter signalled him to ask Jesus whom he meant. He leaned back against Jesus' chest and said to him, 'Lord, who is it?' Jesus answered, 'It is the man to whom I give this piece of bread when I have dipped it in the dish.' Then, after dipping it in the dish, he took it out and gave it to Judas, son of Simon Iscariot. At that moment, after the morsel of food, Satan entered into him. Jesus told him, 'Do quickly what you have to do.' Of course, no one at the table understood why he said this to him. A few had the idea that, since Judas held the common purse, Jesus was telling him to buy what was needed for the feast, or to give something to the poor. As soon as Judas had eaten the morsel, he went out. It was night. When he went out, Jesus said, 'Now is the Son of Man glorified and God is glorified in him. God will, in turn, glorify him in Himself, and will glorify him soon' (13:21–32).

Jesus said to his disciples, 'No one can come to me unless it is granted to him by the Father. . . . It was not you who chose me, it was I who chose you' (John 6:65; 15:16). It is an insult to Jesus Christ to think that he had so little insight into human character that he did not see the quality of someone who was a close disciple of his for the entire period of his teaching. We can right away dismiss the possibility that Jesus Christ was unmindful of the activities or the intentions of Judas and was surprised by them. He knew the kind of men he had chosen; and he loved Judas no less than the other disciples for whose sake he was born and for whom he died. At the least, Judas and Jesus were co-conspirators in a drama of which the chief actor and the director was Jesus himself. Judas seems to have been a willing and a consistent disciple who tried to do whatever Jesus demanded of him, no matter what the cost to himself.

While trying to understand the very special relationship between Jesus and Judas, we need to be on guard about the possibility of jealousy among the disciples who disputed with each other, during the life of Jesus Christ as well as after his death, for exalted positions. In the light of this, all the editorial remarks concerning Judas in the Gospels and other records, influenced as they are by other disciples, are a little suspect. There is also the very real fact of a surface understanding displayed by most of the disciples who had a great difficulty in comprehending the subtle aspects of Jesus' teaching. They did not understand what Jesus had asked Judas to do and for what purpose. In addition, there are suggestions throughout the Gospels, including this chapter, that several things passed between Jesus Christ and certain disciples individually of which the others had no idea.

Among the significant details told about Judas in the Gospels are that he was the chief of the treasury and the keeper of the purse for the community of Jesus. It would certainly be strange for him to have betrayed Jesus for thirty pieces of silver when in his position he could easily have had access to much more money. Very often the Gospels speak symbolically, and one cannot disregard the possibility of spiritual treasures of Christ being guarded by Judas, and possibly by him alone among the disciples. At the Last Supper, which was hosted by Jesus Christ, it appears from the various fragmentary details provided in the Gospels that Judas occupied a place of honour. His feet were also washed by Christ, giving him a part in himself. Also, Judas is the only one who is given a piece of bread by Jesus himself, dipped in a dish which, according to the traditional seating arrangement at a Passover meal, which this one very likely was, was shared by Jesus, Judas and the disciple whom Jesus loved. Also, it need not be forgotten, that Christ himself is the bread from Heaven, as in John 6:35–40, and an ordinary piece of bread when consecrated by him is the very substance of the Son of God.

It may be remarked here, somewhat parenthetically, that the third person sharing the dish with Jesus and Judas was almost certainly Lazarus, for he is the only one about whom the unanimous opinion was that Jesus loved him (see Chapter 11). Besides, this is not surprising: Lazarus was the only one in the circle of Christ who had woken up from the sleep of spiritual death. None of the other disciples can even be told about the state of readiness of Judas and the special task set for him, except Lazarus who alone had successfully undergone the ultimate baptism until death. When Judas left the table, no one besides Jesus and Lazarus had any idea of what was demanded of him, and whether he would be able to accomplish it.

Jesus exhorts all the disciples to put into practice what they know intellectually; however, he knew the kind of men he had chosen and he could not expect them all to carry out his instructions. Not yet, in any case. But the hour of Judas had now come, along with the hour of Jesus. When the hour of Lazarus had come, Jesus had been deeply troubled in spirit; similarly, now at the time of ripening of Judas, he was again troubled, for all his strength was needed for a proper rite of passage of one of his chief disciples from one state of being to another. There is a parable told by Jesus and reported only in Mark (4:26–29) which is relevant here:

> This is how it is with the kingdom of God. A man scatters seed on the ground. He goes to bed and gets up day after day. Through it all the seed sprouts and grows without his knowing how it happens. The earth produces of itself first the blade, then the ear, finally the ripe grain in the ear. When the crop is ready he wields the sickle, for the time is ripe for harvest.

The word which is used in this parable for being ripe is in Greek *paradidomi*, which also means to deliver from one to another, to entrust, to give in trust, to yield, to give up, to commend, to arrive at maturity, to deliver by teaching as well as to betray. It is the same word which is used in John 13:21 above, as well as in John 19:30, when Jesus delivered over his spirit, and in Matthew 25:14 where a man going away on a journey entrusted his funds to his servants.

In the light of the very special status accorded by Jesus to Judas, any ordinary betrayal by Judas, as it is universally understood in the popular Christian tradition, does not make much sense. What is more likely is that knowing that his hour is nigh, Jesus Christ searched for the right person who would be able to hand over the substance of the tradition and continue it. And the substance of the tradition, the very heart of the yoga of Jesus Christ, is to dwell in Christ and to let him dwell in oneself. What is needed for the right transmission therefore is the delivering of Christ himself. If it is the will of the Father that His Word continue to dwell in human beings, the spirit of Jesus who had given flesh to the Word is not free to return home to his Father until he is able to prepare someone else sufficiently so that he could hand over the Logos to him for embodiment. A true witness, or a real believer, is needed to act as a midwife at any birth: earlier John the Baptiser had assisted the incarnation of Christ by being a witness, now a true disciple was needed to release him from the necessity of staying in the flesh, to free him for a different birth for other purposes, perhaps even for his other sheep elsewhere in this or other worlds.

Who will deliver Christ in substance to the successive generations, by embodying the Word and letting it continue to dwell in himself? Whether it is a demand of the Spirit or a necessity of the laws of the world is not clear, but it does appear that transmission in any spiritual school is only from the master to worthy disciples. In a specific spiritual school there can be only one master although others are needed and can help, because no master can work without assistants, and a real master does not work for himself but for God. There can be only one lion in the jungle; if a lion has departed from the mountain, without another lion to take his place, monkeys begin to rule! The urgent question pressing upon Jesus Christ and troubling his spirit is who will continue his work. For the Buddha the question was who among his disciples will receive and transmit the Buddha mind; for the Christ the question now is who will deliver the body of Christ in spirit and in truth?

Each of the disciples must wonder if he is to be chosen by Christ for this most important task. Jesus naturally looks to Judas, the keeper of the treasury of his teaching. But is Judas able? Does he understand to the very core of his being the lesson that Jesus has just tried to demonstrate – only he can be a master who knows how to be a servant? Has Judas completely emptied himself of the whole of himself, of his fears and of his ambitions? Is he completely naked, like a slave, so that he may be clothed with the garments of glory which are not of this world? Every disciple is like a fig tree, as in the parable in Luke 13:6–9, cultivated in the vineyard of Jesus for three years; now it is time for Judas to yield some fruit, or be cut down.

It is always tempting to imagine that there is peace and harmony in the presence of a wise teacher and that his disciples live in happiness; and that, by extension, if we become followers of Jesus Christ and accept him as our saviour, we shall have an easier life. It is never thus: the very presence of a great teacher is a constant question mark placed in front of a pupil, calling for a continual re-examination of the whole of his life – why he lives and how, and at what level of struggle he is engaged. It is not the case that the most advanced disciples have the easiest life;

159

the life and fate of all the apostles gives the lie to that wishful assumption. The more advanced the disciple, the more he is called to suffer; the closer he comes to Christ, the closer he is to Christ's baptism: crucifixion. But in that crucifixion is the way to Eternal Life. A man is drawn to Christ not for solace and comfort for himself, but for Truth and Light, the price for which is his own self. As was said earlier, he who is close to Christ is close to the fire. Still, even at the risk of being burned, a true seeker is drawn to Christ, as a moth to fire, for he knows that he who is far from him is far from the Kingdom.

Jesus said:

'From him to whom much is given much is demanded. More will be asked of a man to whom more has been entrusted. I have come to light a fire on the earth. How I wish the blaze were ignited! I have a baptism to undergo, and what anguish I feel till it is over. Do you think I have come to establish peace on the earth? I assure you, the contrary is true: I have come for dissension' (Luke 12:48–51).

Fundamentally, the dissension that Christ brings is a warfare within one's soul: between the *yes* to the Light one does not know but cannot stay away from, and the *no* to it which keeps one clinging to the darkness which one knows even while abhorring it. The closer one is to the Christ, the greater is the struggle: Christ's own battle was at the highest level. Krishna said in the *Mahabharata* that for a warrior the choice is not between war and peace, but between different levels of war. At a lower level a person is engaged with a smaller devil; a big devil waits for a big soul! The level of the devil with whom the Buddha or the Christ struggles is much higher than the devil who consents to struggle with an ordinary man.

As the chief disciple of Christ, Judas was a big soul, ready to take on a big devil. We cannot but assume that whatever Christ asked Judas to do was for the good of Judas himself – not in any worldly sense but in the realm of the Spirit. Judas was also one of his own sheep, and he was the model shepherd, who had declared:

I know my sheep and mine know me, just as the Father knows me and I know the Father. And for these sheep I give my life. . . . My sheep hear my voice; I know them, and they follow me. I give them Eternal Life, and they shall never perish; no one shall snatch them from my hand. My Father, who has given to me, is greater than all, and from the Father's hand no one can snatch away. The Father and I are one (John 10:14–15, 27–30).

It cannot be the case that the Devil prevailed against the Christ and his Father and snatched Judas from them. Rather, Christ sent Judas to accomplish a particularly difficult task, to test his understanding and strength, as a teacher prepares the students and then sets a graduation examination for them. The question is about the readiness of Judas to assume the mantle of Christ and to continue the bodily existence of the Word of God; the answer will be determined by how he fares in his final test, the awesome baptism of Jesus Christ.

The final test is set for Judas, as it was for Adam, Job, Peter and for Jesus himself, with the help of Satan – which in the original Hebrew means 'adversary', 'opponent'. Satan is the most consistent and reliable servant of God: nobody gets past him who is not really worthy to inherit the Kingdom:

One day, when the sons of God came to present themselves before the Lord, Satan also came among them. And the Lord said to Satan, 'Whence do you come?' Then Satan answered the Lord and said, 'From roaming the earth and patrolling it.' And the Lord said to Satan, 'Have you noticed my servant Job, and that there is no one on earth like him, blameless and upright, fearing God and avoiding evil?' (Job 1:6–8).

With this, God sent Satan to test his servant Job, as he did later to test Jesus Christ (Mark 1:13). No one can come to God without first coming to the Devil. He guards the gate to heaven, and winnows the wheat from the chaff; he is the one appointed by God to be the examiner of souls. As long as one is not willing to encounter the Devil, to know him and be known by him, to test him and be tested by him, one cannot come to the presence of God. No Devil; no God!

Christ having prevailed over Satan had power of him; Satan was now as much a servant of Christ as of God. Just as Satan had started testing Job on the invitation of God, now he – having already put it in the heart of Jesus that Judas was the one to deliver him – waited for the concurrence of Jesus before testing Judas. This is, of course, a necessity for all the disciples; however, Jesus was much less certain about the preparedness of the other disciples:

> 'Simon, Simon! Remember that Satan has asked for you, to sift you all like wheat. But I have prayed for you that your faith may never fail. You in turn must strengthen your brothers.' 'Lord,' he said to him, 'at your side I am prepared to face imprisonment and death itself.' Jesus replied, 'I tell you, Peter, the cock will not crow today until you have three times denied that you know me.' (Luke 22: 31–34).

He knows what Peter is likely to do, as well as Judas, from whom he expects more, but ultimately even Christ would not completely foreclose the possibility that a person might in a superhuman effort overcome himself, and thus overcome the adversary. The opponent, the Satan, is as much within oneself as God is: if God is the *Self*, Satan is the *self*, and the human being is between these two forces, having a choice between serving the self and being estranged from God, or overcoming the self and serving God. When ego is master, there is hell; when ego is servant, there is heaven.

Jesus Christ sends Judas with his special blessings, fortified with his own strength imparted to Judas through the special morsel of bread, to meet his challenger and undergo his final baptism. Christ urges Judas not to hesitate, and to do quickly what he must do to let the son of man yield the Son of Man. All this passed between them, and with the possible exception of the disciple whom Jesus loved, nobody at the table understood it. Judas waits only long enough to eat the piece of bread given to him by Christ, and goes forth to wrestle with Satan, a servant of Jesus but an adversary of Judas. Of course, Judas might fail, and endanger the master who sent him. But the master has no concern for his personal safety or comfort, as he already showed many times, and especially when the hour of Lazarus had come. Now in the hour of Judas also he does not spare himself; he accepts any and all risks for the sake of his disciples' spiritual growth. He would show his love for them until the end, and especially for Judas, his chief disciple and his present hope. In him he hopes to see the glorification, which is to say the manifestation, of the Son of Man, who might in turn pass through the door of I AM, and be included in the glory of God Himself and be known by Him.

Only He who Knows can Love

'My little children, I am to be with you only a little longer. You will look for me; but, as I told the Jews and now I tell you too, "Where I am going, you cannot come." I give you a new commandment: Love one another. As I have loved you, so you too must love one another. This is how all will know you for my disciples – your love for one another' (13:33–35).

'Lord,' Simon Peter said to him, 'Where are you going?' Jesus answered, 'Where I am going you cannot follow me now; but you will follow me later.' 'Lord,' said Peter, 'why can I not follow you now? I will lay down my life for you?' Jesus answered. 'I tell you truly, the cock will not crow before you deny me three times' (13:36–38).

Here begins a long farewell discourse by Jesus Christ, continuing in the next four chapters, a masterpiece surpassing in subtlety and high feeling anything of its kind in the whole of world literature.

Christ places a nearly impossible demand on the disciples: to love one another as he loved them. Earlier they had heard him endorse the traditional and difficult command to love their neighbours as themselves (Matthew 22:39; Leviticus 19:18). Then he gave them a yet harder one to love their enemies (Matthew 5:44); and now the hardest of all, to love one another as *he* loved them. Is this possible? After all, the disciples are hardly able to be like Christ: they do not have his vision, his heart, his mind; a disciple is a son of man whereas Christ is a Son of God. But no matter; Christ summons them to come to maturity in the full measure of himself, to become sons of God like him, begotten by the Spirit. This is a great invitation to the disciples for transformation, by his own example among them, and by the working of the magic of his love in them.

The outstanding feature of the love of Christ for his disciples, as we see throughout the Gospels, and in this chapter as well, is that it is based on awareness and knowledge, and is never sentimental or reactive to mere like or dislike. It is compassionate but hard-headed. As he said, 'Whoever I love, I reprove and chastise. Be in earnest, then, and turn around' (Revelation 3:19).

As is clear in the teaching conveyed by the washing of the feet of the disciples, he is aware of the unity of all being: the master and the disciples are the same in their deepest essence, not higher or lower, for they together serve something much greater than themselves. In that service, they are all related to the Highest Being, from which they are cut off as long as they live only *for* themselves, and act *from* themselves alone.

In the trial of Judas, Christ is aware of his ripeness, and of the necessity of the testing by Satan before he can progress any further. It is not a question of protecting him from Satan, but of preparing him adequately to meet the challenge. There are risks involved, both for the teacher and the pupil, but it is because of his love that Christ does not flinch from the situation which he knows is necessary. His love for the disciples is not for the sake of making their lives easier or more comfortable. Rather it is for the sake of showing them the necessity of suffering, and helping them find courage to sacrifice themselves, as they have to in accepting his baptism.

His love for Peter is not based on any illusion: he knows the limitations of the disciple; yet loves his potentiality which he tries to draw out by compassion and instruction. Peter does not know himself deeply enough: he is not internally unified to come to one single loyalty. He is impatient and proclaims himself ready to die for Christ; but his very over-confidence is a mark of the fact that he has not died to himself and his vanity. He has not yet had a deep engagement with his own denial, his Satan, and come to terms with him, to be delivered by him from himself. Yet, Christ loves him unconditionally, as he loves the others who seek the Spirit.

CHAPTER

— 14 —

I AM the Way and the Truth and the Life

'Let your hearts not be troubled. Believe in God, and believe in me. In my Father's house there are many dwelling places; otherwise I would have warned you. I am going to prepare a place for you; and when I do go and prepare a place for you, I will come back and take you to myself, so that where I am you may also be. And you know the way where I am going' (14:1–4).

Thomas said to him, 'Lord, we do not know where you are going. How can we know the way?' Jesus said to him, 'I AM the Way and the Truth and the Life. No one comes to the Father except through me. If you really knew me, you would recognise my Father also. From now on you do know Him and have seen Him' (14:5–7).

Philip said to him, 'Lord, show us the Father and that is enough for us.' Jesus said to him, 'Philip, here I am with you all this time, and you still do not know me? Whoever has seen me has seen the Father. How can you say, "Show us the Father"? Do you not believe that I am in the Father and the Father is in me? I am not myself the source of the words I speak: it is the Father who dwells in me doing His own work. Believe me that I am in the Father and the Father is in me; otherwise believe because of the works. In truth, in very truth I tell you that he who believes in me will do the works I do, and far greater than these, because I am going to the Father, and whatever you ask in my name I will do, so that the Father may be glorified in the Son. Anything you ask me in my name, I will do' (14:8–14).

In this farewell address, Jesus consoles the disciples who are understandably desolate at the news that he is going away soon. Jesus Christ wishes to reassure the disciples that his physical end is not the end in any final sense, but a change of state, because a person can dwell in many ways and in many places in the universe, and in different states. This is a point which is common to all religions, and which distinguishes them from secular ideologies: there is more to a human being than what meets the eye, not only in terms of *space* but also in *time*; a person has some other, more inner and spiritual, aspect to him than the physical body, and that his existence on earth has some kind of continuity with an existence in another, subtler realm after the death of the physical body. As St. Paul says: 'Indeed, we know that when the earthly tent in which we dwell is destroyed, we have a dwelling provided for us by God, a dwelling not made by human hands, eternal, and in heaven' (2 Corinthians 5:1). The more a person understands the larger picture in which his ordinary living and dying have their proper place, the less he clings to the compulsive wish for a mere continuation of earthly existence, for in God's house there are many places where a soul can dwell – depending upon its quality and spiritual density or lightness. The Christ who had descended into flesh knowingly, intentionally putting upon himself the constraints of the body, is not going to be limited by the laws of the flesh much longer, and would therefore be able to be present in different worlds more freely, and be able to continue giving spiritual courage to the disciples who are following his way. According to St Augustine, Jesus 'prepares the dwelling places by preparing those who are to dwell in them'.

But, most of the disciples do not always understand the subtle teachings of Christ. Thomas is not at all clear about the destination of Christ and does not know what the way is to the goal that Christ sets for each one of them. The goal is the Father and the Christ himself; he would come back, and would keep coming back until they are ready, to 'take you to myself'. The disciples are continually looking outward, as if the goal and the way were outside. And Christ has to remind them repeatedly that the Way and the Truth and Eternal Life are within themselves; if they do not find these there at the threshold of I AM, connecting the higher and the lower worlds within themselves, they will not find them anywhere (see Chapter 11). There is no other way to the Father except I AM, where the Son of Man meets the Son of God, at the very core of the soul, for 'the Kingdom of God is within you' (Luke 17:21).

Philip still, after Christ has been with him for so long, does not understand and asks to be shown the Father externally. He does not see and believe that Christ is in the Father and the Father in him, just as he, Philip, could be in Christ and have the Christ dwell in him. As always, whenever such exalted statements are made by Jesus, he again reminds the disciples that he has become so transparent to the Divine Ground that he who has seen him has seen the Father, for he has nothing of his own, neither the words nor the works. All he says is what the Father tells him to say, and all he does is done by the Father living inside him. Furthermore, any of the disciples can do what Jesus does if he understand him truly and dwells in him.

A disciple can do even greater works if he asks for it in the *name* of Jesus Christ. (See Chapter 6 for a discussion of *name*.) The important point to be emphasised again and again is that a person can do nothing of any value in his own name, which is to say based on his own energy and for his own sake. Jesus Christ himself does nothing in his own name; he speaks and works only in the name of the Father. In spite of the mutual indwelling of the Father and the Son and the essential oneness of their fundamental energy, there is a discernible and proper internal order, so that it is right to say both 'The Father and I are one' (John 10:30) and 'The Father is greater than I' (John 14:28). Similarly, if there is a mutual indwelling of the Christ and a disciple, they are essentially one, but not without hierarchical order. More than anything else, it is a matter of the right flow of energies – from Above downwards, or from the inside outward, or, to use yet another metaphor, from the vine to the branches. As we hear later in this discourse:

Abide in me, as I abide in you. No more than a branch can bear fruit of itself apart from the vine, can you bear fruit apart from me. I am the vine, you are the branches. He who lives in me and I in him will bear abundant fruit, for apart from me you can do nothing. He who does not live in me is like a withered, rejected branch picked up to be thrown in the fire and burnt (John 15:4–6).

167

Those who Love can Come to Truth

If you love me, you will keep my commandments. I will ask the Father and he will give you another guide (paraclete) to be with you for ever: the Spirit of Truth which the world cannot accept, because it does not see it or know it, but you do recognise him because it remains with you and is within you. I shall not leave you orphans: I am coming back to you. A little while now and the world will see me no more; but you see me as one who has life, and you will have life. On that day you will know that I am in my Father and you are in me and I in you. Whoever keeps the commandments that he has from me is the man who loves me; and the man who loves me will be loved by my Father, and I shall love him and reveal myself to him (14:15–21).

Judas (not Judas Iscariot) said to him, 'Lord, why is it that you will reveal yourself to us and not to the world?' Jesus answered, 'If any one loves me, he will keep my word. Then my Father will love him, and we shall come to him and make him our abode. Whoever does not love me does not keep my words; yet the word you hear is not my own but is of the Father who sent me. This I have said to you while I stay with you. But the guide, the Holy Spirit, whom the Father will send in my name will instruct you in everything, and remind you of all that I told you' (14:22–26).

There is a progressive spiral of dedication, action and knowledge, or rather of love, obedience and truth, along which Jesus has been preparing the disciples. Here it is explicitly stated that if a person loves Christ, this love must be evident in the fact that he obeys the commands of Christ. Only to such a person can truth be revealed. The more one knows Christ, the more one is drawn to him; the more one loves him, the more one tries to act according to his instructions; and the more one obeys him, the more one comes to understand him. There is a very similar situation in the *Bhagavad Gita* where there is a subtle interplay between action (*karma*), love (*bhakti*) and knowledge (*jnana*), all under the guidance of the teaching of the integrated intelligence (*buddhi yoga*), each aspect supporting and furthering the other. (In this connection see R. Ravindra: 'Teaching of Krishna, Master of Yoga'; *American Theosophist*, vol 72, 1984). A disciple is thus more and more prepared, until he can recognise and receive the Spirit of Truth, which will dwell in him permanently. The Holy Spirit had descended on the head of Jesus, witnessed by John the Baptiser, and had stayed dwelling in him for ever; now, in due course, she will descend and dwell in the disciples. This is how Christ himself will come again and show himself to them spiritually and dwell in them. It is the Spirit which is eternal, and not the flesh; of course the flesh of Jesus must die according to the laws of the flesh, but those who are prepared and open of heart can see and receive the Word, who will come and dwell in them and then they will understand the subtle truths.

He will reveal himself to them this way, precisely because they would have been readied by the practice of love, obedience and knowledge, and no doubt further shaken into a state of emotional openness by the shock of the death of their master. The question asked by Judas can scarcely be other than a literary device for the author of the Gospel: of course, the world cannot see or recognise the Spirit of Truth; the world has not been prepared. As has been evident throughout the Gospel, the crowds cannot grasp anything subtle. Even the disciples can hardly understand what is being said much of the time, and this in spite of their long training at the hands of the master for whom they gave up their comforts, professions, families, social positions, and everything else. Are the disciples disheartened at the lack of discernible progress in their understanding, and feel themselves to be just like everyone else in the world? Or, is it a case of genuine humility on their part so that they do not even realise their distinctive situation? In any case, spiritual development also has its rhythms and time, as does natural growth: however much water may be applied by the gardener, the fruit ripens only in its season! The hour of these disciples is not yet.

He who Has Nothing will not Die

'Peace is my farewell to you, my peace is my gift to you; I do not give it to you as the world gives peace. Do not let your hearts be troubled and do not be fearful. You have heard me tell you, "I go away for a while, and I come back to you." If you truly loved me you would rejoice that I am going to the Father, for the Father is greater than I. But now I have told you this even before it happens, so that when it takes place you may believe. I shall no longer speak with you, for the Prince of this world is coming. In me he has nothing; but the world may recognise that I love the Father, and I do exactly as the Father has commanded me. Rise up, let us go from here' (14:27–31).

The peace of Christ is the consummation of all spiritual effort and struggle; it is coming to rest in oneness with the Vastness. But only those who have been denuded of themselves can find this peace, for his peace is not like the peace of the world. As he said earlier, as far as the world is concerned he did not come to bring peace but dissension, to bring a separation between those who are blind but wish to see and those who do not, between those who are asleep but seek to wake up and those who love their sleep. And above all, he came to bring this separation and struggle in the soul of his disciples so that their own more spiritual aspirations might be strengthened in the warfare against the parts which deny the Spirit. It is not comfort or ease or happiness in any usual sense; it is, in the words of St Paul, peace 'that surpasseth all understanding' (Philippians 4:7). Only those who obey the law of Christ, and like him are willing to die to themselves, can love him and come to his peace.

The disciples do not have a clear and continuing understanding of the true nature of Christ; in that sense they do not yet believe. They do not realise that the really significant part of Christ cannot die when his body dies; and that the same is true for them as well. They need the assurance from Christ that he is in fact on his way to a higher and more exalted place, in the presence of the Father, and they should not be distressed for his sake nor fearful for themselves. As Krishna says in the *Bhagavad Gita* (2:16), 'The unreal never is: the Real never is not. This truth indeed has been seen by those who can see what is true.' Most of the disciples do not quite see what is true. They do not realise deeply enough that the Prince of this world has sway only on worldly things, things of the flesh, and not on the things of the Spirit. Christ has so completely emptied himself of all the worldly things, which have ultimately to do with fear and desire, that as far as the Prince of this world is concerned Christ has nothing on which he can lay hold: being free of himself, he is free of the rulers of the world.

Naturally, the body of Jesus will be killed according to the laws of the world; but this by no means puts an end to Christ. He took on a body in obedience to his Father; and he will leave it also in obedience to His will. This is how he manifests his love for God, as he has repeatedly said that he who would love him must obey his word. In the entire New Testament this is the only place where Jesus says that he loves the Father; it is only right that he should affirm in the very next breath his total obedience, made even more striking in the context of his imminent death. Having completely denied his self-will, he becomes one with the Father and the source of Eternal Life; in doing His will he leaves nothing in himself for the Prince of this world to take hold of. *Theologia Germanica* (chapter 16) says; 'If the Evil Spirit himself could come into true obedience, he would become an angel [of light] again, and all his sin and wickedness would be healed and blotted out and forgiven at once.'

CHAPTER

—— 15 ——

Right Order – Internal and External

'I AM the true vine and my Father is the grower. He cuts off
any branch in me that does not bear fruit, and any that is
fruitful He trims clean to make it bear more fruit. You have
already been cleansed by the word that I spoke to you. Abide
in me as I abide in you. No more than a branch can bear fruit
of itself apart from the vine, can you bear fruit apart from me.
I am the vine, you are the branches. He who lives in me and
I in him will bear abundant fruit, for apart from me you can
do nothing. He who does not live in me is like a withered,
rejected branch picked up to be thrown in the fire and burnt'
(15:1–6).

Every spiritual teaching recognises a hierarchy of being in the
universe and of the corresponding levels in its microcosmic
counterpart, in an ideal or fully developed human being. It
is important to emphasise that a human being *can* mirror the
large cosmos in *reality*, but does not ordinarily do so in *actuality*.
In other words, he is potentially created in the image of God,
and can in reality be so if he is begotten by God in a spiritual
birth; otherwise a person dies without fulfilling the possibilities
inherent in a human incarnation. It is for the fulfilment of this
potential that a spiritual path or a yoga is needed. For the sake
of following a transformational discipline, a person becomes a
disciple to be created anew, so that the right internal order could
be established in him, and, with his aid, in the cosmos on the
large. So it was with the disciples of Jesus Christ.

What is the right order inside a person as well as in the cosmos on the large? A human being, as well as a society and the
cosmos, is rightly ordered if there is a harmonious exchange

of energies between levels which mutually support each other, higher levels providing the vision and the lower levels carrying out the requisite actions. Within a human being, it is the Spirit that sees and has the right vision, but it is the body-mind which has to carry out the action. Without the Spirit, the psychosomatic complex of a human being is blind, but without the latter, the Spirit is lame. In a rightly ordered situation, the lower levels listen to and obey what is higher than themselves; they receive their instructions and energy from above and act below. Without this order, the flow of energies is interrupted, and one tries to be egoistically self-sufficient, as if one is oneself the source of the energy required for one's actions.

'Every action is really performed by the constituent forces (*gunas*) of Nature,' says the *Bhagavad Gita* (3:27–28), 'But he who is deluded by ego thinks "I am the doer." He who has the true insight into the operations of the *gunas* and their various functions knows that the *gunas* act on *gunas*, and remains unattached to his actions.' Only when one is engaged in action while being mindful of and receiving the energy from above, can one be a link between two levels of being and act without ego. This is possible only when the Son of Man within has been lifted up from the son of man. Then one is rightly ordered, as was Jesus Christ: 'When you lift up the Son of Man, you will come to realise I AM, and that I do nothing by myself. . . . I am not myself the source of the words I speak: it is the Father who dwells in me doing His own work' (John 8:28; 14:10).

If a person is rightly ordered, then he realises what in any case is true: the lower depends on the higher – literally, the lower hangs from the higher, and cannot exist without it. The cosmic tree, in the metaphor used by the *Bhagavad Gita* (15:1–3), has its roots above and its branches below; and the branches cannot live without remaining organically connected with the life-sustaining roots. The same idea is conveyed here in the Gospel: the disciples are likened to the branches drawing their life-giving energy from the vine of Christ with whom they are intimately connected so that the same energy flows in them as in him. Without this connection with the source of life, a branch dies and is cast off.

However, what is natural in the biological realm requires effort and an intentional reversal of natural tendencies in the human sphere: owing to the wilfulness and unconsciousness inherent in human nature, the children of flesh are not, nor do they wish to be, naturally connected with the higher and spiritual parts of themselves. Another way of expressing it is that there is a conflict between the two natures in man, the higher and the lower, or between the law of God and the law of sin. St Paul said: 'I cannot even understand my own actions. I do not do what I want to do but what I hate. . . . I know that no good dwells in me, that is, in my flesh; the desire to do right is there but not the power. What happens is that I do, not the good I will to do, but the evil I do not intend. . . . My inner being agrees with the law of God, but I see in my body's members another law at war with the law of my mind [*nous* in Greek, higher mind, equivalent to *buddhi* in Sanskrit]; this makes me the prisoner of the law of sin in my members. . . . With my mind I serve the law of God but with the flesh the law of sin' (Romans 7:15–25).

The Christ in man is the deepest and the most spiritual part of the soul, the *Atman*, one with *Brahman* – the Son of God, born in him who has been begotten by the Spirit, and one with the Father. A disciple is the human body-mind, under a discipline for letting the Son of Man arise from within his flesh, which in the Gospel in general means the whole of man. It is the Son of Man who can directly perceive the Son of God, through the door of I AM (see Chapter 8), and in the right internal order receives the spiritual energy from him. Then a disciple can say with St Paul, essentially echoing the words and attitude of Jesus Christ himself, that 'I live, yet no longer I, but Christ liveth in me' (Galatians 2:20).

On the other hand, the indication of a branch being alive is that it bears fruit. To bear fruit is also the purpose of the vine: otherwise, the incarnation of Christ is in vain. He needs the disciples as much as the disciples need him in order to engage in divine work and bear fruit. What is the fruit of the vine of Christ? It is the conceiving of the Son of God in a virgin birth in the secret chamber of one's soul and bringing him forth to full maturity in the world. He who is barren of fruit is already withered, and not in living contact with the vine. And he who yields some fruit and is essentially sound is made more and more unified internally and cleansed of extraneous and unnecessary growths and offshoots, his worldly side interests which siphon off the precious sap from the one really necessary work in which the disciple must engage whole-heartedly. 'Whomever I love I reprove and chastise. Be earnest about it, therefore. Turn around!'(Revelation 3:19).

Love from Above, Obedience from Below

> If you abide in me, and my words abide in you, ask for whatever you will, and it will be done. My Father is glorified in this that you bear much fruit and then you will become my disciples. As the Father has loved me, so have I loved you; abide in my love. And you will dwell in my love if you keep my commandments, just as I have kept my Father's commandments and dwell in His love. This I have said to you so that my joy may be in you and your joy may be full. This is my commandment that you love each other as I have loved you. No one has greater love than this, to give his life for those he loves (15:7–13).

If a disciple remains rightly ordered internally, which is to say that he abides in Christ, and Christ – his love and words – abides in him, then he is connected with the Source of all energy. Then he is one with the Vastness, within which he is hierarchically ordered, and is able to accomplish everything he wills precisely because what he wills is not to do his own personal projects but to do that alone which is in harmony with the will of the Source. Christ himself is the model: he loves his disciples as his Father loves him; he obeys the Father, as they must obey him; this is how he dwells in the Father's love, as they must dwell in his. As was remarked in the previous chapter, only once in the entire New Testament, in John 14:31, does Christ say that he *loves* the Father, and that too in the context of his obedience to the Father; otherwise, always he says that he *obeys* the Father. This is how it should be for the Father is greater than the Son: the Father loves and the Son obeys; the Christ loves and the disciples obey.

This is how the disciples manifest their love for him and earn the right and the capacity to stay in his love. There is nothing sentimental about his love; it consists in the call to make one's life *sacred*, which is the same, even etymologically, as a call to *sacrifice* oneself. Those who dwell in his love, merit his baptism

– that of the cross: crucifixion of one's self-will, and yoking it to that of Christ, as he yoked his own to that of his Father. This is the right order; this is how the proper flow of energy is maintained from Above downward. This is why love sustains the whole cosmos, as is said in the *Rig Veda*; and why it is said that 'God is love, and he who abides in love abides in God, and God in him' (1 John 4:16). This mutual indwelling, the constant flow of one spiritual energy, is supported by love from Above and obedience from below. O seeker, lest you be heedless in wishing to dwell in the love of Christ, look closely at your soul and remember that his love is founded on sacrifice: his own and of him who wishes to be close to him. In dying to himself, as a seed dies in the ground, a person bears fruit and proves that he is a true disciple connected as a branch to the vine of Christ. Apart from him, one can do nothing.

In the losing of one's lower self lies the possibility of finding the Eternal Self. Any disciple who accomplishes this, or rather allows this to be accomplished in himself, will have his joy fulfilled and have the joy of Christ in him. This joy is no *pleasure*; it has nothing to do with liking something or not. When John the Baptiser spoke of his joy being complete (John 3:29–30), it was in the certainty of his own personal decrease, but in the realisation of what he had come to do: to assist at the embodiment of the Logos by his witnessing. Jesus Christ speaks of his *joy* only once, in any of the gospels – and that on the eve of his crucifixion. His joy consists in the completion of his work, given to him by his Father; this completion takes place only on the cross: like a virgin fecundated by God he delivers His spiritual son as his mortal body dies. John's joy was complete at the Incarnation, and that of Jesus at the Resurrection. In the maintenance of this cosmic order, sustained by the sacrifice of the self (*purusha yajna* of the Vedas) is the true joy; the disciples may have their joy fulfilled to the extent that they participate in the necessary sacrifice which is love.

On a cosmic scale, Christ is perpetually engaged in a struggle against the forces of darkness; in this struggle his chief force is in his own sacrifice and suffering, by which he lessens the suffering of those whom he loves and wishes to bring into the Light. To the extent that the disciples participate in the suffering of Christ, they help decrease his sorrow and burden. If they are not crucified themselves, he will have to be crucified again and again. It is reported in the Acts of Peter (XXXV) from the second century that Peter while fleeing from Rome and the danger of martyrdom meets Jesus Christ and asks, 'Master, where are you going?' Christ tells Peter that he is going to Rome to be crucified again in the place of Peter. The conscience of Peter is troubled and he returns to the city to die.

Levels of Disciples

'You are the ones I love when you do what I command you. No longer do I call you slaves, because the slave does not understand what his master is doing. Rather I have called you my friends for I revealed to you everything I heard from the Father. It was not you who chose me; it was I who chose you, and charged you to go and bear fruit, fruit that remains, in order that whatever you ask the Father in my name He will give you. This I command you: love one another' (15:14–17).

The condition of the disciples remaining in the love of Christ is submission to his instructions. Without a sincere attempt to put his teaching into practice, there would be no possibility of the spiritual evolution of a disciple, and therefore hardly any point in his being near Jesus Christ. He chooses the few aspirants who are prepared enough to be helped by him out of the many who are called by him – by his words and works. No proselytisation or evangelism is involved here; Jesus Christ is not interested in reward or punishment, but in clear sight in which a disciple sees and understands that if he does not fulfil his deepest spiritual aspirations his own conscience will condemn him.

Of course, the response to the call of Christ is voluntary. However, those who have been blessed by God are also troubled by him; there is a restless urge in them for something they do not know but which would not let them be in peace until they find what calls them; such have no choice but to respond to his call. His call is the call of I AM, the way to an abundant life, to the Vastness. But the way to the mountain-top passes through the valley of the suffering on the cross. A man who has some inkling both looks forward to the baptism of Christ and dreads it. He has no choice but to respond, but he also knows that if he emerges from the fire of Christ he would not be what he is now. He certainly will not be himself, with his personal fears and ambitions; what he might be, if anything at all, he does not know and cannot know. One of the greatest fears a man has is that of a radical transformation of himself. Something in man knows that the way to real life lies on the other side of the death of the imaginary life in which he lives. But he is afraid to die to his fantasy life for he fears that there may be nothing else. The fear of total annihilation guards the way to transformation. The fruit of Eternal Life, the only fruit that remains, and all the treasures of the Father, are there in the chamber whose door is the cross. The cross calls: inviting and frightening.

The awesome price of being a disciple of Christ was understood by Ignatius of Antioch (ca. 110) who exclaimed on his way to martyrdom, 'Now I am beginning to be a disciple.'

Christ chooses those who seek and can bear the light, those who can be helped. These he prepares for understanding truth and withstanding it. And there is a constant testing and selection: the progress of a disciple to a higher level is less a matter of reward for some merit, and more a recognition of his ability to understand and the capacity to suffer. It is not necessary for a disciple to love Christ or to know him; this he cannot in any case do, for he has no internal unity of purpose, and much of himself is not at all interested in following Christ; in fact, all of his worldly being is opposed to the law of Christ. What is necessary is that the material density of the disciple not completely stifle the tiny seed in the depth of his own soul which wishes to grow and emerge into the light; for this he needs to let the Christ love him and know him. If a seeker can abide in the circle of Christ, under his gaze and in his love, he can be helped.

It is less important for a disciple to choose the master, for he does not know what he needs; it is more important to be chosen by Christ and to be on his way. As a disciple progresses, he comes closer and closer to the centre, understanding more and bearing more. From the periphery of the circle where he understands little and works as a *slave*, against the will of most of himself, he moves inward and becomes a *servant*, for he begins to see the need for serving willingly. Still closer to the centre, he becomes a *friend* knowing the mind of the master and participating in it as he lives more and more from his own right mind. Slowly, as a seed grows into a tree, a son of man gives rise to the Son of Man, charged to bear fruit and bring forth the Son of God.

Leave the World in Order to Change It

'If the world hates you, know that it has hated me first. If you were of the world, the world would love its own, but you are not of the world, for I chose you out of the world, therefore the world hates you. Remember what I told you: the slave is not greater than his master. If they persecuted me, they will persecute you also. If they keep my word, they will keep yours too. But they will do these things because of my name, because they do not know the One who sent me. If I had not come and spoken to them, they would not be guilty of sin, but now they have no excuse for their sin. He who hates me hates my Father also. If I had not done works among them such as no one has ever done, they would not be guilty of sin; but now they have seen and still have hated both me and my Father. However, this is to fulfil the word in their law: they hated me without cause' (15:18–25).

A clear distinction is made here between those who are the sheep of Christ and listen to him and follow him, and those who belong to the world and therefore are in enmity to him. Christ and the world here represent two entirely different and opposing tendencies; the world hates Christ and anyone else who follows him. However, the disciples are also *from* the world, even though they are no longer *of* the world, for Jesus Christ has taken them out of the world with his teaching. It is necessary to distinguish at least two different senses in which to understand the usage of 'the world' in the Gospel: there is the sense in which the world is under the sway of the Prince of Darkness, opposing the Light from Above, and enmeshing people in fears and ambitions. There is another sense in which the world signifies mankind and other creatures on earth; after all, it is for the sake of the world that the Father sent his only begotten son. 'Indeed, God so loved the world that He gave His only Son, that whoever believes in him may not die, but may have Eternal Life. God did not send the Son into the world to condemn the world, but that the world might be saved through him' (John 3:16–17). We find in the Gospel the same dual usage of the word 'flesh'. Flesh is in opposition to the Spirit; however, it is also true that the Word became flesh.

Certainly there is no feeling in the Gospel that God regrets having created the world, and wishes to destroy it. Nor is there any sense that he who would follow the path of the Spirit should exit from the world because the world is an unholy mistake. Christ's own incarnation is for the sake of the world; it is for the purpose of establishing the right order, that of heaven, that he came, taught, suffered and died. He draws his pupils out of the world in order that they may be truly able to help the world. This helping is, however, possible only if they themselves are internally rightly ordered, and are not controlled by the driving principles of the world, namely fear and craving. Thus freedom from the world, or from the Prince of this world, is not an abandoning of the world. Furthermore, this freedom is ultimately for the benefit of the world where a proper and just external social order can be established only by those who are themselves internally well balanced and whole. Inner spiritual development therefore far from being opposed to a concern for social justice is a precondition for it. In that sense, only those who have left the world can change it.

This was the case with Jesus Christ, and those of his disciples who were taught by him and succeeded in leaving the world; and they were responsible for one of the most radical social revolutions in history. Most of the early Christians tried to follow Christ in spite of the persecution by the world. After Christianity became associated with an empire, its kingdom became one of this world, often contrary to the kingdom of Christ. It has been said that before the empire it was danger-ous to *be* a Christian; with the empire it became dangerous *not to be* a Christian. With the establishment of the Church as a temporal power, some of those who suffered at the hands of the ecclesiastical authorities, frequently officially declared as heretics, could be said to be persecuted by the world because of Christ's name. Often they seem to be the only ones connected with the springs of the living waters, as was their master Jesus Christ, who himself was regarded as the very Heresiarch by the established religious authorities of his day.

'If you were blind there would be no sin in that. But because you say, "We see," your sin remains' (John 9:41). Blindness to spiritual light is in itself a part of the natural order of things, as was discussed in Chapters 9 and 11, and not a matter of a personal failure or fault. However, to be in the presence of the light and to wilfully close one's eyes to it, claiming that darkness is light, is *sin*, for sin is that which does injury to the soul. Sin is the wilful rejection of the opportunity for the connection with the Source of light. This is what keeps a man tied to the rope of the Prince of Darkness, the ruler of this world. Christ calls and this man hears him; but he turns over in his sleep and refuses to be woken up and covers his ears, adding to the suffering of Christ.

The Eternal Witness from the Beginning

'When the Paraclete comes, the Spirit of Truth who comes from the Father, whom I shall send you from the Father, he will be my witness. You too should bear witness because you have been with me from the Beginning' (15:26–27).

The real witness in a human being is above the mind; as the *Yoga Sutras* (4: 18–21) says, the seer is the *purusha* (Spirit, Self, *Atman*) and it is not limited by the organs of perception, including the mind. In the language of the Gospel, the true witness is the Spirit (*Pneuma*), which comes from God; it is above the soul (*psyche*) or the mind which are above the body (*soma*) or the senses. In other words, a man born of woman cannot be the witness; only the son of the virgin, begotten by God, can see the real Christ, who is the truth. Even John the Baptiser, who was said by Jesus Christ to be the greatest man born of woman, did not recognise him when he encountered him. He never seems to have directly seen the true Christ, and based his testimony on the voice of the one who sent him (John 1:31–34). All the witnesses of the Christ himself in the Gospel have been from the spiritual realm: the Father, I AM, and the Spirit of Truth (John 5:37; 8:18; 15:26). Any other testimony is a testimony to his works.

In the light of the fact that Christ can be witnessed only from the level of the Spirit or above, asking the disciples here to bear witness to him is a call to them to rise from the realm of the world and the flesh to the level of the Spirit. They are already not entirely bound by the world, for he has taken them out of the world; but they do not yet see spiritually. The ideal, microcosmic, man is the one who can see the Son, but from the corresponding level within himself, the level of the Spirit. One cannot see the Son with the two ordinary eyes; the third eye needs to be opened. As Plotinus said, 'to any vision must be brought an eye adapted to what is to be seen, and having some likeness to it. Never did eye see the sun unless it had first become sun-like, and never can the soul have vision of the First Beauty unless itself be beautiful' (*Enneads* I.6.9).

In the practice of meditation and prayer, a person is most directly aware of the fact that the real witness is not the mind, and that the presence of the witness is only in the present, where the dimension of time meets that of eternity, and not in the past or in the future. In this light one would say that the attention of the disciples is not yet completely steady and free of the fluctuations created by fear and acquisition, the chief forces of the world. They must wait until the Holy Spirit descends upon them and remains dwelling in them, becoming one with that part of them which has been with their brother Christ, first born of their common Father, from the Beginning, 'before the foundation of the world' (Ephesians 1:4). In the language of the Gospel, the Beginning is not simply in the past direction of time; rather it is a timeless dimension appearing in time from one present moment to another present moment, as in John 1:1–3: 'In the Beginning was the Word, and the Word was with God. He was present to God in the Beginning. Through him all things came into being, and apart from him nothing came to be.'

CHAPTER

—— 16 ——

The Scandal of the Cross

'I have told you this lest you be scandalised. Not only will they
expel you from synagogues; a time will come when anyone who
puts you to death will think that he is serving God. And they
will do these things because they knew neither the Father nor
me. But I have told you these things so that when their time
comes you may remember my telling you of them. At the
beginning I did not tell you this because I was with you. But
now I am going to Him who sent me, and not one of you asks
me, "Where are you going?" But because I have told you these
things, grief has filled your heart' (16:1–6).

What is the scandal? The scandal of Jesus Christ is that the way
to end suffering is through suffering; the way to end death is
through death. If you wish to find the peace that surpasseth
understanding, embrace suffering; if you wish to find Eternal
Life, die to yourself. That is the message symbolised by the cross
with exquisite agony. The cross is the scandal of the Crucifer,
Jesus Christ. St Paul says: 'We preach Christ crucified: unto the
Jews a scandal, and unto the Greeks a folly. But unto them who
are called, both Jews and Greeks, Christ the power of God and
the wisdom of God' (1 Corinthians 1:23–24).

If anybody wishes to follow Christ for some worldly success, he
is in for disillusionment. In following him one follows the path of
the cross; and he who acknowledges the cross acknowledges that
'whereby the world is crucified unto me, and I unto the world'
(Galatian 6:14). Let no one underestimate the power of the forces
of the world – expressing themselves in one form or another as
the reward of approval by others, or as the fear of disapproval. A
disciple might be able to bear the condemnation by the powers of

the state or of the market-place if he could find a religious solace. But he needs to be deprived of that comfort as well as long as he is still driven by the principle of approval and disapproval. He must be totally denuded of the hold the world has on his soul so that he may find that which cannot be taken away from him by any temptation or by any fear.

The beginning spoken of here is not of the same import as in the last chapter; in this case it is temporal in nature and not eternal, and is used with a different preposition. Jesus could not impart his hard and rigorous teaching to even these disciples earlier, lest they be too shocked and leave, unable to bear it. A teacher has to make a demand on the pupils, but not so much as to break them or discourage them completely. The demand for effort and understanding must correspond to the ability and preparation of the disciples. Many disciples had already abandoned him because they found his teaching difficult to withstand.

> After hearing his words, many of his disciples remarked, 'This sort of talk is hard to bear. How can anyone accept this?' Jesus was quite aware that his disciples were murmuring in protest at this, and asked them, 'Does this scandalise you? What if you see the Son of Man ascending to the place where he came from? The Spirit alone gives Life; the flesh is useless. The words I have spoken to you are both Spirit and Life. This is why I have told you that no one can come to me unless it is granted to him by the Father.' At this many of his disciples broke away and would not accompany him any more (John 6:60–66).

Even now when they hear of the difficulties of the way for which they have been chosen, their hearts are filled with grief and self-pity at the prospect of their own impending suffering. And they do not hear the really important thing about the immediacy and significance of the situation: Jesus Christ himself is soon to be exalted to a yet higher state of being, that of the Father. If they heard it, their self-preoccupation did not leave them free to inquire where he was heading and how they could assist him in his hour. The teacher has taken care of the pupils; but in his own hour of agony and opportunity, none of the pupils know how to be wakefully present and help:

He said to them, 'Pray that you may not be put to the test.'
He withdrew from them about a stone's throw, then went
down on his knees and prayed in these words, 'Father, if
it is thy will, take this cup from me; yet not my will but
thine be done.' In his anguish he prayed with all the greater
intensity, and his sweat became like drops of blood falling
on the ground. Then he rose from his prayer and came to his
disciples, only to find them asleep, exhausted with grief. He
said to them, 'Why are you sleeping? Wake up, and pray that
you may not be subjected to the trial' (Luke 22:40–46).

The Inner Guide

But I am telling you the truth: it is to your advantage that I
go away. If I do not go, the guide (paraclete) cannot come to
you, but if I go, I will send him to you. And when he comes
he will confute the world, and show where wrong and right
and judgement lie. He will convict it of wrong by its refusal
to believe in me; he will convince it that right is on my side,
by showing that I go to the Father when I pass from your
sight; and he will convince it of divine judgement by showing that the Prince of This World stands condemned. I have
much more to tell you, but you cannot withstand it now. But
when he, the Spirit of Truth, comes, he will be your guide
to the whole truth. He will not speak on his own but will
speak only what he hears and will declare to you the things
to come. He will glorify me, because he will take from what
is mine and declare to you. All that the Father has is mine;
that is why I said that he takes from what is mine and will
declare to you (16:7–15).

There is an amazing statement here: Jesus says that it would
be better for the disciples if he went away. As long as he is there
himself the Spirit of Truth cannot enter into the disciples; and
unless the Spirit comes, they cannot really understand; certainly
not the whole truth. On the other hand, his own coming has been
necessary for the calling, sifting and the teaching of the disciples.
Now, his going away is necessary for their further progress.
The disciples have been brought so far by Jesus Christ, but
they are not yet prepared enough to endure the impact of the

whole of his teaching; and he does not want to scandalise them any further lest they abandon the path at this stage. One should not forget that the pitfalls and the snares are there at every step of the way; one needs a knowledgeable guide and a sure foot, still there can be no guarantee that one will not fail. The disciples have come to a temporary plateau in their spiritual education, and they need to consolidate and deepen before the next major ascent.

But the guide himself now stands in the way of their further progress. As long as the king is there, no prince really knows how to be the sovereign; a student cannot really occupy the place where the teacher stands until the teacher himself moves out of the way. The external guide now must make room for the inner guide. And Jesus Christ, in an act of supreme self-sacrifice for the sake of the disciples, lets the wheel of the worldly cause and effect take its course and submits to his death. Neither Christ's incarnation nor his crucifixion was without inner intention and spiritual purpose. He came for the sake of the few who seek the light, he lived for them, and he departed for their sake so that they might find more abundant Life. Of course, there were physical, biological and social causes and conditions for Jesus' birth as well as for his death. Spirit is what has the vision and gives life; the flesh serves the higher purpose if it acts in obedience to the Spirit, otherwise it is useless. Jesus was an obedient servant of Christ, even unto death.

When the inner guide, the Spirit of Truth, is realised in the disciples, all things which now they do not and cannot understand will be clarified for them. He will tell them about the true mark and aim of existence and straying away from it, about justice and right order, about judgement and discernment between the forces of the world and those of the Spirit. Sitting inside them, he will not speak in his own name, or in theirs, as this particular person or that. He will receive his truth and energy from Christ who himself receives these from the Father. This is how the Father and Christ will come to dwell in the disciples. The more the disciples will speak and act from the truth of the Spirit residing in their own inner core, the less will their words and works be from their own egos and the more they will be in the name of the Son and the Father who will be glorified in them.

Death and New Birth

'A little while and you will look on me no longer; and again a little while, and you will see me.' So some of his disciples said to each other, 'What is this that he is telling us? "A little while and you will not look on me, and again a little while and you will see me." And "Because I am going to my Father."' So they kept wondering, 'What is this "little while"? We do not understand' (16:16–18).

Knowing that they wanted to question him, Jesus spoke to them, 'You are asking yourselves about my saying, "In a little while you will not look on me, and again a little while you will see me." In very truth I tell you that you will weep and mourn, but the world will rejoice. You will have pain, but your pain will be turned into joy. A woman has pain when she is giving birth, when her hour has come; but when her child is born, her joy makes her forget her suffering, because a human being has been born into the world. So now you also feel pain; but I will see you again, and your heart will rejoice, and no one can take that joy away from you. And on that day you will have no more questions to ask me' (16:19–23).

The hour of Jesus is nigh, and he is preparing the disciples to understand the real significance of his imminent death. According to the evidence of all the Gospels, Jesus Christ regarded his own death as a necessary rite of passage from one level of being to another. A difficult one, to be sure, but necessary for a new birth in a different body. Two different words are used in the Greek original to convey *looking* on the physical body which the disciples will not be able to do after a short while, and *seeing* the spiritual body soon after. This is already an indication of spiritual progress made by the disciples, even though they have difficulty understanding what Christ is saying precisely: they have acquired eyes adapted to spiritual vision, for the ordinary eyes of the world cannot see the spiritual body. 'A little while now and the world will see me no more; but you see me as one who has life, and you will have life. On that day you will know that I am in my Father and you are in me and I in you' (John 14:19–20).

The crucifixion is here likened to the labour pains of a mother in childbirth, with the emphasis not on the pain and suffering involved but on the new birth. The disciples will be filled with sadness and mourning at the death of Jesus, even though the world, which by its very nature always opposes Christ's teaching as darkness opposes light, will be happy. But soon after, the disciples will see him; more importantly, they will be *seen* by him, and they will rejoice. They will know him and be known by him, from the inside, without them having to say anything or ask any question, because they will be one with him, sons of their common Father. Jesus said: 'The Kingdom is inside you, and it is outside you. When you come to know yourselves, then you will become known, and you will realise that it is you who are the sons of the living Father. But if you will not know yourselves, you live in poverty, and you are poverty' (Gospel of Thomas II, 2:3).

Participating in the Mind of Christ

'In very truth I tell you, if you ask the Father for anything in my name, He will give it to you. Until now you have asked nothing in my name. Ask and you will receive, so that your joy may be fulfilled. I have said this to you in veiled language, but the hour is coming when I shall no longer speak to you in veiled language, but shall tell you about the Father in boldness. On that day you will ask the Father in my name, and I do not say that I shall have to ask the Father for you, for the Father loves you Himself because you have loved me and have believed that I came from God. I came from the Father and have come into the world; now I am leaving the world to go back to the Father' (16:23–28).

'There,' his disciples exclaimed, 'now you are speaking plainly, without talking in veiled language! Now we know that you know everything and have no need for anyone to ask you. By this we believe that you came from God.' Jesus answered them, 'At the moment you believe; but behold, an hour is coming – indeed has already come – for you to be scattered, each to his own, leaving me all alone. Yet I am not alone because the Father is with me. I have said this to you so that in me you may find peace. In the world you find suffering, but have courage: I have overcome the world' (16:29–33).

For the disciples to ask the Father something in the *name* of Christ, they have to participate in his being and power; for this they need to obey his commandments. So far they have not been able to ask anything in his name; but this is what they must learn to do in order to receive from above what they need so that they may be fulfilled. Some aspects of the teaching have been held back from them because they were not prepared to understand them; they have been taught partly through a veiled language. As discussed in Chapter 5, Jesus Christ went out of his way to speak in the presence of crowds in a parabolic language so that they might not hear the real truths, lest they misuse them for egotistic purposes, and harm themselves or others. The disciples have been gradually taught deeper and higher truths; now they are ready to hear and understand the bald truth which could not be communicated to them directly and boldly earlier. It is not only a matter of using a certain kind of language, but also of the quality and intensity of the energy being conveyed, because the teaching is not only words uttered, but a substantial flame passed from one to the other.

A teaching is a baptism; until someone has acquired the requisite armour for protection, and the appropriate inner organ of discernment, to expose them to the baptism of Christ, that of fire, would be folly. Such a precaution has to be taken not only for the sake of guarding the truth but also for protecting the disciples, as a tender plant has to be protected against fierce winds until it grows strong and is able to withstand the elements. But the time is coming when the caretaker will go away, and the young trees will not be tended any more; however, they are getting stronger and can bear the blast of the Spirit.

Suddenly, like an awakening in *satori*, they do *hear* him, and understand him for the first time clearly and directly. His words and teachings have not changed; the disciples have been transformed – now they have a different mind, and behold, they understand, not only what he says, but his mind. In this higher mind to higher mind, *buddhi* to *buddhi*, insight, no words or questions need to interpose; they understand Christ and he understands them because they both participate in one divine mind. It is then no longer necessary for Christ to speak to the Father on their behalf, they can speak to Him and be heard by Him directly, as they have placed themselves in the circle of His gaze and love. They could not have come to the Father directly by themselves, for He is too high: Christ is the way to the Father, and no one comes to the Father except through him. From this shore of the world to that shore of the Father, Christ is the bridge; those who become of one mind and substance with Christ themselves become a part of the bridge linking both shores.

Just as the disciples become of one mind and spirit with Christ, the time comes for them to part company from him on the earthly plane; as he goes to his home, they must go to theirs, to do there what each one must. In him alone is their peace, but they must go and test their understanding and strength in the arena of the world. It was for the sake of the world that they were being prepared, not for an exit from it. But if they do not remain free from fear and ambition, the forces of the world, as much active inside a human being as outside, they will be lost. Then also they would suffer, as does every human being born of a woman, but their suffering would be in vain. But if they remain in Christ while acting in the world, they can help bring about a right order, and their own suffering will be transformed into the peace of Christ.

But this peace is not attained passively; it requires struggling against and conquering the world, which here connotes the active principle of the Prince of this world, the Evil One, and the Prince of Darkness. He is the one, with all his powers of fear and temptation, against whom Jesus had to struggle. He is also the one over whom the Buddha triumphed; and the one who is called the 'enemy' in the *Bhagavad Gita*, who has to be defeated by anyone who would come to Krishna. But have courage: Christ has set an example in conquering the world, and he would help all those who would seriously try: 'Behold, I stand at the door, and knock: if any man hear my call, and open the door, I will come in to him, and will sup with him, and he with me. To him that conquers will I grant to sit with me in my throne, even as I also conquered, and am set down with my Father in His throne' (Revelation 3:20–21).

CHAPTER

— 17 —

The Work of the Father

After these things Jesus looked up to heaven and said: 'Father, the hour has come. Glorify your Son, so that your Son may glorify you; as you gave him authority over all flesh that he might grant Eternal Life to all that you have given him. (Eternal Life is this: to know you, the one true God, and Jesus Christ, the one whom you sent.) I have given you glory on earth by completing the work you gave me to do; and now, Father, glorify me in your presence, with the glory I have with you before the world began. I have made your name known to those you gave me out of the world. They were yours and you gave them to me, and they have kept your Word. Now they have recognised that all that you gave me was from you, for I gave them the words that you gave me, and they accepted them and they know in truth that I came from you, and they believed that you sent me' (17: 1–8).

'It is on their behalf that I ask. I do not pray for the world but for those whom you have given me, since they are really yours (just as all that is mine is yours and all that is yours is mine), and it is in them that I have been glorified. I am in the world no more, but they are in the world as I come to you. O Father most holy, keep them in your name which you have given to me, so that they may be one, as we are. As long as I was with them I guarded them with your name which you have given to me. I kept watch and not one of them perished, except the one destined to be lost – in fulfilment of Scripture. But now I am coming to you; but while I am still in the world, I say all this so that they may have my joy within them to the full' (17:9–13).

This chapter contains what is called the 'high priestly prayer' or the 'prayer of consecration', offered by Jesus Christ at the end of his earthly life, on the eve of his death. It is partly a report by him given to the Father who sent him, and partly a petition on behalf of his immediate disciples and all those who may come to understand the true nature of the Word made flesh. But, however scandalous it may sound, Christ explicitly excludes the *world* from his prayer. His concern is only for those who are already called by God and who seek spiritual light. Such are from the world but not of it; they are strangers in the world of ambition and self-aggrandisement and the related fear, and they seek their true home in a different realm. Even though the pull of the world keeps them weighted down, they wish to soar with Christ who is no longer held down by the world.

To come to *know* the Son and the Father is said to be the essential meaning of *Eternal Life*. This knowledge, of course, is not only mental knowledge, assenting to some statements; nor is it an emotional belief alone. Throughout the Gospel, from the beginning to the end, and from the level of the crowd to that of the most advanced disciples, there are reminders about the immense difficulty of recognising and understanding the real being of Jesus Christ, and therefore of knowing him and believing in him. The knowledge of the Son, and the belief in his name, in the Gospel means a participation in the being of Christ; this is conveyed completely concretely, sensitive vegetarians might even say crudely, by an invitation to eat his flesh and to drink his blood, so that a disciple will become of one substance with him.

'In truth, in very truth I tell you, unless you eat the flesh of the Son of Man and drink his blood you can have no Life in you. Whoever eats my flesh and drinks my blood possesses Eternal Life, and I will raise him up on the last day. My flesh is real food; my blood is real drink. Whoever eats my flesh and drinks my blood dwells continually in me and I dwell in him. As the living Father sent me, and I live because of the Father, so he who eats me shall live because of me' (John 6: 53–57).

Until the Word takes flesh in the body of a disciple and dwells inside him permanently, he cannot be said to *know* the Son in truth, or to *believe* in his name. Unless an aspirant is begotten by the Spirit and is born again, he does not have the right body to embody the Word, nor the right mind to understand him, nor yet the right heart to love him in the face of tribulations. True knowing and seeing of anything is from the inside of that thing, by becoming one with it. As the Gospel of Philip (II, 3: 61) says,

> It is not possible for anyone to see anything of the things that actually exist unless he becomes like them. This is not the way with man in the world: he sees the sun without being a sun; and he sees the heaven and the earth and all other things, but he is not these things. This is quite in keeping with the truth. But you saw something of that place and you became those things. You saw the Spirit, and you became spirit. You saw Christ, you became Christ. You saw the Father, you shall become Father. So in this place you see everything and do not see yourself, but in that place you do see yourself – and what you see you shall become.

As Jesus Christ said earlier, doing the work that his Father gave him to do is his real food; his joy consists in completing this work. It is for this that he came, that is his total *raison d'être*. In finishing this work, he gives glory to God; in this also lies his own glory. This is not a glorification of his personal, historical existence, of some particular individual born at a specific place or time; on the contrary, it is from the limitations of this particularity that he is now to be freed, so that he can return to his Father's side, and have the glory that is his from the Begining, timelessly. That which has this glory is from the Beginning and cannot die, for it is eternal. But God loves the world, that is to say, eternity is in love with time, and for its sake, incarnates Himself from time to time, in an appropriate specific form, with all its restrictions. When the form is broken, He is freed of the limitations and returns to Himself as he is from the Beginning, in His own glory.

In what lies the completion of the work given by the Father? To make His name known to those whom He gave him out of the world. As has already been remarked, *name* (in Greek, *onome*) in the Gospel is not merely an abstract designation of a person, but represents his very being and power. It was with the name of God that Christ protected the disciples and kept them safe. The real name of God was given to Christ by his Father, for He loved him. Without knowing the sacred name, that is without becoming one with it, the disciples cannot dwell in Christ. Nor can Christ himself dwell in God without knowing His real name; as the Gospel of Philip (II, 3: 54) says,

> One single name is not uttered in the world, the name which the Father gave to the Son, the name above all things: the name of the Father. For the Son would not become the Father except he clothe himself with the name of the Father. Those who have this name know it indeed but do not speak of it. But those who do not have it do not know it.

I AM (*ego eimi*) is declared by God to be His most mysterious and sacred name (see Chapters 6 and 8). This is the name, and the power inherent in it, which Christ came to reveal. This revelation of the name of God can be made only to those who have been chosen by God and lifted out of the world by Him through the work of His Son. This rising from the world is the lifting of the Son of Man from the son of man born of flesh. 'When you lift up the Son of Man, you will come to realise I AM' (John 8: 28). Those who are able to approach the awesome name of God, which devours all that is not of the Spirit, qualify to receive it by keeping and attending to the Word of God which is Christ himself. They have eaten the body of Christ and drunk his blood; they almost embody the Word, and are nearly ready to know the name of God in truth.

Consecration in Truth

> 'I have given to them your Word, and the world has hated them because they are not of the world, as I am not of the world. I am not asking you to take them out of the world but to keep them safe from the evil one. They are not of the world, as I am not of the world. Consecrate them in the truth. Your Word is truth. As you sent me into the world, so I sent them into the world. It is for their sakes that I consecrate myself now, in order that they too may be consecrated in truth' (17: 14–19).
> 'It is not for these alone that I ask, but also for those who believe in me through their word, that they all may be one, just as you, Father, are in me and I in you, so that they also

may be in us in order that the world may believe that you sent me' (17: 20–21).

'And I have given them the glory that you gave me, that they may be one as we are one, I in them and you in me, so that they may be perfected into one. Thus the world may come to know that you sent me and that you loved them as you loved me. Father, I wish that wherever I am, those whom you gave me may be with me also, that they see my glory which you have given me because you loved me before the world began. O Father most just, while the world did not know you, though I knew you, these men came to know that you sent me. And to them I made known your name and will continue to make it known so that the love you had for me may be in them and I may be in them' (17: 22–26).

To embody the Word is automatically to invite the hostility of the world, for the *Word* and the *world*, Spirit and flesh, are opposed to each other as principles and tendencies. They are like two poles of a magnet: the more a person belongs to one, the farther he is from the other. However, the world is also the arena of action and the source of the flesh needed for the Spirit to be embodied so that she (as well as *he* and *it*) may act. Freedom from the darkness of the world, in order to come to the light of the Spirit, does not mean an exit from the world (see Chapter 5). It does seem to be true in the Gospel, however, that Jesus Christ is not really convinced that the world itself can be spiritualised, or that the general mass of mankind can come to truth or accept light. It is for the sake of a very select band of pupils that he has been sent by God, and it is only for their sake he lives and is now ready to die. He is an apostle of God for this specific purpose: that his chosen disciples may be consecrated, that is to say made holy – which is the same as made whole – in truth.

In his turn, he also sends his apostles only for the sake of those few who have the potentiality and the yearning for Eternal Life, and are willing to pay the price with their own life. There is an élitism to be sure, but it is not an élitism based on pedigree, economic or class hierarchy, or any worldly affiliations – social, racial or denominational. The élitism of Christ is wholly and exclusively to do with the nearness to him, which is both a nearness to the Kingdom not of this world, as well as the fire which burns all that is of the ego. Those who are willing and able to let themselves be burnt by the fire of the Spirit may draw near to him, from among all the nations of the world, and be elected. Christ said: 'He who is near me is near the fire, and he who is far from me is far from the Kingdom' (Gospel of Thomas II, 2: 82).

As for the others in the world, who neither are called by God nor seek His Kingdom, Jesus Christ does not even pray for them. Lest this be misunderstood as a lack of compassion on his part, one needs to be reminded that the baptism of Christ is that of fire, and that his way is that of the cross (see Chapters 12 and 15). Only those willing to pay the price of admission to the chamber of Eternal Life, a price exacted by the cross which guards the narrow gate opening into the Vastness, can respond to his call. For others, it is mere fantasy. Even among those who embark on the path, very few are able to make a sacrifice of their wordly selves, and thus pay the price. As he said:

> I will choose you one from a thousand and two from ten thousand, and they will stand because they are a single one. The harvest is great but the labourers are few. Beseech the Lord then to send out labourers to the harvest. Many are standing at the door, but it is the single one who will enter the bridal chamber' (Gospel of Thomas II, 2: 23, 73, 75).

It is an act of mercy on the part of Jesus Christ that he does not try to agitate the minds of those who are not his own with rosy promises of heavenly places. Those who are not called by God, nor have the strength to undertake the journey, are spared the test.

His own consecration is for the sake of sacrifice; as is the consecration of his apostles. His incarnation was a sacrifice, as was his crucifixion. From beginning to end, he was the Lamb of God: for the specific disciples at that time and at that place, so that with his own blood he could consecrate them and make them whole and able to sacrifice their lives for the sake of God. For others elsewhere, at other times, again and again he incarnates himself in them to make them lambs of God. This continual consecration is necessary for the maintenance of right order in the cosmos, each lamb of God adding his own sacrifice to that of 'the Lamb slain from the foundation of the world' (Revelation 13: 8).

CHAPTER

— 18 —

The Overwhelming Force of I AM

After these words, Jesus went out with his disciples across the Kidron valley. There was a garden there which they entered together. The place was familiar to Judas as well, the one who was to deliver him, because Jesus had often met there with his disciples. Judas took a detachment of soldiers, together with the police provided by the chief priests and the Pharisees, and went there equipped with torches and lanterns and weapons (18:1–3).

Knowing fully what was to happen to him, Jesus came out to them and asked, 'Whom are you looking for?' 'Jesus the Nazorean,' they replied. He said: 'I AM.' (Now Judas, the one who was to deliver him, was there with them.) When Jesus said 'I AM,' they stepped back and fell to the ground. So he asked them again, 'Whom are you looking for?' 'Jesus the Nazorean,' they repeated. 'I told you that I am he,' Jesus answered. 'If I am the one you want, let these men go.' (This was to fulfil what he had said, 'I have not lost even one of those whom you have given me.') (18:4–9)

Then Simon Peter who had a sword, drew it and struck the slave of the high priest, severing his right ear. (The slave's name was Malchus.) But Jesus told Peter, 'Put your sword back in its sheath. Am I not to drink the cup the Father has given me?' Then the soldiers with their tribune and the Jewish police arrested Jesus and bound him (18:10–12).

A possible meaning of *Kidron* is 'dark'; this is suggestive symbolically for now Jesus himself has to go through the valley of darkness before he can come to the light in the presence of the Father.

In the majesty and all-encompassing being of God, Satan also has his place: as a faithful servant and son of God he guards the gate to heaven, and examines souls on their worthiness for entry. He who would come to God must contend with Satan. Judas had been sent for his trial with Satan, arranged and blessed by Jesus Christ himself, as his final test before he could be begotten by the Father and come to Eternal Life (see Chapters 6 and 13). According to the popular and official Christian tradition, the chief disciple of Christ failed, and Satan overpowered him into betraying his master and friend, the Son of God. Although no consistent or comprehensible motivation is suggested for the heinous crime attributed to Judas, one might imagine that Satan used his ultimate weapons, the very substance and being of himself: forgetfulness and pride. Satan himself in his pride had forgotten his right place in the presence of God, and wanted to be 'like the Most High'. It was for this that he, the first among the angels, was cast out of heaven, and became the embodiment of all the forces adverse to God. It is possible that in a parallel struggle Judas in his self-importance forgot his proper place: regarding himself as equal to Christ he wanted to usurp Christ's special position as the great teacher, and therefore became a willing accomplice in the plot to kill Jesus.

However, as has been suggested earlier also, we must look for a deeper understanding since Judas himself had been chosen, prepared and commanded by Jesus Christ to undertake what he did. Besides, it is hard to imagine that Christ would knowingly let his chief disciple be led astray unto the perdition of his soul, especially when we are again told (John 18:9) that Christ did not lose even one of those given to him by God. Much of the emotional justification for the suggestion that Judas betrayed Jesus Christ into the hands of the authorities rests on the assumption that the Crucifixion was unnecessary, unintentional and evil. This, however, does not seem to be the case. There is an impression left by all the Gospels that Christ was always in charge of the situation and that he intentionally let the drama unfold as it must according to a higher necessity than that of the crowds or of the momentum of the events. He is a victim, as far as the customary judgement goes; but one can hardly have any doubt that he is the director and initiator of the entire play in which he must be the sacrificial Lamb, as ordained from the Beginning, 'the Lamb slain from the foundation of the world' (Revelation 13:8). He must drink the cup of suffering and sacrifice himself for the sake of the world, in accordance with the will of his Father. There is never any doubt in the accounts given in the Gospels that Jesus Christ is fully aware of what is in store for him, and that he understands the necessity of the sacrifice, and in spite of the natural wish of the flesh to be spared the ordeal he submits himself to the will of God.

Furthermore, he seems to have understood his crucifixion as a rite of passage to a higher state of being, an initiation and a payment which alone will bring him to oneness with the Father. As told in Mark 10:35–38, when two of his disciples had asked to be granted to sit on either side of him in his glory, Jesus said 'You do not know what you are asking. Can you drink the cup I shall drink? or be baptised in the same bath of pain as I?' Pain there is, without doubt, as the physical body will be killed, but there is also the joy of the new birth and the nearness of God. 'If you truly loved me you would rejoice that I am going to the Father, for the Father is greater than I' (John 14:28).

In addition to the demand from God for the sacrifice of the Lamb for the sake of the world, and the necessity of his physical death to make possible his birth into a higher state of being, his going away also seems to be required for the sake of his disciples. As he told them, 'It is to your advantage that I go away. If I do not go, the guide (paraclete) cannot come to you, but if I go, I will send him to you . . . I have much more to tell you, but you cannot withstand it now. But when he, the Spirit of Truth, comes, he will be your guide to the whole truth' (John 16:7–13). In the face of the overwhelming inner and cosmic necessity of the sacrifice – for himself, for his disciples and for the world – and the clear prevision and intention of Jesus Christ, the drama of the crucifixion could hardly be made to turn on the betrayal of Jesus by Judas in any ordinary sense. Jesus had to be delivered to the world in order for him to overcome the world and usher in a new stage of development for all those connected with him. Judas played the essential role of handing him over, in complete accord with the intention, wish and demand of Jesus Christ. His act was selfless and in total obedience to his master, even though he might have himself anticipated the blame and calumny which would be heaped upon him by those who judge by appearances and by the flesh alone.

Even though the Greek term translated here as *Nazorean* is a little different from another one usually rendered as *Nazarene*, these two terms have been understood in the Christian tradition from very early on to mean the same thing. In relation to this, there is a suggestive though enigmatic remark in the Gospel of Philip (II, 3:62):

> The apostles who were before us had these names for him: 'Jesus, the Nazorean, Messiah', that is, 'Jesus, the Nazorean, the Christ'. The last name is 'Christ', the first is 'Jesus', that in the middle is 'the Nazarene'. 'Messiah' has two meanings, both 'the Christ' and 'the measured'. 'Jesus' in Hebrew is 'the redemption'. 'Nazara' is 'the truth'. 'The Nazarene', then, is 'the truth'. 'Christ' has been measured. 'The Nazarene' and 'Jesus' are they who have been measured.

Representatives of the political and the ecclesiastical powers, both arrayed on the side of the world, have come to apprehend Jesus Christ. We are told that when Christ said 'I AM', those who had come to arrest him, estimated to be between two hundred and six hundred men in all and some with weapons, stepped back and fell to the ground. What a manifestation of the tremendous force inherent in the divine name I AM! (See Chapters 4 and 6.) I AM is not a designation or an identification of a particular person, Jesus of Nazareth, as is implied by the usual translations of *ego eimi* in this context, in which a non-existent predicate is supplied by the translators, wresting the original to yield an ordinary commonsense meaning. But we are in the presence of something wholly extraordinary, and incomprehensible by any usual standards: a display of the state of identity of the Son with the Father, made possible by his participation in the mysterious and sacred name of God Himself. Even those who are unsympathetic and hostile to the teaching of Christ are struck by the force of the name *ego eimi* and cannot stand their ground. It is said that when Moses had used the secret name of God in front of the Pharaoh, even the mighty Pharaoh retreated and fell down speechless.

The Trial of Peter

They led him first to Annas, the father-in-law of Caiaphas who was the high priest that year. It was Caiaphas who had proposed to the Jews the advantage of having one man die for the people (18:13–14).

Simon Peter, in company with another disciple, kept following Jesus closely. The disciple, who was known to the high priest, stayed with Jesus as far as the high priest's courtyard, while Peter was left standing at the gate. The disciple known to the high priest came out and spoke to the girl at the gate and brought Peter in. This servant girl who kept the gate said to Peter, 'Are you too one of this man's disciples?' 'I am not,' he said. Since the night was cold, the servants and the guards who were standing around had made a charcoal fire to warm themselves by. Peter joined them and stood there warming himself (18:15–18).

The high priest questioned Jesus about his disciples and about his teaching. Jesus answered: 'I have spoken openly to the world. I have taught always in the synagogue or in the temple where all the Jews come together. There was nothing secret about what I said. Why do you question me? Question those who heard me when I spoke. Obviously, they should know what I said.' At this reply, one of the guards in attendance slapped Jesus in the face, exclaiming, 'Is that any way to answer the high priest?' Jesus said, 'If I have said anything wrong produce the evidence, but if I spoke the truth why hit me?' Annas next sent him, bound, to the high priest Caiaphas (18:19–24).

All through this Simon Peter had been standing there warming himself. They said to him, 'Are you not a disciple of his?' He denied it and said, 'I am not.' One of the high priest's slaves, who was related to the one whose ear Peter had cut off, said, 'Did I not see you with him in the garden?' Peter denied it again, and just then a cock began to crow (18:25–27).

The fact that Jesus taught openly for all to hear, at least until he turned away from the crowds completely and spoke only to a select band of his disciples, does not mean that there were not varying levels of understanding among his audience. Even if they all heard the same words, they understood them differently. Also, on many occasions, Jesus went out of his way to speak in parables, although still in public places and openly, so that the unprepared might not understand him and misuse subtle truths for egoistic purposes (see Chapters 5 and 12). Furthermore, even to his closest disciples he had said that there were many things which he did not tell them earlier, and many more which he could not tell them even on the eve of his death because they could not bear them; the presence of the Spirit of Truth dwelling inside them is necessary for them to understand the true significance of the Christ and his teaching (John 16:4, 12–13). There may be nothing secret in what he said, in the sense of anything behind closed doors, but his teaching deals with the most mysterious and subtle truths, requiring for their comprehension the most strenuous attention of mind, heart and body, and above all an election by God himself. Therefore, he and his teaching are naturally veiled from those who are only of the flesh: the more anyone is at home in the world, the less he understands the Word incarnate or his words.

Sooner or later, all the disciples have to pass through their trial; now it was the turn of Peter. His denials cannot be fully understood at the obvious surface level, any more than the betrayal by Judas can be. There is no suggestion in the Gospel account that the authorities were trying to arrest Jesus' disciples as well; in fact, we are told that one of the disciples was known as such and could move about freely. Peter had shown his impatience and lack of unity (see Chapter 13) and had claimed more for his loyalty than he possessed. At the time of the arrest of Jesus, Peter displayed not only an impetuous nature in cutting off the ear of Malchus, but also by that very act he showed a lack of confidence in his master, assuming that his own common sword of ordinary metal was superior to Christ's 'sword of the Spirit, the word of God' (Ephesians 6:17). Peter forgot that he who was protected by the power of the most sacred name of God could not be harmed by any worldly force, save to the extent that it was necessary for the purposes of teaching and for the sake of the sacrifice for those whom he loved. He did not really understand Christ or believe in him. That lack of trust and that forgetting were Peter's real inner denials; what he said to the servant girl or to the guards was relatively superficial.

However, in the presence of the majestic display of power of I AM (*ego eimi*) by Christ, it is entirely appropriate that Peter should say 'I am not' (*ouk eimi*). That is the right human counterpoint to the divine point made by Christ. One might allow oneself to imagine that Peter, like St Ignatius (see Chapter 15)

would not regard himself a proper disciple until the moment
of his martyrdom for the sake of Christ. It is true after all (see
Chapter 1) that out of all the disciples called by Christ, only Peter
seems to have been struck right from the start by the terrifying
distance between the greatness of Christ and his own smallness;
he had said, 'Depart from me, O Lord, for I am a sinful man'
(Luke 5:8). It was owing to the solidity of his knowledge of his
nothingness that he was given a new name by Jesus: he was now
to be called Peter, the Rock-man. Is he here again aware of the
immense gulf between what he is and what he needs to be in
order to be a disciple of Christ in truth and spirit? Is his denial
really an acknowledgement of this distance?

Nevertheless, it is true that Peter was warming himself with
the guards at the same time as one of them was slapping Jesus
Christ. Certainly, Satan defeated Peter through his forgetfulness;
but it is not clear whether the other main weapon of Satan was
Peter's excessive pride, or the obverse of the same coin, excessive
humility.

The King of the Inner Kingdom

At daybreak they brought Jesus from Caiaphas to the
praetorium. They did not enter the praetorium themselves, for they had to avoid ritual impurity if they were
to eat the Passover supper. Pilate came out to them. 'What
accusation do you bring against this man?' he demanded.
They retorted: 'If he were not a criminal, we would certainly
not have handed him over to you.' At this Pilate told them,
'Take him yourselves then and pass judgement according
to your own law.' But the Jews answered, 'We are not
permitted to put anyone to death.' (This was to fulfil what
Jesus had said, indicating the sort of death he was to die.)
(18:28–32)

Then Pilate went into the praetorium and summoned
Jesus. 'Are you the King of the Jews?' he asked him. Jesus
answered, 'Do you ask this on your own, or have others been
telling you about me?' 'Am I a Jew?' Pilate exclaimed. 'It is
your own people and the chief priests who have handed
you over to me. What have you done?' Jesus answered, 'My
kingdom is not of this world. If my kingdom were of this

world, my subjects would be fighting to save me from being handed over to the Jews. But as it is, my kingdom is not of here.' At this Pilate said to him, 'So, then, you are a king?' Jesus replied, 'It is you who say I am a king. The reason I was born, the reason why I came into the world, is to testify to the truth. Everyone who is of truth listens to my voice.' 'Truth!' said Pilate. 'What does that mean?' (18:33–38)

After this remark, Pilate went out again to the Jews and said to them, 'For my part, I find no case against this man. Remember that you have a custom that I release someone for you at Passover. Do you want me, then, to release for you the King of the Jews?' They shouted back, 'We want Barabbas, not this man!' Barabbas was an insurrectionist (18:39–40).

The real charges which the religious leaders have against Jesus Christ are blasphemy and disregard of convention and authority: he, a mere man, declared himself to be one with God, and seemed cavalier towards the Sabbath laws and the social and ecclesiastical hierarchy. He was an insurrectionist of the Spirit and Truth, not satisfied with external authority in these matters and continually appealing to the inner experience of the Son of Man, I AM, and the Son of God. Not an egotist at all, he would submit only to the inner authority of truth – the voice of the Father dwelling inside him, telling him what to say and what to do. It was this inner kingdom of which he was the king; a kingdom in the world but not of it. Having conquered this kingdom in battle with Satan, he could hardly be deflected from the truth by the Sanhedrin! No threat, nor any temptation could make him deviate from what he knew in his soul to be true, right and necessary.

Jesus was no political insurrectionist. Having rejected sovereignty over the whole world, he had chosen what was true and abiding: mastery over himself. This was not the first nor the last time in history that there had been a collusion between the political and religious powers for getting rid of troublesome elements which prick the conscience of those who would rather rule than serve, and who would rather sleep than wake up. In this instance, however, the struggle is largely between the forces of tradition and churchly authority, co-opted by darkness inherent in all flesh, and the forces serving inner freedom and Light. Pilate himself is shown as an unwilling but necessary pawn in this; on purely political grounds, which was all that interested him in this matter, he found no case against Jesus, and seemed anxious to release him. (It may be remarked incidentally that from quite early on in the Christian tradition, and not entirely without an eye on political considerations, Pilate himself was largely exonerated of any responsibility for killing Jesus. Pilate and his wife Procla even qualified as saints in the Coptic and Ethiopic hagiography, having their feast celebrated on 25 June!)

The whole *raison d'être* for the incarnation and teaching of Jesus Christ, and now of his death, was to testify to the Truth. He had said that the Word of God was Truth, which is what he embodied himself, and with which he consecrated himself and his disciples so that they could understand more and more the true name of God, and dwell in its power and being. However, there was only a small group of people who seemed to understand him and to follow in their lives the implications of his teaching. Hardly anyone even in this small group stood by him until the end. Nevertheless, it was for their sake that he died, a death which he said was necessary for the Spirit of Truth to come and reside in them. Abandoned by the world and by his own friends and followers, he stood by the will of his Father until death.

Given the choice between Jesus and Barabbas, which literally means 'the son of the father', the crowd prefer Barabbas. Each person, whenever he comes to himself, is on the cross, and at a crossing; for a few moments he can decide whether to follow the son of the father or the Son of the Father.

Which do you choose?

CHAPTER

— 19 —

The Crown of Thorns and the Inner Kingdom

Then Pilate took Jesus and had him scourged. The soldiers wove a crown of thorns and fixed it on his head, throwing around his shoulders a cloak of royal purple. Repeatedly they came up to him and said, 'All hail, King of the Jews!', slapping his face as they did so. Once again Pilate went out and said to them, 'Look here, I am bringing him out to you to make you understand that I find no case against him.' When Jesus came out wearing the crown of thorns and the purple cloak, Pilate said to them, 'Behold the man.' As soon as the chief priests and the temple guards saw him, they shouted, 'Crucify! Crucify!' Pilate told them, 'Take him yourselves and crucify him; I find no case against him.' 'We have our law,' the Jews responded, 'and according to that law he must die because he made himself God's Son.' When Pilate heard this kind of talk, he was more afraid than ever (19:1–8).

Going back into the praetorium, Pilate said to Jesus, 'Where do you come from?' But Jesus would give him no answer. 'Do you refuse to speak to me?' Pilate demanded. 'Do you not know that I have the power to release you and the power to crucify you?' Jesus answered, 'You would have no power over me whatever unless it were given you from above. That is why he who handed me over to you is guilty of a greater sin' (19:9–11).

After this, Pilate was eager to release him, but the Jews shouted, 'If you free this man, you are no friend of Caesar's. Anyone who makes himself a king is challenging Caesar.' Pilate heard what they were saying, then brought Jesus outside and took a seat on a judge's bench in the place called the Stone Pavement – 'Gabbatha' in Hebrew. (It was the Preparation Day for Passover, and the hour was about noon.) He said to the Jews, 'Look at your King!' At this they shouted,

'Away with him! Away with him! Crucify him!' 'What!' Pilate
exclaimed. 'Shall I crucify your King?' The chief priest replied,
'We have no king but Caesar.' In the end, Pilate handed him
over to be crucified; so they took Jesus. And carrying the cross
by himself, he went out to what is called the Place of the Skull
(in Hebrew, 'Golgotha'). There they crucified him, and two
others with him: one on either side, Jesus in the middle. Pilate
had an inscription placed on the cross which read: 'Jesus the
Nazorean, the King of the Jews.' This inscription, in Hebrew,
Latin and Greek, was read by many of the Jews, since the place
where Jesus was crucified was near the city. The chief priest of
the Jews tried to tell Pilate, 'You should not have written "The
King of the Jews". Write instead, "This man claimed to be the
King of the Jews."' Pilate answered, 'What I have written, I
have written' (19:12–22).

Jesus Christ is subjected to total ignominy and mockery by the
soldiers. In the process, however, they provide a strong visual
symbol of the way of Christ: the crown of thorns. He who would
be king of the inner world, a king of himself, must wear a crown
of thorns in the world, the world that laughs at and mocks the
concerns of the Spirit. Jesus Christ never claimed or wished to be
the king in this world. The kingdom that he was concerned with
is an inner one, too subtle and disturbing for a mind which has
not been nourished at all by the life-giving waters from heaven.
Such a mind and heart cannot make any place for the teaching
of Christ and has to eliminate the one who disturbs the sleep of
man.

The powers of the state, personified by Pilate, can be neutral
in this case, because no political insurrection is at issue. But
even these powers are essentially helpless in the presence of the
fanatical forces of the theologians and the leaders of organised
religion who have been deeply offended by him who would
appeal to inner experience rather than to external authority, to
living God rather than to scripture and tradition. Since by his
very presence Jesus Christ poses a threat to the authority and
importance of the priests and the scribes, they are naturally
against him, and keep attributing to him egoistic claims of
a special relationship with God (John 5:18, 8:53, 10:33). They
would be right in condemning anyone who proclaimed himself
to be a son of God. That would in fact be blasphemy. Even if
such a person were not put to physical death, as the ancient law

demanded (Leviticus 24:16), he would in any case die a spiritual death, because proclaiming oneself represents the very epitome of spiritual darkness. No one can make himself a son of God; if he has denied himself, he may be begotten by God and made His son (see Chapters 10 and 18). He can empty himself of the world in him, with its attendant fears and ambitions, and if he is acceptable to God he will be filled by Him with Himself.

The real sin of the accusers of Jesus Christ lies not in their understanding of blasphemy, nor in their hard-heartedness in demanding the full punishment for it, but in their blindness because of which they cannot discriminate between blasphemy and consecration. Furthermore, there is a continual suggestion in the Gospel of a wilful clinging to this blindness on the part of the religious authorities. It is owing to this that their sin is greater than that of Pilate, who merely carried out what, out of weakness and fear, he could not resist. He who did nothing for his own glory, and claimed no authorship or credit for his words or works, could hardly be accused of indulging in self-will and making himself equal to God. The very vehemence of their hostility to Christ is an indication that the contemporary ecclesiastical powers were co-opted by the larger forces of darkness which inevitably must struggle against any attempt to bring light.

If the priests and the scribes, often pious and learned in the Scriptures, could not understand where Christ comes from, it is difficult to expect that the Roman governor would. Much of the time, even the chosen disciples of Christ did not understand this, for they too constantly tried to see the things of heaven with the eyes of the earth. It is no wonder that Jesus kept silent in the face of Pilate's question about his origins. He had been emphasising the truth of his real paternity to those who might be expected to understand, but in vain. He could tell his earthly origins, but that was not of much importance; as he had said, 'It is the Spirit that gives Life; the flesh is useless' (John 6:63). As for his spiritual origins, what could he now say? Either he tells the truth, and provides a superficial proof of his guilt of the charges against him, or he tells a lie. Like the sacrificial lambs being led at that very moment to be slaughtered for Passover, the Lamb of God makes no effort to defend himself and lets himself be sacrificed – to make possible a spiritual passing over for his disciples. Behold the man (*ecce homo*) sacrificing himself for those whom he loves, so that they may wake up and see.

Pilate is not aware of being a player in a cosmic drama, in which he has his own specific role. He thinks he has the power to release Christ or to kill him, as does every man about his own inner Christ. Willy-nilly, each one of us lets Christ be crucified; and this power too is given us from above, and is a part of the natural order of things. It is sometimes the case that an occasional person, with effort and grace, overcomes the worldly forces within him pressurising him to hand over Christ to be crucified, and stands firm against himself and conquers the world. Such a person may still be *in* the world, but he is no longer *of* it; he becomes a brother of Christ, a son of their common Father.

The others, in one form or another, deny their own deepest truth and crucify it; in total disregard and betrayal of their tradition and heritage, they embrace Caesar and reject Christ, shouting 'We have no king but Caesar.' In this, of course, they speak the truth. But in that very fact lies the need for the incarnation and sacrifice of Christ: the hearts of men are devoted to Caesar, and Christ suffers because the work of the Father is not done. The more they are for Caesar and opposed to God, the more he has suffer; when they declare themselves totally on the side of Caesar and no one else, if God still loves the world He has no choice but to offer the ultimate sacrifice – of Himself incarnated in His Son – to help turn at least some of them around. Of course, what is eternal does not die; that cannot be crucified. What is killed, however, is the opportunity offered by God in an embodied form at a particular place and time. He sent His own Son as a messenger to call men to Him; and we men killed the messenger so that our sleep might not be disturbed. However, in that very death, for them who will participate in that death in spirit and truth, lie the seeds for the tree of Eternal Life.

Delivering the Spirit to the One Whom He Loved

After the soldiers had crucified Jesus, they took his garments and divided them four ways, one for each soldier. There was also his tunic; but this tunic was woven in one piece from top to bottom and had no seam. So they said to one another, 'We should not tear it. Let us throw dice to see who gets it.' (The purpose of this was to have Scripture fulfilled: 'They divided my garments among them; for my clothing they cast lots.') And this was what the soldiers did (19:23–24).

Near the cross of Jesus there stood his mother, his mother's sister – Mary of Clopas – and Mary Magdalene. Seeing his mother there with the disciple whom he loved, Jesus said to his mother, 'Woman, here is your son.' In turn he said to the disciple, 'Here is your mother.' And from that hour the disciple took her into his own. After that, Jesus realising that everything was now finished, said to fulfil the Scripture, 'I thirst.' There was a jar there full of common wine; so they stuck a sponge soaked in this wine on some hyssop and raised it to his mouth. When Jesus took the wine, he exclaimed, 'It is finished'; and bowing his head, he handed over the Spirit (19:25–30).

Since it was the Day of Preparation, the Jews did not want to have the bodies left on the cross during the Sabbath, for that Sabbath was a solemn feast day. They asked Pilate that the legs be broken and the bodies be taken away. Accordingly, the soldiers came and broke the legs of the men crucified with Jesus, first of the one, then of the other. When they came to Jesus and saw that he was already dead, they did not break his legs. One of the soldiers thrust a lance into his side, and immediately blood and water flowed out. (This testimony has been given by an eyewitness, and his testimony is true, so that you may believe.) These events took place for the fulfilment of Scripture: 'Break none of his bones.' There is still another Scripture passage which says: 'They shall look on him whom they have pierced' (19:31–37).

Afterwards, Joseph of Arimathea, a disciple of Jesus (although a secret one for fear of the Jews), asked Pilate's permission to remove Jesus' body. Pilate granted it, so they came out and took the body away. Nicodemus (the man who had first come to Jesus at night) likewise came, bringing a mixture of myrrh and aloes, weighing about a hundred pounds. They took Jesus' body, and in accordance with Jewish burial custom bound it up in wrappings of cloth with perfumed oils. In the place where he had been crucified there was a garden, and in the garden a new tomb in which no one had ever been buried. Because of the Jewish Preparation Day they buried Jesus there, for the tomb was close at hand (19:38–42).

The seamless garment that Jesus wore, given to him with everything else by his Father, indicates his priestly function, serving as a link between mankind and God. A similar function was served by Adam and Moses who, according to an ancient Rabbinic idea, received seamless tunics from God. Christ is both a king and a priest, although in neither case in the usual worldly sense. He is neither in the line of Pilate representing Caesar, nor in the line of the high priest shouting for the crucifixion of Jesus; instead, he 'is a priest for ever, one who has become a priest not according to a system of earth-bound rules, but by the power of life that cannot be destroyed' (Hebrews 7:16–17). From the Beginning, without the beginning of days or the end of the earth, the Son of God remains a priest for ever. Above all, he is the high priest because he sacrifices himself for his flock, setting an example, and laying down a way from There to here, so that those who would tread his path, the path of the Crucifer, may be able to ascend from here to There.

All the disciples of Jesus have abandoned him, except the one whom he loved who is standing near the cross with the mother of Jesus and some other women from his circle. These women and this particular disciple seem to have more trust in him as the Son of God, and more affection and concern for him, than the others who are all disheartened and uncertain about the way and the teacher. It is remarkable that the close disciples of Jesus do not even bury him, thus not fulfilling the most minimal obligations of friendship in such situations. The two persons who are specifically said to have been responsible for his burial are Joseph of Arimathea and Nicodemus; they were both members of the Sanhedrin, the very council which condemned Jesus to death. They were secret admirers and followers of Christ, even though they could not forsake all their worldly connections and ambitions to follow him everywhere. In this hour, they discharge their debts to him with dignity and propriety, and one imagines that they had worked hard inside the council to avert the crucifixion of Jesus. He is buried in a tomb in which no one has been buried before. Always with an eye to symbolic detail the author of the Gospel underscores the perpetual, moment-to-moment, freshness of Eternal Life; it is right that he who can say 'Before Abraham came to be, *I AM*' emerges from a virgin womb, and enters into a virgin tomb.

Only one disciple was there at the cross; he is not named but is designated as 'the one whom Jesus loved'. One person alone is so identified in the Gospel, by practically everyone including Christ himself (John 11:3, 5, 11, 36), namely Lazarus. He is the only one who has been resurrected from the dead, and should be expected to be free of the ultimate fear, that of death, which might have kept the other disciples away. Furthermore, Lazarus is the brother of another person near the cross: Mary Magdalene, if she is identified with Mary of Bethany keeping the perfume for the day of Jesus' embalming (John 12:3–7), an identification made in the Western Christian Church for centuries. It may also be remarked here that there is a divergence of opinion about the number of women near the cross as mentioned in the Gospel text above. The number varies from two to four; three has been accepted here, largely on the basis of a remark in the Gospel of Philip (II, 3:59): 'There were three who always walked with the Lord: Mary his mother and her sister and Magdalene, the one who was called his companion. His sister and his mother and his companion were each a Mary.'

What is the final act of Jesus on the cross before he realises that everything is now finished? It is tempting to interpret the scene in very human filial terms as Jesus making arrangements for the care of his mother after his death. This may well be true; but there is nothing in the Gospel to prepare us for this perspective. The last we heard of Jesus' mother was in the second chapter, where he was if anything a little curt with her; there has been no hint anywhere of him having much ordinary care or concern for her as his mother, or for that matter even for himself. Wholly dedicated to the teaching, he would not allow a prospective disciple to go and bury his father, or to take leave of his family. In order to follow him, the disciples had to leave and deny their mother and father and their own selves (Luke 9:59–62; 14:26):

He was still addressing the crowds when his mother and his brothers appeared outside to speak with him. Someone said to him, 'Your mother and your brothers are standing out there and they wish to speak to you.' He said to the

one who had told him, 'Who is my mother? Who are my
brothers?' Then extending his hand towards his disciples,
he said, 'There are my mother and my brothers. Whoever
does the will of my heavenly Father is brother and sister
and mother to me' (Matthew 12: 46–50).

The disciple who is loved by Christ could hardly be loved out of
any human weakness or a personal liking on the part of Jesus.
In any master–disciple relationship, personal and subjective like
or dislike has no place; the master loves the disciple not for his
own pleasure, nor for the sake of the ego enhancement of the
disciple. To the extent the disciple dedicates himself to trying
sincerely to do the work that the master assigns him to do, in
this case to crucify his self-will to the will of the Father, to that
extent he is loved by Christ. In his last act of teaching, Jesus
Christ acknowledges the beloved disciple as his spiritual son,
and therefore his brother, for everyone who is begotten by the
Spirit is a son of God. As at Cana, when Jesus transformed water
into wine, similarly in his last hour on the cross, his two mothers were present. Not only Mary, the earthly mother of Jesus,
but also *Shekinah* (feminine in Hebrew, translated into *Pneuma*
which is neuter in Greek, further translated into masculine
Spiritus in Latin), the heavenly Mother of Christ (see Chapter
1). Whatever the role of the earthly women at the cross, it was
to his heavenly Mother, the Eternal Virgin, that he introduced
his beloved disciple. Jesus was begotten by God at the moment
of the descent of the dove on his head as witnessed by John
the Baptiser; thus the Holy Spirit had entered into him and
stayed dwelling inside him. Now the time has come for Jesus
to deliver voluntarily the Spirit to the one he loved and who
had made himself worthy. And from that moment, the beloved
disciple took her into his own, and she dwelt inside him, and
his transformation is complete. Now, Jesus and his beloved are
no longer master and disciple, nor even only friends; they are
full brothers – born of the same heavenly Father and of the same
heavenly Mother.

Now the work of Jesus Christ is completed. But something is
still unfinished. He says, 'I thirst' – a cry that has reverberated
not only through the corridors of history, but in the souls of all
those who have heard his voice down the ages. But in the final
act of mockery, his thirst for the liberation of the spirit of man is

met with some cheap wine! In the midst of his total humiliation by the world, he knew with certainty that he had done what he came to do; for that moment in time, his work was finished. But throughout time, any time, his work needs to be carried out, for he still thirsts. If no true disciples respond to his call and accomplish his work and drink the cup of his suffering, he will have to come again and be crucified again; and again. He said, 'I stood in the midst of the world and I appeared to them in flesh; I found all of them drunken; I found none among them thirsty. And my soul was pained for the children of men, for they are blind in their hearts, and they do not see that they came empty into the world seeking also to leave the world empty. But now they are drunken. When they shake off their wine, then they will repent' (Gospel of Thomas II, 2:28).

CHAPTER

—— 20 ——

I Sleep, but My Heart Waketh

Early on the first day of the week, when it was still dark, Mary Magdalene came to the tomb. She saw that the stone had been moved away from the tomb; so she went running to Simon Peter and to the other disciple (the one whom Jesus loved) and told them, 'They took the Lord from the tomb, and we do not know where they put him!' (20:1–2)

At that, Peter and the other disciple started out on their way to the tomb. They were running side by side, but then the other disciple outran Peter and reached the tomb first. He stopped and looked in and saw the wrappings lying there, but he did not go inside. Then Simon Peter came, following him, and he went into the tomb. He observed the wrappings lying there and the piece of cloth that had covered the head, not lying in the wrappings, but rolled up in a place by itself. Then the disciple who had arrived at the tomb first went in. He saw and believed. (Remember that as yet they did not understand the Scripture that Jesus had to rise from the dead.) With this the disciples went to their own place (20:3–10).

Meanwhile, Mary stood beside the tomb weeping. Even as she wept, she stooped to peer inside, and there she saw two angels in dazzling robes. One was seated at the head and the other at the foot of the place where Jesus' body had lain. 'Woman,' they asked her, 'why are you weeping?' She told them, 'Because they took my Lord away and I do not know where they put him.' She had just said this when she turned around and caught sight of Jesus standing there. She did not realise, however, that it was Jesus. 'Woman,' he asked her, 'why are you weeping? Who is it you are looking for?' Thinking that he was the gardener, she said to him, 'Sir, if you are the one who carried him off, tell me where you have laid him and I will take him away.' Jesus said to her, 'Mary!' She turned to him and said, in Hebrew, 'Rabbuni!' (which means 'master'). 'Stop touching me,' Jesus told her, 'for I have not yet ascended to the Father. Go to my brothers and tell them, "I am ascending to my Father and your Father, to my God and your God!"' Mary Magdalene went to the disciples. 'I have seen the Lord!' she announced, reporting what he had said to her (20:11–18).

The eternal dying in time is already in the realm of paradox. 'It was not only when he appeared that he voluntarily laid down his life,' says the Gospel of Philip (II, 3:53, 56), 'but he voluntarily laid down his life from the very day the world came into being. . . . Light and darkness, life and death, right and left, are brothers of one another. They are inseparable. Because of this neither are the good good, nor the evil evil, nor is life life, nor death death. For this reason each one will dissolve into its original nature. But those who are exalted above the world are indissoluble, eternal. Those who say that the Lord died first and then rose up are in error, for he rose up first and then died.'

Mary Magdalene was among the very few disciples and friends at the cross; she was the first one to be at the tomb after his burial where she realised that the stone at the entrance of the tomb had been moved away. She was the only one to see the angels seated at the place where Jesus had been laid, and the first one to see the risen Christ, and perhaps the only one to touch him after his resurrection. She clearly had an unusually close relationship with Jesus Christ, a relationship in which the direct connection between them transcended physical death. However, consistent with the lack of interest of the Gospel writer in ordinary historical details, he does not tell us very much about her, nor about her relationship with Jesus, even though she, with the sole exception of Jesus' mother, is the only other woman in the Gospel to play any role at all. It is possible that she is the same as Mary of Bethany, sister of Lazarus, who anointed the feet of Jesus with expensive perfume. We learn from the other canonical gospels that Jesus had cast seven devils from her, and that she was one of the women who accompanied him, along with other disciples, as he journeyed through towns and villages teaching about the Kingdom of God (Mark 16:9; Luke 8:2).

Among the non-canonical gospels, the Gospel of Peter (51)

calls her 'a disciple of the Lord'. Levi, one of the disciples, says to Peter in the Gospel According to Mary (BG 8502, I, 18), 'If the Saviour made her [Mary Magdalene] worthy, who are you indeed to reject her? Surely the Saviour knows her very well. That is why he loved her more than us.' Finally, the Gospel of Philip (II, 3:63–64) has this to say:

> And the companion of the Saviour is Mary Magdalene. But Christ loved her more than all the disciples and used to kiss her often on her mouth. The rest of the disciples were offended by it and expressed disapproval. They said to him, 'Why do you love her more than all of us?' The Saviour answered and said to them, 'Why do I not love you like her? When a blind man and one who sees are both together in darkness, they are no different from one another. When the light comes, then he who sees will see the light, and he who is blind will remain in darkness.'

It is clear that Mary was no ordinary associate of Jesus; she was very close to him and intimate with him, no doubt corresponding to her quality of being. Just as there is the male disciple whom Jesus loved, usually left unnamed in the Gospel except when he is identified as Lazarus (John 11:3, 11), Mary is the female disciple who Jesus loved. If this Mary is the same as Mary of Bethany, as is generally accepted in the Church tradition, then the two disciples whom Jesus loved were brother and sister. If the earlier Judaic and the subsequent Christian traditions had been more hospitable to the idea of feminine greatness, no doubt we would have heard much more about Mary as well as other female disciples of Christ.

There can hardly be any doubt about the love of Mary for Jesus Christ, and also about her sensitivity. When other disciples are in hiding somewhere, she is at the tomb of him whom she loved. When Peter and the other disciple peer in the tomb, what they see are wrappings; when Mary looks there she sees angels! Peter seems unaffected by what he saw; the other one, because he is loved by Christ, did understand something, but surprisingly both of them returned to their place as if nothing special had happened. Not so with Mary: she is heartbroken, but she is searching for Christ, looking everywhere and asking everyone who might know about him. She sought and she found; she was there when he was crucified, and she is there now when he rises from the dead. He has undergone enough transformation that she has difficulty recognising him, until he calls her by her name. In her response, there is not the least hint of fear or hesitation; there is only pure joy, and she bursts out with a term of endearment, *Rabbuni* – my dear Rabbi! The translation of the Aramaic word *Rabbuni* as 'Master' ignores the feeling of tenderness associated with this diminutive of *Rabbi*.

John the Baptiser had witnessed Christ into incarnation; Mary Magdalene witnesses Jesus into resurrection.

It is difficult to read this chapter in the Gospel without wondering if Mary was the feminine balance to the masculinity of Jesus, the *yin* to his *yang*, as Radha to Krishna. How can one not be reminded here of the Song of Songs, the book which the great Rabbi Aqiba had declared to be the holiest of the holies, and about which he had said that all the ages were not worth the day when this book was given to Israel?

> I sleep, but my heart waketh:
>   it is the voice of my beloved that knocketh . . .
> By night on my bed I sought him whom my soul loveth:
>   I sought him, but I found him not.
> I will rise now, and go about the city
>   in the streets, and in the broad ways I will
>   seek him whom my soul loveth:
>   I sought him, but I found him not.
> The watchmen that go about the city found me:
>   to whom I said, 'Saw ye him whom my soul loveth?'
> It was but a little that I passed from them,
>   but I found him whom my soul loveth:
>   I held him, and would not let him go . . .
> I am my beloved's, and my beloved is mine . . .
>   (Song of Songs 5:2; 3:1–4; 6:3)

Now, however, Jesus Christ has already gone beyond the level of materialisation at which Mary is; he has a far subtler body now than hers. Every religious tradition maintains that there is more to a human being than his physical body, and that this non-physical aspect survives the physical death in some form. In some traditions, especially among the Hindus and the Buddhists, the supra-physical substance is spoken of in terms of two or three subtler bodies associated with the physical, earthly body but not bound by it. The subtler or lighter the body, the higher it can ascend. Immediately after the crucifixion of Jesus, his next higher body is still hovering within the earth's atmosphere, and is able to make contact with and be seen by those who had been intimately associated with him before the death of his physical body. However, this seeing is not quite the ordinary seeing, any more than the subtle body is the ordinary body. Not everybody can see the risen Christ; a special sort of connection with him and sensitivity is needed – precisely of the kind made possible by eating his flesh and drinking his blood, that is by keeping his words and dwelling in his love. Those who love him, and more importantly those who are loved by him, are the ones who can see him. As Christ said, 'Whoever keeps the commandments that he has from me is the man who loves me; and the man who loves me will be loved by my Father, and I shall love him and reveal myself to him' (John 14:21). It is no wonder that Mary is the first one to see him risen; and we are told later (John 21:7) that it was the male disciple whom Jesus loved who first recognised him at the shore of the Sea of Tiberias.

This level of the subtle body is said to exist within the environs of the departed person's friends, and loved ones, and even his belongings – particularly if he is attached to them – from three to forty-nine days. After that period, either the subtle body dissolves, or is reborn in some suitable form according to the deep-seated tendencies clinging to it. But if a person has attained, through spiritual practice and grace, yet subtler bodies, they will ascend higher at the end of this period, depending on their levity and freedom from bondage to the world. This is rare; but one would naturally expect that Christ would ascend higher, right up to the highest level – of the Father. After a few days, his intermediate subtle body, in which he could still appear to his disciples on the earth, would dissolve because he would have no more need of it.

The departed soul can be assisted in its spiritual journey by those who remain behind by prayer and meditation, thereby generating the fine substance of subtle attention and higher feeling which is what the soul needs for its food. But the soul can also be hindered in its upward journey by clinging on to it through fear or craving, making it heavier and more and more bound to the world. It is now not the time for an earthly

219

connection between Jesus and Mary; the subtler body of Christ can still be dragged down into the world below, interfering with his ascension, if Mary's attention and equilibrium falter, yielding to desire and attachment, for he has not yet ascended to the Father. She must stop touching him, and let him be free of the world. Because he has overcome the world, he is poised to ascend to the highest level, that of oneness with the Father. The message from the risen and still rising Christ that Mary is vouchsafed, not only for herself but for all who would truly be his disciples, is the same he gave from the cross to the other disciple whom he loved: do not rest until you, male or female, become my brothers, so that *your* God is the same as *my* God, and *your* Father is *my* Father. He invites all who hear, be they from here or there, then or now, not in his own name but that of God, 'to share the likeness of His Son, that the Son might be the first-born of many brothers' (Romans 8:29).

The Spirit of Truth as the Subtle Body of Christ

On the evening of that first day of the week, even though the disciples had locked the doors of the place where they were for fear of the Jews, Jesus came and stood before them. 'Peace be with you,' he said. And when he had said this, he showed them his hands and side. At the sight of the Lord the disciples rejoiced. 'Peace be with you,' he said again. 'As the Father has sent me, so do I send you.' Then he breathed on them and said: 'Receive the Holy Spirit. If you forgive men's sins, their sins are forgiven; if you hold them bound, they are held bound' (20:19–23).

It happened that one of the Twelve, Thomas (this name means 'twin'), was absent when Jesus came. The other disciples kept telling him, 'We have seen the Lord!' His answer was, 'Unless I see the holes from the nails, and put my finger into the holes from the nails, and put my hand into his side, I will not believe.' Eight days later, the disciples were once more in the room, and this time Thomas was with them. Despite the locked doors, Jesus came and stood before them. 'Peace be with you,' he said; then to Thomas: 'Put your finger here, and examine my hands, and take your hand and put it into my side. And do not become unbelieving but believing.' Thomas answered with the word, 'My Lord and my God!' Jesus told him, 'You have believed because you have seen me. Blessed are they who have not seen and yet have believed' (20:24–29).

Jesus performed many other signs as well – signs not recorded here – in the presence of his disciples. But these have been recorded so that you may believe that Jesus is the Christ, the Son of God, and so that, believing, you may have life in his name (20:30–31).

Only for the sake of easier specification of various subtle bodies, and not in order to impose an alien schema on the Gospel account, one may borrow the terminology developed in the spiritual tradition of Tibetan Buddhism. Four different bodies (*kayas*) are distinguished: the highest one, which encompasses the other three and transcends them, is called *Svabhavikakaya*, the essential body of intrinsic nature (*svabhava*). The first of the other three is *Dharmakaya*, which is the Body of *Dharma* or Truth, the absolute Buddha-nature. Next, less subtle, is *sambhogakaya*, the body of experience or enjoyment; this is the body which communicates the dharma, and is shown in the Tibetan tradition as manifesting in the form of peaceful or wrathful deities corresponding to the state of mind of the person. The lowest, that is the grossest, is *nirmanakaya*, in which a person is physically manifested on earth. A similar point of view, sometimes more elaborated and sometimes less, can be found in many other traditions, as well as in the writings of St Paul (see 1 Corinthians 15:40–44; 2 Corinthians 12:2–4). It may also be remarked here that the tripartite division of Spirit (*pneuma*), soul (*psyche*) and body (*soma*) in the New Testament more or less corresponds to *Dharmakaya*, *sambhogakaya* and *nirmanakaya*. The Father, who encompasses all there is and is still beyond, would thus correspond to *Svabhavikakaya*.

In those spiritual traditions where the actual science and practice of being has not been lost, either in rationalist theology without experience or in enthusiastic confession of faith without the sword of insight, the main concern is with the inner alchemy so that the finer and finer gold of the three interior bodies may be distilled from the lead of the gross one. But, always one needs to remain on guard and not be misled into a superficial mode by the use of words like 'body' or 'Father';

otherwise, one will be hindered by the finger pointing to her and not see the celestial maiden whom mortals call the moon.

At the death of the physical body (*nirmanakaya*) of Jesus Christ, his higher bodies are not destroyed. From the minimal description given in the Gospel, it appears that it was the soul (*sambhogakaya*) of Jesus Christ who met Mary Magdalene and some of the other disciples. This is the body which is said to have extrasensory perceptions, such as in clairvoyance, and the ability to go through any resisting material and to have instantaneous locomotion across vast distances. Those who had shared intimacies with Jesus Christ, and had eaten his flesh and drunk his blood, a ceremony which might in fact have been undertaken in the spirit of such practices as swearing 'blood brotherhood' or making oaths 'by blood', would be aware of the presence of his subtler body which could communicate with them, even though those outside the intimate circle of the departed might have absolutely no idea or sense of such a presence. The important point is that this entity, *sambhogakaya*, is not something diffuse or formless; it is a definite body, belonging to a particular individual, with a definite form and shape; those who can see it look at it as on an ordinary body but with many radically different characteristics and abilities.

However, the body higher than this one, namely the *Dharmakaya* (Spirit), does not have the characteristics of shape and form, particularity and individuality, like the lower bodies. As the *sambhogakaya* is intimately connected with feelings and emotional sensitivity, the *Dharmakaya* is closely connected with insight and breath. No doubt this is the reason why in practically all ancient, especially scriptural, languages the word for 'spirit' is very close to the one for 'breath'. In the light of the difference of individuality in the two bodies, whereas it makes sense to speak of *my* or *your* soul (*sambhogakaya*, self, *buddhi*), it does not make much sense to speak of *my* Spirit (*Dharmakaya*, Self, *Atman*) as distinct from *yours*. This is the very point of demarcation which is indicated by the upper-case first letter: self and soul are individual and personal, but Self and Spirit are supra-individual. Similarly, the Son of Man arises from a son of man, as Spiritual Body from the natural body, but is not bound by it. God is still beyond: as long as a person's father is different from the Father of Christ, and his god different from Christ's God, he is not related to a very high divinity; it is a god within the realm of his own psyche, corresponding to his own world of fear and ambition, made in his own image. The more his self is cast in the likeness of Christ, the more his God is the same as the One God, as Jesus asked Mary to go tell the disciples.

Now he comes to them himself, and breathes into them the Holy Spirit; this is the subtler body (*Dharmakaya*, the Body of Truth), which he is able to bequeath to them because he himself is ascending higher still, to the Father, the *Svabhavikakaya*. Until now, he himself needed to retain connection with this subtle body in order to remain incarnated and act with wisdom and insight on the earth. He can breathe the Spirit of Truth into them only from a position higher than the Spirit, as he transcends It. What seemed strange earlier, now becomes clear: 'If you loved me you would rejoice that I am going to the Father, for the Father is greater than I. . . . I am telling you the truth: it is to your advantage that I go away. If I do not go, the guide [paraclete, Spirit of Truth] cannot come to you, but if I go, I will send him to you' (John 14:28; 16:7). When the disciples are guided by the Spirit of Truth, they would naturally be filled with discernment as well as compassion. Then what they judge as bound, is in fact bound; and where their mercy and guidance can help, they will help to bring men to the right mark of their existence. And at that time, they would be aware that they in fact can do nothing in their own name; they must act in the name of and in connection with the Christ, as he himself acted in the name of the Father and in obedience to His will.

Thomas wants to have a direct contact with the risen Christ himself, and would not accept the second-hand testimony of his fellow disciples. That seems right enough, but what sort of evidence is Thomas looking for? Not any soul-to-soul communication with Christ, or subtle understanding. He did not have the Holy Spirit breathed into him; and thus did not have the beginnings of a new man in him. All he could ask for and understand was a gross, physical proof: holes created by the nails in the hands of Jesus. The risen Christ meets him at the level where Thomas still is, and invites him to examine the holes made by the nails; however, he appeals to Thomas' higher mind, asking him to look at a deeper level and not stay fixed on the surface. Christ's words touch Thomas to the core; he realises that he in fact has no need to touch Jesus and to examine the physical holes. And suddenly, he truly sees Jesus Christ, for the first time;

and as he sees him, he sees the Father. The disciple who did not know (John 14:5) where Christ was going now has a direct perception of him ascending to and arriving in God. Christ further underscores the necessity of understanding, and thus believing, even more subtly. Even though Thomas did not have to make a physical examination of the holes in Jesus' hands, he still had to be reminded by the presence of the *sambhogakaya* of Christ. A subtler, more universal and more inner understanding and believing is at the level of the Spirit, the Buddha-nature (*Dharmakaya*); blessed are they who live from that level.

The Gospel writer is not interested in producing a complete catalogue of all the signs performed by the risen Christ, any more than in providing a full record of all the works done by him in the flesh. It is not a disinterested collection of historical data that engages him; he has a clear purpose which he wishes his writing to serve: to help the reader believe that Jesus is the Christ, the Son of God. It has already been remarked on several occasions that *believing* in the Gospel is akin to *seeing, recognising* and *understanding,* and that only those can believe, who have been chosen and called by God, and stay in the love of Christ by obeying his commandments. The Gospel writer is attempting to help us understand the true nature of Christ which he had from the Beginning, and to enable us to follow the Crucifer, with all the literary skill and wisdom at his disposal. Some form is needed for us to make a connection with That which is beyond all forms; but the end is not the form.

Other forms, developed beside the River Yangtze or Ganga rather than by the River Jordan, expressed in the feminine mode of the Mother and the Daughter rather than the masculine one of the Father and the Son, may be utilised by other writers of genius at other times and places to convey the Unsayable. A great form, which is as much a text, as a system of ideas, or a work of visual art or a piece of music, both reveals and veils the Truth: it has the purpose of transporting a soul to the One who calls from above the forms; but the beauty and the charm of a form have their own seductions and can easily turn an aspirant into an adherent. Some sort of flesh is required for the incarnation of the Logos; but, as Christ said, 'It is the Spirit that gives Life; the flesh is useless' (John 6:63).

Naturally, the Gospel writer must use the language, symbols and metaphors appropriate to the people and the times for which he is writing. For other readers, who are far from the writer in time, space and cultural background, it is necessary to try to listen to the eternal truths and principles with an inner ear that can hear behind the surface, temporal and contingent, meanings of his words and images. Otherwise, even if one can find the Jesus of history and touch the holes made by the nails in his hands, one would see through a glass darkly and would not awake to the Christ of eternity. Only when a man has been lifted up above his surface self to the Son of Man in himself can he meet the Son of God; and the meeting takes place at the threshold of I AM, in the eternal now.

This particular cycle in the descent and ascent of Christ is now over. The Gospel had opened with the theme of a new creation, parallel to the old one; as there was the old Adam, now a new Adam is to be born, a child of God 'begotten not by blood, nor by carnal desire, nor by man's willing, but by God' (John 1:13). We are told in Genesis (2:7) that 'The Lord God formed man out of the dust of the earth and breathed into his nostrils the breath of life. Thus the man became a living creature.' Jesus Christ chose the disciples from among men and breathed the Spirit of Truth, his own subtle body, into them, so that they might have eternal and abundant Life. The old Adam was given control over external nature; the new being has control over his inner nature. For his teaching to be lived in full, so that his disciples may have new life, he himself had to die to the world. And he warned the disciples about the inevitability and the necessity of them also drinking the cup of suffering for the sake of the new birth.

Whereas there is nothing sentimental or soft or easy about his teaching, ultimately it is full of true hope: as he said,

'In very truth I tell you that you will weep and mourn, but the world will rejoice. You will have pain, but your pain will be turned into joy. A woman has pain when she is giving birth, when her hour has come; but when her child is born, her joy makes her forget her suffering, because a human being has been born into the world. So now you also feel pain; but I will see you again, and your heart will rejoice, and no one can take that joy away from you' (John 16:20–22).

CHAPTER

— 21 —

A New Beginning

After this, Jesus again showed himself to his disciples, at the Sea of Tiberias. This is how the appearance took place. Assembled were Simon Peter, Thomas (the 'Twin'), Nathanael (from Cana in Galilee), Zebedee's sons, and two other disciples. Simon Peter said to them, 'I am going fishing.' 'We will join you,' they replied and went off to get into the boat. All through the night they caught nothing. Just after daybreak Jesus was standing on the shore, though none of the disciples knew it was Jesus. He said to them, 'Children, have you caught anything to eat?' 'No,' they answered. 'Cast your net to the starboard side,' he suggested, 'and you will find something.' So they cast the net, and took so many fish thay could not haul the net in. Then the disciple whom Jesus loved exclaimed to Peter, 'It is the Lord!' On hearing it was the Lord, Simon Peter threw on some clothes – he was stripped – and jumped into the water (21:1–7).

Meanwhile the other disciples came into the boat, towing the net full of fish. Actually they were not far from land – no more than a hundred yards. When they landed, they saw a charcoal fire there with a fish laid on it and some bread. 'Bring some of the fish you just caught,' Jesus told them. Simon Peter went aboard and hauled ashore the net loaded with large fish – one hundred and fifty-three of them! In spite of the great number, the net was not torn. 'Come, and eat your meal,' Jesus told them. Not one of the disciples dared to inquire, 'Who are you?' for they knew it was the Lord. Jesus came over, took the bread and gave it to them, and did the same with the fish. (This was now the third time that Jesus revealed himself to the disciples after his resurrection from the dead.) (21:8–14).

One cycle has now ended and another is beginning in a ceaseless exchange of energies between levels, the cosmic *yajna* and sacrifice. Sacred work is necessary in order to be able to receive energy from above for the maintenance of the cosmos, both on the scale of an individual human being and on the large scale, inner and outer, but it is constantly threatened by forces of forgetfulness and destruction. One deviates continually from the freedom of the path of the cross – crucifixion of oneself to the world and of the world to oneself – and returns to fear and self-importance. The lamb of Christ, within each human being and in the society, is always menaced by the wolf of the world; the lamb is weak and needs to be nourished and cared for. It was in order to call his sheep, who had strayed and had been lost, and to show them the right path that Christ had come into the world and had died on the cross. Now he is not here in the flesh, but that very freedom from the restrictions of the physical body allows him to dwell inside every disciple in the Spirit.

However, the inner Christ has to be realised and embodied each time anew; it is the essence of Eternal Life that it lies in a dimension other than that of time, intersecting with time only in the present now. It does not continue in time, but is reborn afresh from one living moment to another. Eternity is not an extension of time; although manifesting in history, eternal life has no history. What is from the Beginning is always fresh and at the beginning. So it is in Peter, as it is in everyone – in the moment when he comes to himself, and realises that on his own resources, without maintaining an active contact with Christ, after a whole night's toil he has obtained nothing. Whatever treasures one may be fishing for, and it can just as well be through ordinary fishing as through any other activity since all action is sacred if done as a sacrifice, one catches nothing of real substance, a substance that can last, without help from Above.

Peter is again at the beginning, in a situation highly reminiscent of the occasion when he first met Jesus Christ: same sight, but fresh insight, similar words, but newer depths and larger responsibility. There is a repetition to be sure, but less in a circle, more in a spiral; each time one is at the beginning-point of the new cycle, it is at a different level. What had struck Peter the most when he had first encountered Jesus Christ, as recounted in Luke 5:1–11, was Jesus' uncanny ability to predict the precise location for casting the nets so that an enormous quantity of fish could be caught. At this, Peter had realised the wide gulf between the greatness of Jesus and his own smallness, and had fallen on his knees, saying, 'Depart from me, O Lord, for I am a sinful man.' Christ had reassured him, 'Do not be afraid; henceforth you will catch men.' With that, he and his friends had brought their boats to land, abandoned everything, and had become the followers of Jesus.

Since then, the disciples have been chosen by Christ, prepared and given the Spirit by him, and sent to do God's work so that his thirst would be quenched. Peter is among those disciples; and he seems to have qualities of leadership because many of the other disciples naturally follow him; but something deep within him still does not believe. This is quite understandable and universal: at each level, there is a struggle between the part that wishes to serve God and the part that wants to escape from the responsibility and the suffering inherent in following the path of the Crucifer. Jesus himself had wished to be spared the cup if it were possible, but had overcome himself, and thus the world, and submitted to the Father: 'Not my will, but thine, be done' (Luke 22:42). But Peter still needs help from Above, for he forgets – himself, his connection with Christ and the charge given to him when he received the Holy Spirit; he relies on his own resources and those of his friends. Again and again, in spite of their wishes to the contrary, they abandon their link with Christ and launch their boats on their own on the uncertain seas of the world. Christ, however, does not abandon them, nor does he lose hope. He knows that without remaining connected to him, as branches on a vine, they can do nothing; he comes to them at a time when, even in the most ordinary sense, having caught nothing after a long night's labour they are open to a miraculous contrast of his abundance with their own poverty.

However, even the miraculous catch of fish does not strike Peter or jog his memory. The disciple whom Jesus loved is the first one to recognise the risen Christ standing on the shore. This is to be expected, because he reveals himself only to those whom he loves. It is not that Christ did not love the others; but the beloved disciple is special – not in any subjective like–dislike sense, but precisely because he lives not from his personal being but from that of Christ. This is how the remarkable reluctance of the Gospel writer in naming the beloved disciple can be understood. His own name now does not designate the really significant centre of the beloved disciple's new being, because he lives in the name of Christ. To name him as this or that, son of so and so, as the crowds tried to do with Christ, is to specify him and to reduce him.

Peter, on the other hand, still lives from his own ego-centre and self-will. He had been tempted earlier by Satan to deny Christ; here he turns away from him in forgetfulness. And the reminder that Christ is here brings out in Peter the shame of his nakedness which he hurriedly tries to cover. But, Peter cannot hide from Christ; on the contrary, his conscience is aroused, and he comes to his right mind, as if awoken from sleep, and remembers his master. With his characteristic impetuousness, but also childlike simplicity and exuberance, he jumps into the water to approach Christ – although it is far from certain that he arrived before others in the boat!

In spite of the large number of fish they caught, what they are fed is the fish and the bread already laid out for them, from Above. (It is interesting to note that the scene depicted here is the basis for some early representations of the eucharist to show the bread of sacrament accompanied by fish rather than wine.) One cannot help wondering if the charcoal fire, on which the sacred meal was cooked by Christ for his disciples, reminded Peter of the other charcoal fire by which he was warming himself with the soldiers at the same time as one of their company was slapping Jesus at his trial. Certainly, what follows gives every indication that Peter was touched to the core, and was humbled; and prepared to listen and to speak to Christ from a different level of understanding.

Meanwhile, the risen Christ has undergone further changes since he revealed himself last to the disciples, but nobody dared to question him, no doubt owing to the tremendous force emanating from him. Besides, what can one ask of a person who already knows the mind of the speaker before the words are uttered?

The Lamb of Christ among the Wolves of the World

When they had eaten their meal, Jesus said to Simon Peter, 'Simon, son of John, do you love me more than these? 'Yes, Lord,' he said, 'you know that I love you.' At which Jesus said, 'Feed my lambs.' A second time Jesus repeated the question, 'Simon, son of John, do you love me?' 'Yes, Lord,' he said, 'you know that I love you.' 'Tend my sheep,' Jesus told him. A third time Jesus asked him, 'Simon, son of John, do you love me?' Peter was hurt because he had asked a third time, 'Do you love me?' So he said to him, 'Lord, you know everything. You know well that I love you.' 'Feed my little lambs,' Jesus said. 'I tell you this in very truth: when you were a young man you fastened your belt and went about as you pleased; but when you are older you will stretch out your hands, and another will tie you fast and carry you off against your will.' (What he said indicated the sort of death by which Peter was to glorify God.) After these words, Jesus said to him, 'Follow me' (21:15–19).

The risen Christ needs Peter, and through him symbolically everyone else who would respond, to carry on his and his Father's work, and, of course, Peter needs the Christ to have any significance to his existence. Christ knows this and comes to Peter where he is, and appeals to his highest conscience. Peter also knows his need; but he is not completely self-possessed and in spite of himself ends up forgetting his link with Christ, and his own real situation and need. Perhaps this is why he is addressed here after the manner of his human parentage, as Simon, son of John, rather than Peter, a name which Jesus had given him to mark an important realisation on his part of his own nothingness.

Does he love Christ more than these? The Gospel writer is a subtle artist, and he leaves it teasingly ambiguous as to what "these" refer to: Does Simon love Christ more than these things, such as the boat, the fish, the business? Does he love Christ more than he loves the others, the fellow disciples and friends? Does he love Christ more than the others do? Is Peter sure that there is nothing in the world – possessions, relatives, friends – which his heart values more than Christ? Is anybody sure? How could he know, how could anyone know, that he loves Christ more than other people do, except in one's own competitive fantasy of being more ardent than anyone else? There is hardly a person who would not hesitate before giving a confident answer to any of these questions, dealing as they do with the crucified Christ on the one hand and acquisitiveness, need for approval and the

230

wish to be more important than fellow human beings on the other. The entire man is in question; whom would he choose: himself or Christ? The many wolves of the world prowl in the same space of the heart where the little lambs of Christ also play.

'Peter, Peter,' Christ might have cried, 'how long will you crucify me?'

In his trial by Satan (see Chapter 18), Peter was alone, and he was defeated, for he relied upon himself. Again, he is on trial this time not by the Lucifer but by the Crucifer. Peter does not rely on his own knowledge of himself, which has been far from luminous in the past. He does not declare confidently that he loves Christ more than these; he surrenders his heart and soul to Christ, and lets himself be known by him and be judged accordingly, hoping that Christ will in fact find that Peter loves him. The self-willed and self-confident Simon has truly deepened. In an acknowledgement of Peter's insight that it is better to be known by Christ than to know oneself, he is charged by Christ to feed his sheep.

But Peter's trial is not over quite yet, nor is any other disciple's. Without reference to any of these – things or persons – does Peter in fact love Christ? Peter again lets Christ be the seer of his heart. A third time again Christ asks the same question – in order to burn it on the soul of Peter, lest the demon of forgetfulness overtake him again. Peter is conscience-stricken; he is hurt not because Christ does not trust him but because he realises that Christ knows everything and he is afraid that he may be found wanting, and not worthy of the Holy Spirit breathed into him by Christ. However, as Peter dispossesses himself he is owned by Christ and made his very own, and charged by him to tend to his little lambs. The lamb of God, within oneself as well as outside, is always weak and needs to be nourished, and protected from the wolf of the world, also within oneself as well as outside. Only in an extraordinary state of watchfulness, described as the rule of Immanuel in new Jerusalem, can there be friendship between the wolf and the lamb (Isaiah 11:1–6; 65:17–25). Peter is summoned to that watchfulness, an awakening from sleep and forgetfulness. When Shiva performs his eternal dance of liberation, he steps on the head of Muyalaka, the demon of forgetfulness.

'If anyone wishes to come after me, let him deny himself, take up his cross, and follow me' (Mark 8:34). Before Peter is anointed as a disciple of Christ, he is warned and called to drink the cup of suffering, and to endure the cross. When he was young, he could preen himself and do as he wished. As he matures internally and grows older, he will no longer be free to do what he wishes according to his self-will; he must submit himself to the will of another, for he will no more be his own man; he will be owned by Christ and by God. One who is born of the Spirit does not proclaim himself, for 'this man has now become another and is neither himself nor his own' (Plotinus, *Enneads* vi.9.10). A spiritual son of Christ, he will be his brother, born of the same Father and Mother; he must engage in their work however much against his own will, and obey them even unto death, as did his master Jesus. Peter has to understand truly that in following the Christ he follows the cross, and that only the lamb can be the king and wear the crown.

Let Not Him Who Seeks Cease until He Finds

Peter turned around at that, and noticed that the disciple whom Jesus loved was following (the one who had leaned against Jesus' chest during the supper and said, 'Lord, which one will deliver you?'). Seeing him Peter said, 'Lord, what about him?' 'If I will that he abide until I come, what is that to you?' Jesus replied, 'Your work is to follow me.' This is how the word got around among all the brothers that this disciple was not going to die. As a matter of fact, Jesus never told him that he was not going to die; all he said was: 'If I will that he abide until I come, what is that to you?' (21:20–23).

It is this same disciple who is the witness to these things; it is he who wrote them down; and his testimony, we know, is true. There are still many other things that Jesus did. Yet, if they were written down in detail, I doubt there would be room enough in the entire world to hold the books to record them (21:24–25).

Peter follows Christ knowing that he must be crucified to the world, and the world to him. However, he is concerned about his friend, the disciple whom Jesus loved, and wants to know what will happen to him. Or, perhaps, he hopes that the beloved disciple will share some of the responsibility that Christ has asked him to undertake, for lurking behind his *yes* to Christ, there may still be a little *no*. But the work that the other disciple must do is not the same as what Peter must do. Each disciple has to discover his own particular way of serving God, corresponding to his essential being and capacities. If necessary, the beloved disciple can remain, waiting until Christ comes and calls him for a specific task. Or, the beloved disciple, according to his inner calling, may remain contemplatively abiding in Christ until his life's end. This is no concern of Peter; he must do what is demanded of him. Peter and the beloved disciple are very different from each other: among the male followers of Christ, Peter is to the beloved disciple what Martha is to Mary among the women – one of them is more inclined to *doing* and the other to *seeing*. But both are needed by Christ; furthermore, they both need each other; in addition, they need other fellow disciples and, further, their own pupils to carry out together the work of their common Father.

Having prepared others to continue the sacred work that must be done for the maintenance of the cosmos, inner as well as outer, Jesus can now let go of this responsibility which had bound him to the earth, and ascend higher to the Father. Such work is constantly needed, because the forces of destruction and misunderstanding are large and ever-present. As is clear from the Gospel, even during Christ's own life, in his very presence, his sayings and teachings are often misheard and taken wrongly. His own close disciples are not free of such misunderstanding, not to speak of those who do not wish to receive the Light or those who oppose him. The distortion, misunderstanding and opposition to Truth are natural and to be expected; great insights are very difficult to maintain, and require a continual struggle with oneself. Spiritual blindness is the world; Christ needs to keep dying on the cross because we keep sleeping. 'And they heard a voice from the heavens saying, "Have you preached to those who sleep?" And a response was heard from the cross: "Yes"' (Gospel of Peter 10).

Those who sleep and will not awaken, continually crucify Jesus Christ. However, those who wish to wake up must struggle in the midst of this world of sleep; this is how they can participate in the suffering of Christ and lessen his sorrow. With the aid of the words of the sages and the Scriptures, we may be brought to the original vibration of the Word, not *original* in the sense that it was actually, physically, articulated two thousand years ago, but that it was and is in reality from the *Source*, from the *Beginning*.

Death can overtake a person any moment, and in that sense the end of the world is always nigh. When one is aware of it, one is at the crossing, having to choose between Christ and the world, between the crown of thorns and the crown of power and possessions. It is fitting that the very last words of the risen Christ reported in the Gospel be underscored, for they are addressed not only to Peter but to all who would hear: 'Your work is to follow me.'

Each one of us must begin anew, perhaps again and again, if we wish to come to the deathless Beginning. Jesus Christ said, in a non-canonical saying found on some papyri discovered in Oxyrhynchus in Egypt at the end of the last century: 'Let not him who seeks cease until he finds, and when he finds he shall be astonished. Astonished he shall reach the Kingdom, and having reached the Kingdom, he shall rest.'

BIBLIOGRAPHY

Translations of Canonical Christian Sources have been adapted from
the following:

The Anchor Bible: The Gospel According to St John, Introduction, transla-
tion and notes by Raymond E. Brown, Doubleday & Co., Garden City,
New York, vol. 29 (1966), vol. 29A (1970).
The Four Gospels, translated by E. V. Rieu, Penguin Books, Harmonds-
worth (1952).
The Four Gospels and the Revelation, translation by Richmond Lattimore,
Hutchinson, London (1980).
The Holy Bible, the Authorized King James Version, World Publ. Co., New
York (n.d.).
The New American Bible, Thomas Nelson Publishers, Nashville (1971).
The New English Bible with the Apocrypha, Oxford University Press and
Cambridge University Press (1970).
The New Testament, Greek and English (3rd edn), American Bible Society,
New York (1971).

Translations of Non-canonical Christian Sources have been adapted
from the following:

The Nag Hammadi Library in English, Gen. Ed. James M. Robinson,
Harper & Row, New York (1977)—used for The Gospel of Thomas,
The Gospel of Philip and The Gospel of Mary.
The Secret Sayings of Jesus, Robert M. Grant in collaboration with David
Noel Freedman, with an English trans. of The Gospel of Thomas
by William R. Schoedel, Doubleday & Co., Garden City, New York
(1960)—used for The Gospel of Peter, The Oxyrhynchus Papryi, and
The Gospel of Thomas.

Translations of Non-Christian Sources have been adapted from the
following:

The Bhagavad Gita, translation by Juan Mascaro, Penguin Books,
Harmondsworth (1962).
The Bhagavad-Gītā, translation by R. C. Zaehner, Oxford University
Press, London (1973).
The Principal Upanisads, translation by S. Radhakrishnan, George Allen
& Unwin, London (1953).
The Yoga-Sūtra of Pātañjali: a New Translation and Commentary, Georg
Feurstein, Wm Dawson & Sons Ltd, Folkestone (1979).
Effortless Being: The Yoga Sūtras of Patanjali, translation by Alistair
Shearer, Wildwood House, London (1982).

Commentaries and Studies

The Gospel according to St John (2nd edn.), C. K. Barrett, SPCK, London
(1978).

Essays on John, C. K. Barrett, SPCK, London (1982).

The Anchor Bible: The Gospel According to St John, Introduction, translation and notes by Raymond E. Brown, Doubleday & Co., Garden City, New York, vol. 29 (1966), vol. 29A (1970).

The Gospel of John, R. Bultmann, English translation, Oxford University Press (1971).

The Interpretation of the Fourth Gospel, C. H. Dodd, Cambridge University Press (1953).

The Fourth Gospel (2nd edn.), E. C. Hoskyns, ed. F. N. Davey, Faber, London (1947).

The Gospel of St John, John Marsh, Penguin Books, Harmondsworth (1968).

Five Gospels: An Account of How the Good News Came to Be, John C. Meagher, Winston Press, Minneapolis (1983). Attention is also drawn to an article by this author, 'John 1:14 and the New Temple', *Journal of Biblical Literature*, 88 (1969):57–68.

The Composition and Order of the Fourth Gospel, D. Moody Smith, Yale University Press (1965).

Johannine Christianity: Essays on its Setting, Source and Theology, D. Moody Smith; University of South Carolina Press (1985).

The Spiritual Gospel, M. F. Wiles, Cambridge University Press (1960).

Relevant Publications by the Author, R. Ravindra

'Time in Christian and Indian Traditions', *Dalhousie Review* 51 (1971) 5–17.

'Self-surrender: Core of Spiritual Life', *Studies in Religion*, 3 (1974) 357–363.

'Is Religion Psychotherapy?—An Indian View', *Religious Studies*, 14 (1978) 389–397.

'The Dimensions of the Self: *Buddhi* in the Bhagavad Gita and *Psyché* in Plotinus', *Religious Studies*, 15 (1979) 317–332 (with A. Hilary Armstrong).

'Perception in Yoga and Physics', *Re-Vision: Journal of Consciousness and Knowledge*, 3 (1980) 36–42.

'Ancient Wisdom in a Changing World', *American Theosophist*, 71 (1983) 331–337.

Whispers from the Other Shore: Spiritual Search East and West, Quest Books, Wheaton, Illinois (1984).

'Teaching of Krishna, Master of Yoga', *American Theosophist*, 72 (1984) 55–61.

'Physics and Religion', *The Encyclopedia of Religion*, eds. M. Eliade et al., Macmillan Press, New York (1987), vol. 11. pp 319–23.

'In the Beginning is the Dance of Love', in *Origin and Evolution of the Universe: Evidence for Design?* ed. John M. Robson, McGill-Queen's University Press, Montreal (1987).

'Yoga: the Royal Path to Freedom', *The Theosophist*, vol. 110, April, 1989, pp. 247–56.

Science and Spirit, Paragon House, New York (1991).

INDEX OF REFERENCES

(NEW TESTAMENT ONLY)

Matthew

	Chap.	Page
1:23	8	103
3:11–12	3	45
4: 8–11	6	71
5:44	13	163
7:6	11	140
7:21–7	8	106
7:29	7	95
10:38	12	152
11:25	6	69–70
11:28	1	20
11:28–30	8	107
12:30	Int.	6
12:46–50	19	212–13
13:13–15	5	67
	12	149
13:55	7	84
15:10	1	17
16:24	5	58
22:14	1	25
	12	149
22:21	12	144
22:39	13	163
23: 2–28	7	85
25:14	13	158
26:38–43	11	137
26:39	4	53

Mark

	Chap.	Page
1:13	13	161
2:27	5	61
3:33	1	28
3:35	1	28
4: 9–12	5	66
	12	149
4:26–9	13	158
6: 3	6	77
	7	84
6:14–16	1	22
6:51–2	6	72
8:34	21	152

	Chap.	Page
10:35–8	18	199
14:33–6	5	63
	12	146–7
16: 9	20	216

Luke

	Chap.	Page
1:13–17	1	22
1:15	1	23
1:28–38	1	16
1:44	1	22
1:46–7	1	16
4: 5–13	11	140
5: 1–11	1	28
	21	227
5: 8	18	203
7:28	1	22
8: 2	20	216
8:10	12	149
9:23	6	68–9
	15	152
9:46–8	6	70
9:57–62	6	68–9
9:59–62	19	212
11:23	Int.	6
	7	95
11:27–8	1	19
12:48–51	13	160
12:49–50	3	45
13: 6– 9	13	159
14:26–7	7	86
	12	152
	19	212
15:22–4	11	138
16:20–5	11	131
17:21	14	166
18:10–14	9	120
18:17	6	70
18:18–19	Int.	4
	7	86
	7	92
	8	98

	Chap.	Page
	10	126
22:24	13	154
22:31–4	13	161
22:40–6	16	184–5
22:42	21	238

John

	Chap.	Page
1: 1	Int.	3
1: 1–3	15	182
1: 1–5	1	13
1: 4–14	12	148
1: 6–9	1	14
1:10–13	1	16
1:11	7	91
1:12–13	5	63
1:13	20	225
1:14	1	17
	6	79
	8	97
1:15	1	19
1:16–18	1	19
1:19–34	1	20–1
1: 3–34	15	181
1:35–51	1	24–5
2: 1–11	2	31
2:12–25	2	33
2:21	8	97
2:24–5	4	54
3: 1–21	3	38–9
3: 4	1	17
3:13	Int.	3
3:16	Int.	3
3:16–17	15	180
3:22–36	3	41–2
3:27	Int.	3
3:29–30	15	176
4: 1–3	4	46
4: 2	1	26
4: 4–16	4	47–8
4:16–18	4	50
4:19–24	4	51

	Chap.	Page		Chap.	Page		Chap.	Page
4:21	Int.	12	8:12	12	152	12:17	11	131–2
4:23	Int.	12	8:12–20	8	99	12:20–36	12	144–5
	7	93	8:15	8	97	12:24–6	11	133
4:24	Int.	17	8:18	15	181	12:25	7	92
	7	93	8:21–30	8	101–2	12:37–43	12	148
	8	97	8:28	4	53	12:40	12	149
4:25–42	4	52–3		15	173	12:44–50	12	151
4:34	11	134		17	194	13: 1–17	13	153
4:43–54	4	55	8:31	8	99	13:18–32	13	155–6
5: 1–9	5	57	8:31–47	8	105	13:21	13	158
5: 8	8	105	8:37	4	47	13:33–8	13	163
5:10–17	5	59		7	89	14: 1–14	14	165
5:18	5	62	8:44	10	125	14: 5	20	223
	19	207	8:48–59	8	108	14: 6	Int.	3
5:19–30	5	62–3	8:50	4	53	14:10	Int.	3
5:25	11	137	8:53	19	207		4	53
5:31–47	5	64–5	8:58	6	75		7	91
5:37	15	181	9: 1–7	9	111		15	173
5:38	8	105	9: 8–17	9	113–14	14:15–17	1	27
6: 1–13	6	68	9:18–34	9	116–17		6	75
6:14–15	6	70	9:35–41	9	118	14:15–26	14	168
6:16–21	6	71	9:39–41	10	122	14:19–20	16	188
6:22–34	6	74	9:41	15	181	14:21	20	219
6:35–40	13	157	10: 1–21	10	121–2	14:23	8	99
6:35–42	6	76	10:14–15	13	124–5	14:24	Int.	3
6:43–52	6	78	10:22–42	10	160–1	14:27–31	14	169
6:51	6	70	10:26	10	122	14:28	14	167
6:53–7	17	192	10:27–30	13	160–1		18	199
6:53–8	6	78	10:30	Int.	3		20	223
6:59–60	6	81		4	53	14:31	15	175
6:60–6	16	184		8	100	15: 1–6	15	172
6:61–71	6	81–2		10	127	15: 4–6	14	167
6:63	6	79		14	167	15: 7–13	15	175
	19	208	10:30–9	4	53	15:14–15	8	107
	20	224	10:33	19	207	15:14–17	15	177
6:65	13	156	11: 1–10	11	129	15:16	1	25
7: 1–13	7	84	11: 3	19	212		13	156
7:14–32	7	87–8	11: 5	19	212	15:18–25	15	179
7:16	Int.	11	11:11	19	212	15:22	3	44
	5	64	11:11–16	11	129	15:26–7	15	181
7:17	Int.	7	11:17–44	11	134–6	16: 1–6	16	183
7:23–24	9	116	11:36	19	212	16: 4	18	202
7:33–36	7	90–1	11:45–57	11	138–9	16: 7–8	20	223
7:37–52	7	92–3	11:46–53	10	127	16: 7–15	16	185
7:50	3	41	12: 1–8	12	142	16:16–23	16	187
7:53	8	96	12: 3–7	19	212	16:20–2	20	225
8: 1–11	8	96	12: 9–19	12	143–4	16:23–33	16	188–9

	Chap.	Page
17: 1–6	8	102
17: 1–13	17	191
17: 4–6	12	150
17: 9	1	25
17:14–26	17	194–5
17:21–3	10	128
18: 1–12	18	197
18: 9	18	198
18:13–27	18	200–1
18:28–40	18	203–4
18:36	1	20
	2	34
	6	71
	12	144
19: 1–22	19	206–7
19:23–42	19	209–10
19:30	13	158
19:39	3	41
20: 1–10	20	215
20:11–18	9	115
	20	215–16
20:19–31	20	220–1
21: 1–14	21	226
21: 7	20	219
21:15–19	21	229–30
21:20–5	21	232

Acts

	Chap.	Page
28:26–7	12	149

Romans

	Chap.	Page
6: 3–8	7	94
7:14–25	3	25
	15	174
8:14–17	5	63
	8	102
8:15	5	63

	Chap.	Page
8:29	20	220
11: 8	12	149

1 Corinthians

	Chap.	Page
1:23–4	16	183
2:14	6	82
2:16	8	109
3:18–19	8	109
4:20	12	150
10: 3–4	6	76
15:35–44	2	36–7
15:40–9	6	79–80
	9	221

2 Corinthians

	Chap.	Page
5: 1	14	166
5:17	9	114
12: 2–4	20	221

Galatians

	Chap.	Page
2:20	6	80
	7	91
	15	174
4: 6	5	63
5:18	1	20
6:14	4	53
	8	110
	16	183

Ephesians

	Chap.	Page
1: 4	15	182
4:13	6	81
	8	107
4:22–4	8	109
5:14	8	109
	11	136
6:10–12	6	83

	Chap.	Page
	9	112
6:17	18	202

Philippians

	Chap.	Page
2: 7	4	53
4: 7	14	170

Timothy

	Chap.	Page
5: 6	11	130

Titus

	Chap.	Page
3: 5	13	155

Hebrews

	Chap.	Page
5: 1–10	10	126–7
7: 3	8	103
7:16–17	19	211

James

	Chap.	Page
4: 4	8	106–7
	9	113

1 John

	Chap.	Page
2: 3–6	8	106
4:16	15	176

2 John

	Chap.	Page
1: 9	8	105

Revelation

	Chap.	Page
3:19	13	164
	15	174
3:20–21	16	190
13: 8	12	152
	17	196
	17	198

INDEX

Abba 63
Abraham 28, 72, 110, 131
Abram 28, 72
Absolute, the 24
action 59, 50, 168
Acts of Peter 176
Acts of Thomas 134
Adam 161, 211, 225
adharma 41
Aenon 42
amartia 23, 44, 59, 98
Amen 122, 146
Analogue, Mount 130
Anchor Bible 8, 73
Andrew 27–8, 70
Aqiba, Rabbi 93, 218
Arjuna 20, 29, 40, 88, 110, 123
asmita 77, 88
Atman 3, 22, 39, 40, 64, 77, 97, 128, 133, 174, 181, 222
Augustine, St 166
authority 86–9, 99, 117, 136, 204, 207
avatara 123
avatars 16, 20

Babylon 53, 77
Baptiser, John the 10, 11, 14–15, 19, 32, 46, 65, 158, 168, 176, 181, 213, 218
   and his disciples 25
   discusses Jesus 41–2
   different level from Jesus 43
   function 22
   self-knowledge 21, 27
baptism 104
   of Jesus 25, 34, 46, 50, 140, 160, 164, 175, 177, 189, 196
   of John and Jesus, contrasted 22, 45
Barabbas 205
Beginning 3, 182, 193, 211, 224, 227, 234
being, new 39, 109
belief 10

believing 15, 224
beloved disciple 9, 181, 213, 228, 232–3
Bethesda 57, 58, 137
Bhagavad Gita 2, 3, 14, 20, 22, 27, 30, 40, 41, 50, 51, 56, 59, 60, 62, 66, 100, 110, 119, 122, 123, 149, 168, 170, 173, 190
Bhagirth 26
bhakti 168
birth,
   new 16, 39, 67, 133, 188
   spiritual 172
   virgin 10, 16–17, 102, 115, 134, 174
blasphemy 53, 110, 126–7, 204, 207–8
blindness, spiritual 111–13, 119, 122, 138, 148, 181, 208
bodhisattvas 61
body
   as temple 34–5, 97
   different levels 218–14
Boehme, Jacob 91
blood 79–80
Brahman 3, 14, 77, 128, 174
Brahman
   gate 24
   world 24
bread 75–6, 79, 157
Brihadaranyaka Upanishad 35, 130
brother, of Christ 209, 213, 232
Brown, Raymond 8, 73
Buddha 136
Buddha, the 11, 60, 65, 104, 146, 159, 190
Buddha-nature 221, 224
buddhi 22, 39, 40, 51, 174, 189, 222
   and John the Baptiser 22, 46
buddhi yoga 40, 42, 168

Caesar 144, 209, 211
Caiaphas 154
Cana 10, 31–3, 213
chakras 94

240

charioteer   123–4
Choruses from the Rock   18
Chosen One   126
Christ, the inner   227
  mind of   109–10
Christianity   4, 6–7, 63, 180
Church, the   180
Clement of Alexandria   9
Commandments, Ten   19
cross   151, 175–8, 183, 196, 205, 212,
  227, 232
crown of thorns   207
Crucifer   152, 183, 211, 224, 228, 231
crucifixion   27, 94, 124, 126, 146–7,
  152, 153, 160, 175–6, 186, 188, 196,
  198–9, 211, 218, 227

dark night of the soul   36, 45
Darkness, Prince of   130, 147, 179,
  181, 190
Daumal, René   130
death   130, 140, 142, 148, 234
development, stages of   138
devil   54, 95, 108, 112–3, 125, 144,
  146, 148, 154, 160–1
dharma   19, 41, 61, 140, 221
Dharmakaya   222–4
disciple   117
  levels of   178–80
discipleship   105–8
'Dry Salvages'   92
dying   132, 146

Eckhart, Meister   64, 89, 102, 103
ego   57–58, 77, 107, 115
ego eimi   73, 77, 99, 102, 115, 123,
  194, 200, 202
Egypt   104
Eliot, T.S.   18, 92, 141
Emmanuel   103
Enneads   90, 102, 149, 182, 232
esoteric message   64–7, 76–7, 140
Eternal Life   14, 36, 40, 44, 49–50, 54,
  75, 80, 108, 122, 146, 166, 171, 183,
  192, 195–6, 198, 209, 211, 227
eucharist   229
Evil One   190
exclusivity   43

flesh   19, 79, 80, 113, 169, 180, 186,
  192, 195
Four Quartets   92
fruit of the vine   174

Gabriel   16
Ganga   26, 224
garment, seamless   211
gender   14, 102, 127
Gethsemane, Garden of   137, 146,
  155
Gita Govinda   128
Gitanjali   58
Gospel of Mary   29, 216
Gospel of Peter   216, 233
Gospel of Philip   17, 152, 193, 194,
  200, 212, 216, 217
Gospel of St John
  date of   9
  source of   5
  writer   9
Gospel of Thomas   45, 136, 137,
  154–5, 188, 196, 214
gospels,
  canonical   8, 216
  synoptic   8, 32, 132
Ground, Divine   167
  of Being   151
gunas   173

hara   94
heart, simple   70
Heaven   3, 40
Heresiarch   180
Herod, King   22
hierarchy of being   172
  according to the *Bhagavad Gita*   22
  spiritual, in Gospel   81, 103
Hindu tradition   2
hollow men   47, 85
Holy Spirit   4, 11, 16–17, 23, 31–2,
  168, 181, 213, 223, 231

I AM   10, 37, 53–4, 72–3, 76, 77,
  79, 87, 88–92, 99–104, 110, 113, 115,
  118, 123–4, 126, 134, 136–8, 154,
  163, 166, 173–4, 177, 181, 194, 200,
  202, 211, 225
Ignatius, St of Antioch   178, 202

Immanuel 231
incarnation 17, 152, 153, 158, 172, 176, 180, 186, 196, 218
indwelling 80, 167, 175
inner crowd 69
Intelligence, the 13, 14
Isha Upanishad 132
Israel (Jacob) 28, 72
Israel (place) 23, 29, 218

Jacob 28, 48, 49–50, 72
Jacob's ladder 29
Jacob's well 48
James, brother of Jesus 27, 77, 84
James, son of Zebedee 27
Jerusalem 12, 20, 27, 34, 51, 86, 124
Jesus,
  and Nicodemus 38–41
  and the Samaritan woman 47–54, 97
  and the woman caught in adultery 96–9
  after the resurrection 220–6
  arrest 197
  as the vine 172–4
  baptism by John 15
  calls his disciples 25
  cleansing the temple 33
  example 154–5
  feeds the five thousand 68–70
  gives sight 111–20
  going away 165–7, 187–8
  his peace 169–71
  joy 176
  love for his father 170–1, 175
  meaning of his name 72–3, 132
  mission 102, 117
  nourished by doing God's will 54, 56, 193
  obedience 175
  priestly function 211
  purpose 153–4, 195
  raising of Lazarus 129–37
  receives the Holy Spirit 11, 15, 23, 31
  reveals himself to his disciples 102
  teaching on the Sabbath 59–62
  trial and crucifixion 203–6

jnana 168
John, son of Zebedee 9, 27
Jordan, River 224
Joseph of Arimathea 29, 150, 211
Joseph, father of Jesus 10, 77, 79, 90, 154
Joses, brother of Jesus 84
Joshua 72, 132
Journey of the Magi 141
Judas, Iscariot 82–3, 143, 155–62, 164, 169, 198, 199, 202
Jude, brother of Jesus 77, 84

kalos 123
Katha Upanishad 124
kayas 100, 221
karma 20, 60–1, 168
Kidron 197
king 204, 207, 211, 232
  of Israel 144
kingdom, inner 204, 207
Kingdom, the 12, 195
  of God 20, 39
  of Heaven 104
kingship 70–1
kinship
  in Jesus' circle 27–8
  Father and Son 128
koan 18
koilia 93
kishas 100
Krishna 3, 11, 14, 20, 27, 29, 40, 50, 56, 59, 61, 62, 66, 83, 88, 100, 110, 119, 123, 128, 148, 160, 170, 190, 218

Lamb of God 10, 23, 25, 35, 40, 122, 196, 198–9, 208
lamb, sacrificial 10, 23, 208
Lao Tze 11
Last Supper 157
Lazarus, brother of Mary and Martha 10, 127, 129–37, 142, 144, 146, 147, 150, 157, 162, 212, 216, 217
Lazarus the leper 131
Levi, the disciple 216
Light 14, 130, 147–8, 160, 176, 179, 204, 233

logos 13, 72
Logos, the 16, 19, 63, 91, 99, 130, 133, 158, 176, 224
love, for Jesus 168, 175
Lucifer 81, 231

Mahabharata 83, 160
Mahapurusha 101
Malchus 202
manas 22, 46
manipura chakra 93
manna 75
Mara 146
Martha, sister of Lazarus 133, 136, 142, 233
Mary, mother of Jesus 10, 15, 16–17, 22, 32, 77, 79, 84, 90, 154, 213
Mary Magdalene 143, 212, 216–18, 222
Mary, sister of Lazarus 131, 133, 136, 142–3, 150, 212, 216–20, 233
messiah 53, 66, 71, 89–90, 144, 147
metanoia 45, 106, 132
mind,
   how to lose 109–10
   right 5
Mosaic law 88
Moses 19, 63, 65, 73, 75, 131, 200, 211
mother 28, 32
Muyalaka 231
mystery, spiritual 17–18

name,
   new 28
   of God 53, 72, 194, 202
   of the beloved disciple 228–9
   significance of 72, 167, 189, 193
Nathanael 27, 29–30
Nazarene 199
Nazareth 29
Nazorean 199
Nicodemus 17, 38–41, 51, 89, 95, 126, 139, 150, 211
nirmanakya 221
nous 174

One, the 2, 12
onome 72, 193

ouk eimi 202
Oxyrhynchus papyri 104, 234

parables 66, 76, 119, 149, 201
paradidomi 158
Passover 10, 23, 69, 157, 208
Patanjali 77
Paul, St 11, 20, 28, 44, 63, 72, 73, 75, 79, 81, 91, 94, 107, 109, 112, 136, 149, 150, 155, 166, 170, 174, 183, 221
peace, of Christ 170, 190
Peter 72, 155, 161, 162, 164, 176–177, 202, 203, 216, 217, 227–34
Phaedo 24–8
Pharaoh 200
Pharisees 97, 136
Philip, the disciple 27–8, 69, 166
Philo 72
Pilate 144, 154, 204–5, 207–8, 211
Plato 124
Plotinus 90, 102, 149, 182, 232
Pneuma 17, 40, 89, 181, 221
prakrita 2, 22, 59, 112
prayer, Vedic 129
preparation 26, 69, 72, 140, 150, 151
price, of discipleship 178
Prince of this world 170, 180, 190
Procla 205
Prologue to the Gospel 13–14
Psalms 35, 36
psyche 89, 92, 97–8, 113, 133, 147, 181, 221–2
purusha 100, 181
purusha yajna 176

Radha 128, 218
resurrection 84, 115, 134, 136, 176, 216, 218
rhuh 17
Rig Veda 176

Sabbath 59, 61, 115, 204
sacrifice 35, 92, 152, 175, 196, 199, 202, 209, 226
sahasrara chakra 24
Salim 42
salvation 147
sambhogakaya 221–4

samskrita 2, 112
sanatana dharma 2
Sanhedrin 39, 88, 131, 150, 204, 211
Satan 161, 162, 164, 197–8, 203, 204, 229, 231
satori 189
Saul 11, 28, 72
Saviour of the World 54
Scriptures 65, 109, 136, 147, 208, 233
Self 2, 162, 222
Septuagint 73
Shatapatha Brahmana 11
sheep 121–4, 125, 127, 138, 159, 160, 179, 227
shekinah 17, 32
shepherd 121–4
Shiva 26, 231
Silesius, Angelus 7
Siloam 113
Simon, brother of Jesus 77, 84
Simon Peter 27–8, 201, 203, 229–30
sin 5, 10, 97, 106, 109, 130, 132, 181
sin, original 130
Sinai, Mount 19
slave 106–7, 178
soma 181, 221
Son,
   of common Father 18, 209
   of God 15, 16, 29, 64, 80, 81, 102, 113, 118, 123, 124, 127, 133, 134, 137, 138, 139, 163, 166, 174, 179, 204, 211, 224, 225
   of Man 29, 30, 64, 80, 81, 102, 107, 115, 118, 123, 124, 134, 138, 146, 147, 148, 162, 166, 173, 174, 179, 194, 204, 222, 225
Song of Songs 128, 218
sonship 63, 126
Source, the 175, 181, 234
spirit, source of 93–94
Spirit, the 8, 15, 16, 22, 65, 82, 90, 108, 113, 133, 137, 158, 163, 168, 169, 170, 172, 173, 180, 181, 182, 185, 186, 189, 192, 194, 195, 196, 202, 204, 205, 207, 213, 222, 223, 224, 225, 227, 228, 232
Spiritus Sanctus 17
svabhava 221

Svabhavikakaya 221, 223
svadharma 27

tabernacle 124
Tagore, Rabindranath 58
Tantra 80
Tao 14
temple 34
Teresa, St of Avila 102
Theologia Germanica 41, 171
Thomas, brother of Jesus 134
Thomas, disciple of Jesus 166, 223–4
time 13, 104, 110, 136, 166, 182, 227
torah 61
Torquemada 7
tree, cosmic 173

Upanishads 35, 57, 77, 128

Vastness, the 2, 6, 12, 127, 170, 175, 177, 196
Veda 11, 12
Vedas 19, 20, 176
vine 173, 176, 228

water 48–50, 94
Way, the 166
Wheel of Dharma 140
Will,
   of God 86, 151
   of Heaven 3
   of the Father 126, 205
witness 10, 14, 15
Word, the 3, 13–4, 16, 113, 124, 158–9, 161, 169, 180, 191–2, 194, 195, 202, 233
World 192, 195, 232

Yahweh 73, 77, 132
yajna 30, 122, 226
Yangtze, River 224
Yehoshua 72, 132
YHWH 73, 77
yoga 2, 24, 40, 61, 91, 107, 110, 151, 158, 172
Yoga Sutras 77, 88, 110, 151, 181
yoke 91, 107

Zen 18, 94